D1483350

A Manual for Repertory Grid Technique

A MANUAL FOR
REPERTORY GRID TECHNIQUE

FAY FRANSELLA
Royal Free Hospital School of Medicine,
University of London, London, England

and

DON BANNISTER
High Royds Hospital, Menston,
Ilkley, West Yorkshire, England

1977

ACADEMIC PRESS

London   New York   San Francisco

A Subsidiary of Harcourt Brace Jovanovich, Publishers

ACADEMIC PRESS INC. (LONDON) LTD.
24/28 Oval Road
London NW1

United States Edition published by
ACADEMIC PRESS INC.
111 Fifth Avenue
New York, New York 10003

Library of Congress Catalog Card Number: 77-71817
ISBN Casebound edition: 0-12-265450-1
ISBN Paperback edition: 0-12-265456-0

PRINTED IN GREAT BRITAIN BY THE LAVENHAM PRESS LIMITED, SUFFOLK

Preface

Grids are like people. They come in many shapes and sizes; they ask questions and give answers; they can be studied as a group or individually, on one occasion or successively over time; they can be used well or distorted out of all recognition. So we make no attempt to be definitive. Our aim is to inform both those familiar with grids who want to know more, and those for whom grid technique is a vaguely interesting but ill-defined notion. The information given is both general, in terms of grid development, reliability and validity, and specific, in terms of grid forms, measures, underlying assumptions and common pitfalls.

No specialised knowledge is required, only a willingness to contemplate a few simple statistical ideas. George Kelly, in fact, described a very simple method in 1955 for "going beyond words". His Rep Test enabled him to see how one idea has linkages with a number of other ideas, and how one person can be seen as similar to some people and yet different from others. These linkages are such that the person may not be able easily to put them into words. The first part of the book deals with the development of grid technique from its inspired beginnings to the many forms now used and dwells at some length on how the grid form of measurement differs from other methods in more common use today.

At first sight, this volume may appear to be large rear and little front. There is as much appendix as there is book. But we feel that one major contribution this book makes is to give the reader the first published annotated bibliography on grid usage. The list is not definitive, nor was it planned to be so. The general rules were to give later rather than earlier references, those citing novel rather than repetitious usage, and theory related rather than grid for grid's sake usage. Some attempt has been made to cluster the papers under specific headings, but the distribution is of necessity rather arbitrary as in many cases papers could be placed under several headings. There is considerable overlap between the annotated bibliography and the references. But there is reason in this apparent paper foolhardiness. This is a manual and not a general text, so we felt it important that the grid user should be able to lay hands on a reference quickly.

Likewise, Brenda Morris' chapter may seem oddly placed in the Appendix, but we wanted it to stand out clearly on its own as showing the grid to be a living tool—something to be used as well as talked about.

Our general aim has been to give readers enough knowledge to set about designing their own grids for their own specific purposes while making them aware of their underlying assumptions and limitations. We hope that the extensive bibliography will enable those interested to extend their enquiries further. In places it may seem as if we are obsessed with certain ideas—like range of convenience—and this is probably true. It comes from many years of advising students and professionals alike in the design of grids and, in particular, in dealing with problems that arise because of ignorance of some of the basic requirements of this form of measurement. We hope that those who read this book will overcome such problems and that they will be able to enjoy exploring the personal worlds of others, leading eventually to a greater understanding of those others and themselves.

March, 1977   FAY FRANSELLA

Acknowledgements

The authors and the publisher wish to thank the following for their kind permission to reproduce material quoted from other volumes:

John Wiley & Sons Inc. for quotations from "Clinical Psychology and Personality: The Selected Papers of George Kelly" edited by B. A. Maher; Rand McNally College Publishing Company for a quotation from "Personal Construct Systems in Psychotherapy" by A. W. Landfield; and W. W. Norton & Co., Inc. for quotations from "The Psychology of Personal Constructs" by George A. Kelly.

Contents

Figures

Tables

1

The Basis of Repertory Grid Technique

A scientist's inventions assist him in two ways: they tell him what to expect and they help him to see it when it happens. Those that tell him what to expect are theoretical inventions and those that enable him to observe outcomes are instrumental inventions. The two types are never wholly independent of each other, and they usually stem from the same assumptions. This is unavoidable. Moreover, without his inventions, both theoretical and instrumental, man would be both disoriented and blind. He would not know where to look or how to see.

G. A. Kelly
(Selected Papers, 1969, p. 94)

Let us suppose that Fred supposes that people with *cold eyes* tend to be *mean with their money*. Let us suppose also that Fred is a psychologist—presumably one who believes in fixed personality traits of genetic origin. Fred will undoubtedly yearn to give his notions a statistical foundation, so it will not surprise us when he sets out to survey his landscape of people and judge them, in each case, in terms of the dimensions *cold-eyed—warm-eyed* and *mean—generous*. He may then cast his observations on say 100 people into the form of a chi-square which may appear as follows.

	cold eyes	warm eyes
mean	28	19
generous	2	51

chi-square $= 36.9$ (p<.001)

We can view these data in two ways.

We can look upon them as telling us something about the nature of eye temperature and miserliness in people. We can say (given the customary cavils about experimental design) that at a given level of significance, *cold—warm eyes* are related to *miserliness—generosity*. We can proceed from there to offer explanations to account for the relationship, formulate consequent hypotheses and design further experiments to test them.

Alternatively, we can look at these data as information about the mind of Fred. The significant association found could be looked on as a sign that for Fred the constructs of *cold-eyed—warm-eyed* and *mean—generous* are related. We could go on to discuss further constructs of Fred which might be interlinked and the total construct system of which these constructs are a part. We could consider what lines of action Fred might be prompted to take, viewing people thus; what kind of validating or invalidating experiences might strengthen or modify his mode of construing and so forth.

One approach does not deny the usefulness of the other and construct theory takes the first into account in concerning itself with validation. Construing is the lively way in which we go about trying to anticipate events—real events in the outside world.

However, if we consider the second approach for a moment and comment on the data as revealing aspects of Fred's personal construct system, then in his chi-square we have the beginnings of repertory grid technique. Many such chi-squares can constitute a grid. Behind each single act of judgement that a person makes (consciously or unconsciously) lies his implicit theory about the realm of events within which he is making judgements. Repertory grid technique is, in its multitude of forms, a way of exploring the structure and content of such implicit theories. Each of us has many such implicit theoretical beliefs about billiards or love affairs or accounting or children or God. In turn, our smaller theories (e.g. construct sub-systems) are linked into the overall theory that we call a personal construct system.

In using the metaphor of "theory", we are not arguing that such theories are formal and articulated. They may be verbal or non-verbal or pre-verbal, they may be tightly structured or loosely structured, they may be easily testable or almost too tangled to test, they may be idiosyncratic or commonly held. But they *are* theories in the sense of being networks of meaning through which persons see and handle the universe of situations through which they move. In this sense, a person's theories—his personal construct system— might be referred to in other psychological approaches as his "personality", his "attitudes", his "habits", his "reinforcement history", his "information coding system", his "psychodynamics", his "concepts", his "philosophy" or his "central nervous system".

Kelly (1955 and 1969) argued that it would be convenient and useful to see personal construct systems as being made up of hierarchically linked sets of bipolar constructs—*nice-nasty, here-there, two stroke-four stroke, ugly-beautiful, alkali-acid, past-future, master-servant, odd-even* and so forth and so on. Thus, a dictionary is a record of how verbalised constructs are publicly related. The difficulties of exploring construct systems, by grid or any other means, forces us to focus more heavily on verbalised and easily accessible constructs. But we should never assume that a construct is the same as its verbal label. A construct is a discrimination, *not* a verbal label. We should accept that in talking about an individual's personal construct system, we are talking about his stance towards the world, we are talking about him as a *person*. Thus, Kelly describes a construct in the following terms (1969).

"A construct is like a reference axis, a basic dimension of appraisal, often unverbalised, frequently unsymbolised, and occasionally unsignified in any manner except by the elemental processes it governs. Behaviorally it can be regarded as an open channel of movement, and the system of *constructs* provides each man with his own personal network of action pathways, serving both to limit his movements and to open up to him passages of freedom which otherwise would be psychologically non-existant."

Suppose I am haunted by the feeling that the more people know my secrets the less I will be liked. This can be summarised in diagrammatic form.

knows my secrets	*v.*	does not know my secrets
does not like me	*v.*	likes me

It is possible to demonstrate by the mathematics of a grid that these particular constructs are linked for me in this way. But even when the argument is supported by the mathematics of a grid investigation, it is necessarily an oversimplification of the probable state of affairs. We are singling out a pair of constructs from what is a very complex network. The value and meaning of these constructs can only be ultimately assessed in terms of their location within this entire network—which is a changing network anyway. But suppose that the grid has revealed this aspect of my construing to you, then you may use it as a source of information about me, either as it presents itself or as subsumed under some higher order construction of your own, such as that it is essentially "neurotic" (*versus* "normal").

However, I may use this revelation about my construct system to see to what degree I think my interpersonal relationships are limited by this mode of construing, this kind of anticipation of how other people will respond to me. Yet more aspects of my construing may need examining in order to locate other constructions which I place upon the world, which in some way, contradict or cut across this belief that the more people know my secrets the less I will be liked. It may be that even while believing this I make special and exceptional cases out of psychotherapists or priests or women. It may be that if I am drunk I believe I have a licence which takes away the effect of the ruling. It may be that I am changing my secrets and believe that they are becoming less objectionable. It may finally be that I am ceasing to operate the construction as a self-fulfilling prophesy and new evidence may yet become available to me which radically alters this aspect of my interpretative system.

The purpose of grids is to inform us about the way in which our system is evolving and its limitations and possibilities. The results of the grid have often been looked on as a map of the construct system of an individual, a sort of idiographic cartography as contrasted with, say, the nomothetic cartography of the semantic differential (Osgood *et al.*, 1957). To the extent that a grid gives us a map of an individual's construct system, it is probably about as accurate and informative as the maps which Columbus provided of the American coastline. At that, it may be a good deal more sensitive to the nature of the person than the kinds of psychological instrument we have tended to use to date.

The grid is perhaps best looked on as a particular form of structured interview. Our usual way of exploring another person's construct system is by conversation. In talking to each other we come to understand the way the other person views his world, what goes with what for him, what implies what, what is important and unimportant and in what terms they seek to assess people and places and situations. The grid formalises this process and assigns mathematical values to the relationships between a person's constructs. It enables us to focus on particular subsystems of construing and to note what is individual and surprising about the structure and content of a person's outlook on the world. Yet the information it gives us is not novel or some peculiar product of our "scientific method". It is a formalised version of the kind of information we are always seeking about each other, the kind of understanding we are always in process of gaining about each other.

THE GRID AS PART OF PERSONAL CONSTRUCT THEORY

Psychologists often behave as if all that is needed for effective research or applied work is a single idea and an instrument. They ignore the fact that behind any single idea are whole series of assumptions and underlying any instrument yet a further series of assumptions. The assumptions underlying the "instrument" may well contradict the assumptions implicit in the "idea". Thus grid method is frequently brought into play, quite without relation to its parent theory. It has often been looked on as some sort of measure of "attitudes" or "meaning" or "personality" or "concepts" and it has achieved a status as a sort of rich man's semantic differential.

Yet psychologists who use the grid thoughtfully will find themselves assuming the truth of many of the assumptions of personal construct theory, even when they are ignorant of the theory as such. A skeleton outline of personal construct theory and its main contentions is given in Appendix III. Here attention is drawn only to those aspects of the theory from which the grid is directly derived and where the relationship between theory and instrument needs to be borne in mind.

GRIDS—A MEASURE OF WHAT?

The model underlying construct psychology is explicitly the idea of "every man his own scientist". Kelly believed that we strive to make sense out of our universe, out of ourselves, out of the particular situations we encounter. To this end each of us invents and re-invents an implicit theoretical framework which, be it well or badly designed, is our personal construct system. In terms of this system we live, we anticipate events, we determine our behaviour, we ask our questions. It is in terms of this same system that we evaluate outcome and elaborate changes in the interpretative system itself. Thus we are "scientists" who derive hypotheses (have expectations) from our theories (our personal construing). We subject these hypotheses to experimental test (we bet on them behaviourally, we take active risks in terms of them). We observe the results of our experiments (we live with the outcomes of our behaviour). We modify our theory (we change our minds, we change ourselves) and so the cycle continues.

Kelly devised repertory grid technique as a method for exploring personal construct systems. It is an attempt to stand in others' shoes, to see their world as they see it, to understand their situation, their concerns.

GRIDS ARE ABOUT CONSTRUCTS

Kelly offers several definitions of a construct. For example, a construct is "a way in which two or more things are alike and *thereby* different from a third or more things". This definition manifests itself directly in one of the procedures for eliciting constructs for grids. At another time Kelly said "a construct is a way of transcending the obvious". Here Kelly is stressing that when we make a new abstraction out of events we are escaping from the limitations of the "facts" of earlier abstractions.

In all his definitions, Kelly retains the essential notion that constructs are bipolar. His argument is that we never affirm anything without simultaneously denying something. This makes the notion of a construct quite different from the notion of a concept. When we say that Bill Bloggs is *honest* we are not saying that Bill Bloggs is *honest*, he is not a *chrysanthemum* or a *battleship* or the *square root of minus one*. We are saying that Bill Bloggs is *honest*, he is not *a crook*. We do not always, or even very often, specify our contrast pole but Kelly's argument is that we make sense out of our world by simultaneously noting likenesses *and* differences. It is in the contrast that the usefulness of the construct subsists. The bipolarity subsists in the construct itself not in the two sets of elements that are sorted by the construct. *North-South* is an axis of reference so that elements which in one context are *North,* in another context become *South.* The essence of a construct is that it is a moveable feast. It is a vehicle whereby we move from one situation to another.

It is this very bipolarity that makes the designing of grids possible. Suppose we try using "concepts" to build a grid and start with the concept *honest.* We could designate some of our acquaintances as *honest* and leave the rest outside the concept. Then we might go on to the concept *cruel* and put some of our acquaintances under that heading leaving the rest outside once more. All we can now do is to make some statement about class inclusion or exclusion. We can make statements about the number of people who are in one category and who are or are not in another. We cannot directly examine the *relationship* between the concepts except in terms of overlap.

We may use a simple bipolar grid where we allot each of our elements to one pole of the construct or the other or we rank our elements from most like to the most opposite or we rate them on, say, a seven point scale. In every case it is the dimensionality, the bipolarity of the construct, which enables us to arrive at some kind of matrix of the pattern of interrelationships between constructs.

It is this capacity of the grid to look at the *relationship* between constructs that enables us to go beyond the issue of whether the person's construing is "correct" or "incorrect". If we limit ourselves to the idea of the concept, then we are liable to end up working in terms of some such notions as "over-inclusion" and "under-inclusion". But to say that a person's concepts are over-inclusive or under-inclusive, inevitably involves us in the argument that there is a correct and right level of inclusion of objects within the concept, whether we define "right" in terms of normative standards or some set logic. We can, if we wish, compare a person's manifest relationships between constructs in grid form, with normative standards or with any other standards we care to erect. But we are not limited to this venture, we can consider the person's construct system as a system *within itself* and move from there to issues such as communicability and so forth.

RANGE OF CONVENIENCE

All grids involve a consideration of the issue of range of convenience. Kelly argued that a construct (or a subsystem of constructs) operates always within a context and that there are a finite number of elements to which it can be applied by a given person, at a given time (note the range corollary of the theory—Appendix III). This is something we recognise very readily in speech when we categorise furniture as *antique* or *modern* or numbers as *prime* or *non-prime* while it bends our minds to consider antique or modern numbers and prime or non-prime furniture. Obviously, the range of convenience of our constructs can be, and sometimes is, extended, as in poetry, intoxication and inspiration. But for a given act of construing at a given time, the range of convenience of our constructs is always limited. From this argument about the nature of construing, Kelly derived a prime rule of grid construction. For given persons completing a grid, all elements must be within his range of convenience. Otherwise we are inviting him to commit a nonsense. For example, he may sort his people into *attractive* and *unattractive*. But, because we have not allowed him to tell us that, for him, *attractive-unattractive* is a construct whose range of convenience is *limited to women*, then what he may do is to put some of his women into *attractive*, some of his women into *unattractive* and all his men into *unattractive*. He is forced to do this because we have left him no alternative. Obviously, when we come to relate the construct *attractive* to others in the grid, we will be bound to produce a distorted picture of his system.

It is interesting to note that in constructing the semantic differential, Osgood ignored the range of convenience rule and this enabled him to make some interesting statements about precisely those constructs which have the most *enormous ranges of convenience*. His famous trio of *good-bad, active-passive* and *weak-strong* are essentially what Kelly called major superordinates. Osgood thereby created endless arguments about what was happening to meaning as he was measuring it—Brown's (1958) question "is a boulder sweet or sour?" and arguments centering on problems such as scale-concept interaction (Levy, 1972).

INDIVIDUALITY COROLLARY

This corollary states simply that "persons differ from each other in their construction of events". Nobody has ever responded to a stimulus. They respond to what they *perceive* the stimulus to be. The aim of grids is to add to our capacity to explore the individual worlds of meaning in terms of which we live. Even the most "public" of constructs (e.g. those of mathematics or science) are personal in that each of us must individually give them a meaning and make them part of our total system. "Public" constructs may have consensus support, repeatedly demonstrated predictive implications and often rehearsed meanings as emphasised in Kelly's Commonality Corollary. Thus neither construct theory nor grids are exclusively concerned with those ambiguous constructs about feeling and relationship that people most often refer to as "personal".

COMMONALITY COROLLARY

This reads "to the extent that one person employs a construction of experience which is similar to that employed by another, his processes are psychologically similar to those of the other person". This is the contrast pole of the individuality corollary but, in the context of the total theory, it reminds us that the grid is most useful when it follows through the lines of implication of a construct. At the level of the exact relationship between two constructs, two people may appear to be construing in a very similar way, but if the lines of implication of these constructs are followed through for the two people, radical differences may occur. These differences can also be seen at group level. For example, Fransella and Bannister (1967) showed that both Labour Party and Conservative Party supporters saw a positive relationship between the constructs *proud of being British* and *likely to vote Conservative*. If we follow the relationships through the network, we then find that for Labour Party supporters *proud of being British* relates positively to *prejudiced* while for Tory party supporters it relates negatively to *prejudiced*.

SOCIALITY COROLLARY

This reads "to the extent that one person construes the construction processes of another he may play a role in a social process involving the other person". A key implication of this corollary is that to construe the constructions of another person is not simply to hold or mimic those constructions. If I point out to you that two aspects of your way of interpreting your world are contradictory I am certainly not simply reproducing your constructions but I am construing them. This is one of the relatively unexplored aspects of the theory in grid terms.

ORGANISATION COROLLARY

This reads "each person characteristically evolves for his convenience in anticipating events, a construction system embracing ordinal relationships between constructs". Here Kelly is pointing to the fact that construct systems are hierarchical with constructs standing to each other in what he terms, subordinate and superordinate relationships. This is something that is recognised in formal logic in that *modes of transport* subsume *boats* which subsume *sailing boats* which subsume *dinghys* which subsume *Mirror dinghys* and so forth. It is recognised in common argument when we talk of important ideas, central ideas, the main features of this or that as contrasted with detail, trivia and so forth. However, standard use of grids may, in some cases, have lead to the impression that constructs are to be seen in terms of a Euclidean geometry, lying flat and side by side rather than being seen as pyramidal in relationship to each other. Grid studies such as those of Hinkle (1965), Landfield (1971) and Fransella (1972) have focussed on the organisational qualities of construct systems.

KINDS OF CONSTRUCT

Construct theory offers a mode of categorising constructs as pre-emptive (if this is a lie it is *nothing but* a lie), constellatory (if this is a lie then it is also *unfair, punishable,* a *sure sign of moral decay* and so forth) or propositional (this may be considered, *as if it were,* among other things, a lie). If grid method has been used largely within the context of personal construct theory, we might well have seen the development of forms of grid designed to elucidate these modes of using constructs and their implications. In fact, since the grid has been used so often outside the context of the theory, these possibilities have been little explored and only in relatively rare studies like that of Levy (1956) has such a focus been taken.

CONSTRUCTS IN TRANSITION

Not only have grids been used frequently outside the context of personal construct theory, they have been used in the context of other theories. A theoretical assumption underlying most tests used in psychology is that there are stable and unvarying features of the person and that these are our primary concern. Kelly argued that "man is a form of motion" and offered a number of constructions designed to deal with the idea of constructs in transition. His notion of *hostility* (the attempt to extort validational evidence in favour of a type of social prediction which has already been recognised as a failure) and aggression (the active elaboration of one's perceptual field) and guilt (the awareness of dislodgement of the self from one's core role structure) are examples. These are all designed to cast light on the way in which our construct systems change and resist change as we experience varying validational fortunes. If we examine the history of grid usage, we find that a notion such as cognitive complexity—simplicity (Bieri, 1955) has been extensively explored although it tends to contradict some of the tenets of construct theory. It assumes that the whole construct system has a single structural quality whereas construct theory argues for different structural qualities between subsystems. More importantly such work presents complexity—simplicity as a kind of static trait and this is antithetical to construct theory arguments. Had grids developed more centrally out of construct theory, we might more readily be elaborating forms of the method designed to detect, explore and assist people whose constructs are in transition and who are dealing with their own guilt, hostility and aggression.

CONCLUSIONS

Although it is an often repeated truism that the grid is a method not a test, it is still a largely ignored truism.

This is exemplified in our constant failure to recognise that the use of a grid involves all the kinds of problems that we confront in designing an experiment. Whatever the question being experimentally asked, to use a grid is to involve the researcher in a whole series of problems. These concern the nature of the elements to be used, forms of construct elicitation and the format (e.g. ranking, rating or bipolar allotment) in which the subject is to respond. Additionally there are a multiplicity of ways in which grid data can be analysed and many kinds of inference it is legitimate to draw from them. Yet whether the focus of concern is with an individual case in psychotherapy or large scale research, grids tend to be too readily used and the user is often buried in the mountains of data which are generated.

The potential usefulness of grid method has been amply demonstrated in practice and can reasonably be argued in principle. The great advantage of the grid is that data from a single individual can be subjected to many of the kinds of group statistics which we have hitherto reserved for populations of subjects. Cluster analysis methods, t-tests of group differences, correlational consistency measures, significance of correlation methods, co-efficients of concordance and a range of other measures are technically feasible. They are potentially rich in the light they may throw on the underlying structure and manifest content of the construing which underlies the person's grid responses. The use of group statistics within the population of responses of a single person enables us to establish the meaningfulness of the single grid in that it can be readily shown that a given grid is most unlikely to have been produced randomly. The pattern of associations within the responses is demonstrably *meaningful*, in statistical terms, however difficult its psychological meaning may be to interpret (Draffan, 1973).

Though the grid was logically derived from construct theory, it is illogical to argue that it must be used only within the context of the theory. What can be argued is that any psychologist using the grid should be aware of the assumptions underlying it and should make these assumptions clear to his audience. Thereby the researcher will be involved in an internal and public dialogue with personal construct theory and it is in *this sense* that the method cannot be separated from the theory.

British empiricism is still a strong tradition and it seems to have lead many psychologists to value instruments more than they value the ideas and arguments from which the instruments derive. A most tragic example of this has been the enormous concentration of interest in "the intelligence test", while virtually ignoring the fascinating issue of the nature of thinking. It would be sad if the grid were to become a vastly popular instrument with virtually no attention being paid to construing.

2

Constructs and Elements

> Thus, for any of us, the sharing of personal experience is a matter of *construing* the other person's experience and not merely a matter of having him hand it to us intact across the desk. The psychology of personal constructs therefore lends itself quite conveniently to the handling of the theoretical problem of gaining access to private worlds. (Kelly, 1955, p. 200).

This chapter is concerned with some issues you need to consider about constructs and elements before you design your grid. More detailed discussion about some of the difficulties surrounding these issues can be found in Chapter 8.

There is no such thing as an element that is *only* an element or a construct that is *nothing but* a construct. Thus, *father-not father* can be used as a dimension along which other people are placed, as being *father-like* or *not father-like*. But "father" can also be an element construed in terms of, say, the dimension *strong in character-weak in character*.

CHOICE OF ELEMENTS

Elements are chosen to represent the area in which construing is to be investigated. If it is interpersonal relationships, the elements may well be people. These may be presented in the form of unspecified acquaintances or they may be people named to fit specific role titles. The twenty-four role titles suggested by Kelly are as follows:

1. A teacher you liked (Or the teacher of a subject you liked).
2. A teacher you disliked (Or the teacher of a subject you disliked).
3. Your wife or present girl friend.
3a. (for women) Your husband or present boy friend.
4. An employer, supervisor, or officer under whom you worked or served and whom you found hard to get along with (Or someone under whom you worked in a situation you did not like).
5. An employer, supervisor, or officer under whom your worked or served and whom you liked (Or someone under whom you worked in a situation you liked).
6. Your mother (Or the person who has played the part of a mother in your life).
7. Your father (Or the person who has played the part of a father in your life).

8. Your brother nearest your age (Or the person who has been most like a brother).
9. Your sister nearest your age (Or the person who has been most like a sister).
10. A person with whom you have worked who was easy to get along with.
11. A person with whom you have worked who was hard to understand.
12. A neighbour with whom you get along well.
13. A neighbour whom you find hard to understand.
14. A boy you got along well with when you were in high school (Or when you were 16).
15. A girl you got along well with when you were in high school (Or when you were 16).
16. A boy you did not like when you were in high school (Or when you were 16).
17. A girl you did not like when you were in high school (Or when you were 16).
18. A person of your own sex whom you would enjoy having as a companion on a trip.
19. A person of your own sex whom you would dislike having as a companion on a trip.
20. A person with whom you have been closely associated recently who appears to dislike you.
21. The person whom you would most like to be of help to (Or whom you feel most sorry for).
22. The most intelligent person whom you know personally.
23. The most successful person whom you know personally.
24. The most interesting person whom you know personally.

Obviously the grid designer can modify these as much as he wishes to meet the requirements of his particular situation. Some examples of different elements that have been used are: occupations (Shubsachs, 1975), feelings (Fransella and Adams, 1965), situations (Fransella, 1972), diseases (Orley and Leff, 1972), rooms (Honikman, 1976), photographs of people (Bannister, 1962a), Rorschach cards (Salmon, Arnold and Collyer, 1972), shops (Hudson, 1974), foreign countries (Lemon, 1975), classes of spirit in Ganda mythology (Orley, 1976), brightly coloured stand-up models (Salmon, 1976). There are many more besides these that have been used and who can say how many there are that *could* be used?

One particularly useful type of element is that described by Ryle and Lunghi (1970). Each element is a relationship between two people. For instance, Fay's relationship to Don, Don's relationship to Fay; Fay's relationship to her husband, his relationship to her. The number of elements in this "dyad" grid will partly be determined by the number of people considered to be important in that person's life. Ryle and Breen (1972b, 1972c) have also described the double dyad grid in which two people (e.g. a married couple) construct the dyad grid jointly. But the elements remain single relationships as in the dyad grid.

There are two important factors to be kept in mind when selecting the type of element to be used in a grid.

(a) *the elements must be within the range of convenience of the constructs to be used.* Constructs are discriminations we make between people or events or things in our lives. But each applies only to a limited number of people, events or things. So it is no use constructing a grid consisting of constructs to do with the youth-of-today and having one or two old people in among the elements—they would be outside the range of convenience of the youth-of-today type of construct. For example, it may be impossible to construe grandad as either *commercial pop fan* or *progressive rock fan*. Alternatively, if you want to find out what are a homosexual's views of sex, then you will need both sexes represented in the elements. But if you want to find out a homosexual's views of some aspect of homosexuality—for example, sexual positions—then clearly the elements would need to be homosexuals only. Range of convenience of specific constructs cannot always be accurately assessed by the good sense of the examiner. The subject needs to be given the opportunity to *say* when a construct is inapplicable to an element.

(b) *the elements must be representative of the pool from which they are drawn.* "If the test is to indicate how the subject develops his role in the light of his understanding of other people, it is necessary that the other people appearing as elements in the test be sufficiently representative of all the people with whom the subject must relate his self-construed role" (Kelly, 1955, p. 230). Kelly developed the use of the role title list to ensure adequate element representation.

This assumption of representativeness of elements was investigated by Mitsos (1958). He elicited constructs from one group of people using role titles and from another using lists of names of personal friends. When retested three months later, the group using role titles produced significantly more identical constructs than did the group using friends. But Mitsos pointed to a factor possibly influencing the results. People with role titles are likely to provide the *same* people to fit them on a second occasion, whereas, after three months, friends can change. Pedersen (1958) had indeed found that 77 per cent gave the same people to fit role titles after an interval of one week. To investigate this, Mitsos repeated the procedure with the "friends" group after another three months (six months after the original testing) using the elements of the second occasion. The same level of construct repetition was found.

Salmon (1976) discusses at length the problems involved in selecting elements with children and describes some of the methods that have been used. Barton, Walton and Rowe (1976) do the same for the mentally handicapped (see p. 55 for details).

THE ELICITATION OF CONSTRUCTS

Kelly states six assumptions that underlie his original Role Construct Repertory Test (Rep Test), but which are equally applicable to subsequent grid modifications and to construct elicitation in general.

(a) the constructs elicited should be *permeable*. This means that the person is able to apply the constructs elicited to people and interpersonal situations other than the three elements from which the construct has been elicited. "We hope that the subject reveals, in taking the test, those channels through which new experiences, as well as old, may run". (Kelly, 1955, p. 229).

(b) pre-existing constructs should be elicited. While the person may, on occasion, develop a new construct during the process of elicitation, it is assumed that this does not often happen and that there is "some lingering degree of permanence in the constructs".

(c) the verbal labels attached to the constructs should be communicable. That is, the examiner has some reasonably accurate idea as to what the subject is getting at. It is often necessary for the examiner to test out the accuracy of her understanding by conversing with the subject.

(d) the constructs elicited should

"represent the subject's understanding, right or wrong, of the way other people look at things. If the subject gives only responses which describe his relationship to other people as if they were unthinking animals, the test has failed to elicit *role constructs*. The subject's measure of understanding of other people may actually be inadequate or preposterous; but, if it is the basis of a real social interaction with them, it is indeed related to his role construct system". (Kelly, 1955, p. 230).

(e) the subject should not dissociate himself entirely from the elements or from the constructs elicited. He must be able to see *himself* somewhere along the construct dimensions.

(f) the constructs elicited should be explicitly bipolar. By stating what a person or thing is, one is also stating that which he or it is not.

METHODS OF CONSTRUCT ELICITATION

By triads of elements

Kelly (1955) originally described 6 ways in which one can elicit constructs.

(i) *The Minimum Context Card Form*

The person is first asked to give names to role titles as, for example, listed by Kelly. They are then presented with three of these elements and asked to specify *some important way in which two of them are alike and thereby different from the third*. Having recorded the reply, they are asked in what way the third person differs from the other two people (if they have not indicated which two people are alike they are asked to do so). The answer to the question concerning the difference is the *contrast pole*. As many triads of elements are presented to the subject as the administrator thinks appropriate. There are no set rules. There are only questions of "sample size" in the number of constructs to be examined.

(ii) *The Full Context Form*

In this form, all elements, written on separate cards are spread out in front of the person. They are asked to think of important ways in which groups of the people are alike. When the first two cards are selected, they are asked in what way they are alike. As subsequent cards are added, the person is occasionally asked whether it is still the same category as for the first two cards. If one is taken away, the person is also asked if the same category is still being used.

(iii) *The Sequential Form*

Here, the elements are presented as in the Minimum Context Form (that is, as triads rather than as a group), but they are presented systematically by changing one in the triad each time. For example, having been presented with 1, 2 and 3, number 1 is removed and number 4 substituted for it and so on.

(iv) *The Self-Identification Form*

The elements are presented as in the Sequential Form, but the element "myself" is always included in the triad. This ensures (as far as possible) that all constructs elicited are personally relevant.

(v) *The Personal Role Form*

This is similar to the Self-Identification Form, but the instructions now are: "suppose that the three of you were all together by yourselves for an evening. What kind of place might it be? What would happen? How would you yourself be likely to be acting? How would each of the others be likely to be acting?" Many other situations or conditions could be used and it allows the subject greater flexibility of reply.

(vi) *Full Context Form with the Personal Role Feature*

For this method, all element cards are laid out before the person. When all the cards have been sorted into piles, the "myself" card is placed by each pile and the Personal Role questions asked for each. These are posed in the form "Suppose you were to spend an evening with this group, what would be likely to happen?" and so on.

The Personal Role forms seem to be a way in which subject and examiner can discuss how the subject sees his own and others' personal interactions. It is in the course of this conversation that the subject will reveal the construct dimensions he uses which can be noted by the examiner.

Kelly based his triad method for eliciting constructs on his theory as to how constructs are first formed. But since one is eliciting constructs already established in the person's repertoire there is no reason why *three* elements need be used. The triad is not even necessary to ensure obtaining the opposite of the emergent pole given. Epting and his colleagues (1971) found that a more explicit contrast was obtained by asking the person for the opposite to the likeness pole of the construct than by asking them how the third person in the triad was different from the other two. There is nothing sacrosanct about the triad. It is equally reasonable to use two elements for elicitation or more than three as in Kelly's Full Context Form.

By dyads of elements

Although many people use triadic elicitation methods, some have indeed found this too complex a cognitive task for certain groups. Salmon (1976) cites a study by Allison (1972) in which two elements at a time are compared rather than three, as this seemed an easier task for children.

In their dyad grid, Ryle and Lunghi (1970) use interpersonal relationships as elements. The elements might thus be self-to-Peter, Peter-to-self, self-to-Paul, Paul-to-self, and so on. Because it was found too difficult a task for the subject to be presented with triads of such elements, Ryle also suggests presenting only two at a time. The method of elicitation involves asking for some important way in which the relationship of self-to-Paul is similar to or differs from the relationship to Peter-to-Self, and so on.

By laddering

This is a procedure described by Hinkle (1965) for eliciting increasingly superordinate constructs; that is, constructs of a higher order of abstraction than those elicited from triads or dyads of elements. This procedure involves first eliciting constructs in the usual manner and then asking the person to say by which pole of each construct they would prefer to be described. Hinkle's standard instructions are:

"Now on this construct you preferred this side to that side. What I want to understand now is why you would prefer to be here rather than there . . . What are the advantages of this side in contrast to the disadvantages of that side as you see it?" (Hinkle, 1965, pp. 32-33).

The answer given is another construct superordinate to the first and which also has a preferred side. The question "why" is again asked about the preferred side of this new construct. The question "why" is asked of each new construct until the person is unable (or unwilling) to produce more.

For example, with different types of camera lens as elements, the laddering was carried out from the elicited construct *shows more than can be seen by the naked eye—shows what can be seen with the naked eye*. The preference was for lenses showing more than can be seen by the naked eye and, when asked why, she replied that one *might see something new* whereas there was no chance of seeing something new with the other type of lens. Why was it important *for her* to have a chance of seeing something new? You *might stumble across a mystery—something you could not explain*. Why was this important? It *put you in your place* whereas otherwise you could *think you were master of everything*. Why was it important to be put in your place from time to time? Because *only God has the answer to everything and you need to be reminded of that.*

As the organisation corollary would lead one to expect, as this questioning is repeated with each successive subordinate construct there is an increasing tendency for the same superordinate constructs to be eventually reached.

A person can be encouraged to ladder "downwards" by asking such questions as "how do you know when a person is X?" or "what would be evidence that a person is X?". Honikman (1976) did this in his study of people's views on living-rooms. By asking why a particular room was considered say, *formal,* he found the answers always ended up with physical characteristics, e.g. rough bricks.

Sometimes it is difficult to make out precisely what the person is trying to convey as they go "up" the ladder. In these cases, the following comments can be useful.

(i) You can say "I think I understand what you mean, but, just to make sure, would you please say what you had in mind again". Very often, in repeating the discrimination, the person will be able to tighten up his construing and rephrase the construct in half-a-dozen words.

(ii) If you are in doubt whether or not you understand the construct, the stated opposite pole of the construct will often clarify it for you.

(iii) If in doubt, or you feel the words are too vague, you can ask whether he is really saying X, when you are pretty sure that X is not the case. By being given an indication of what the construct is not, the person is often able to tighten sufficiently to tell you what it really is.

By constructing pyramids

This is another way, suggested by Landfield (1971), of avoiding the more formal approach of Kelly's Minimum Context Form of elicitation. In this pyramid procedure, the person may first be asked to think of someone he knows, with whom he feels most comfortable and whose company he most enjoys. The name is unimportant to the interviewer, but it is useful to know whether the person being thought of is male or female. It is important that the person understands that he has only to focus on one aspect of the acquaintance. He should also

"be encouraged to say whatever comes into his mind and not to be concerned if he gives repetitive responses later in the procedure. When the client feels he should react more rapidly or finds it difficult to think of the most appropriate words or expressions, he is reassured by being told that the task is a new experience and most people have this difficulty (which is true)". (p. 135).

When the person has named the characteristic he is asked to state what kind of person would represent the opposite of that characteristic. When the two construct poles have been elicited, the interviewer returns to the first pole and asks what kind of person an X is. In Landfield's example, the construct first elicited was *open-closed*. When asked what kind of person an *open* person is, the client answered that "he is willing to listen to you". He was then asked to state what kind of person does not listen to one. And the reply was "someone not interested in me". The reply to the question about what kind of person a *closed* person is was "somebody people do not like" and this in turn is "someone that does not like me". Schematically the pattern is thus:

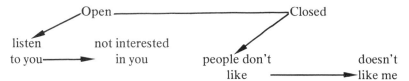

A third level can then be elicited by asking about each construct pole at the second level; for example, "how would you know that a person is not listening to you". One is here eliciting increasingly subordinate (concretistic) constructs.

Other pyramids can be formed by this method of elicitation and the constructs, as with the other forms, put into some form of grid. This procedure has much in common with Hinkle's laddering, with Hinkle taking the person "up" a ladder and Landfield taking him "down". Both methods can also become an integral part of psychotherapy as both parties learn from the experience. Both can also be used as part of any general interviewing procedure.

The self characterisation

This last example of methods for eliciting constructs is self-characterisation. It is by no means as structured and "tidy" as those previously mentioned. But as a means of coming to understand something of the constructs used by another to construe the world it is well worthy of consideration. The instructions for this are:

"I want you to write a character sketch of Harry Brown, just as if he were the principal character in a play. Write it as it might be written by a friend who knew him *intimately* and very *sympathetically,* perhaps better than anyone ever really could know him. Be sure to write it in the third person. For example, start out by saying 'Harry Brown is . . .'."

The person would, of course, substitute his own name for the mythical Harry Brown. Kelly chose the words with care. "Sketch" was to suggest that general structure rather than elaborate details were to be described. Emphasis on the third person was to indicate that it was not to be a chronicle of faults or virtues, but rather to be a view of the whole. Other phrases were calculated to reduce the threat implicit in such an activity, to enable the person to give speculations as well as facts.

If particular areas of life are of interest then the wording can be altered.

For instance, the sketch can be of the person as he was before being ill, as he will be after this episode in his life, as he will be after this period of his education, or in ten years time, or in a particular professional role (e.g. Psychologist), or whatever. Of all methods of elicitation mentioned so far, this imposes the least structure or restrictions on the individual.

When thinking about eliciting constructs, it must never be forgotten that all of us do it all the time, whether in the more structured interview situation or in plain everyday conversation and discussion.

TO ELICIT OR TO SUPPLY CONSTRUCTS?

Quite a literature has developed over the question whether or not supplied or provided constructs give the same answers as do elicited constructs. Bear in mind here that one is essentially supplying the verbal label to which the person will attach his personal construct; what is essential is that the labels be meaningful to the subject. Provided labels may range from those that are identical with those normally used by the subject to constructs that are gibberish to him. These could be constructs with verbal labels in a foreign language or constructs from specialised subsystems containing jargon. All constructs are "personal" in the sense that the person is able to place the construct's dimension over events and make something of them. Kelly's Individuality Corollary states that "Persons differ from each other in their construction of events". Another's constructs may not be precisely as useful to you as your own are.

There seems to be no need to be pedantic. For some purposes, it is best to supply construct labels, at least in part. People may not give you constructs which you have reason for suspecting are very important to them. This is particularly so in the field of clinical work. You may be testing out an idea about why a person is behaving as she is. It may be vital for you to supply her with certain constructs which will then be given personal meaning by being related to those elicited from her. It is, for example, usual to supply constructs to do with various aspects of the self (e.g. like me in character, like I'd like to be in character, as others see me, etc.). For some experimental purposes, for example in the study of language, it is necessary to compare the relationship between specific verbal labels. In such cases it is clearly essential to supply these labels. If you are in doubt about what kind of constructs are applicable to a certain group of people, it is common practice to collect a sample of constructs from a comparable group or the group itself. You are then fairly safe in assuming that the most commonly used constructs for that group will be meaningful to the individual. But as they have been selected from a common elicited pool they are not, in any simple sense, either "provided" or "elicited".

If there is some doubt about the meaningfulness of a construct for an individual you can then refer to the individual. Salmon (1976) recommends that the meaningfulness of a provided construct for a child be tried out. She gives the example of the child whose difficulty in accepting a new sibling is under investigation. The psychologist may wish to supply the construct *feels jealous of the baby-is glad about the baby*. The meaningfulness of this construct can be tested by asking the child directly whether it makes sense. For instance, by saying "do you know what I mean when I say . . .?".

A more detailed discussion of the differences that have been obtained using elicited and provided constructs and the suggested reasons for these differences can be found in Chapter 8, pp. 106-107 and in the concluding chapter.

TYPES OF CONSTRUCT

Methods of modification

Not all constructs elicited are useful in a particular grid format. Kelly (1955) quotes Hunt as having suggested ways of dealing with this problem. Hunt's suggestions are as follows:

(i) *Excessively permeable constructs:*
"These two are alike, they are both men". The examiner may record the response but say "That is *one* way in which they are alike. Can you tell me some psychological characteristic in their both being men that makes them alike, or can you tell me any *other* way in which they are alike?" (Such a construct discrimination would not always be rejected. To say that two elements are alike because they are men and the third is different because she is a woman is a vitally important difference. You may well decide to accept such a construct and use it in the grid you are designing because of its important implications.)

(ii) *Situational constructs:*
"These two are alike; they're both from the same town." The procedure described in (i) can be used.

(iii) *Excessively impermeable constructs:*
The person may say, "These two are tool makers and the other is a die maker". Again, the same procedure as above can be used.

(iv) *Superficial constructs:*
"They both have the same colour eyes". Again, proceed as above.

(v) *Vague constructs:*
"They're both O.K." The examiner can ask the person to explain further and to give possible examples of other people who are O.K.

(vi) *Constructs which are a direct product of the role title or element:*
"Both are hard to understand". The examiner may then say "Is there something about their being hard to understand which seems to be alike?"

These are just some ways of dealing with such constructs. But it must always be borne in mind that what seems superficial or vague to you as examiner may be neither superficial nor vague to your subject. An easy relationship and a free-flow of discussion between examiner and subject is the best basis for construct elicitation.

Classification

Landfield (1971) has provided the first attempt at the systematic categorisation of elicited constructs. He provides 22 categories, each with a definition and examples. For example, Social Interaction is defined as "any statement in which face-to-face, ongoing, continuing interaction with others is (clearly) indicated". Examples of active statements concerning social interaction are *aggressive, brotherly, engaged* and *extrovert.*

Landfield has done some work on examining the implications of these categories. That is, relating them, for instance, to sex of subject and to likelihood of change in therapy. Landfield also reports some interscorer reliabilities for the different categories. What he is doing here is putting the commonality corollary into effect; "to the extent that one person employs a construction of experience which is similar to that employed by another, his psychological processes are similar to those of the other person". But the use of similar verbal labels does not necessarily mean similarity of construing. This may be part of the reason why Fransella (1972) found that a substantial minority of constructs of a British sample appeared to fit several categories. It is often said that Americans and British do not speak the same language although they use the same words.

But in spite of some difficulties in using the categories as they at present exist, Landfield has made a most important contribution to our understanding of construct classification. As an example of possible use, Fransella (1972) found that, for a sample of 19 stutterers, 11.6 per cent of constructs fitted the "high social interaction" category and 27.6 per cent the "low social interaction" category. This makes an interesting comparison with some of Landfield's data showing that, for 30 college students, 11 per cent of the constructs were in the "high social interaction" category and only 1 per cent in the "low" category. This difference can be explained on common sense grounds as those with communication problems are likely to be conscious of, hence construe, relationships in which they play a subordinate role.

Liftshitz (1974) used a construct classification system in studying the differences between the construing of social worker trainees and their supervisors. She showed that the trainees more often use concretistic constructs (e.g. age and sex) and supervisors more abstract constructs.

Whole figure constructs

It is possible to use people in a grid, either as elements or as constructs. Elements can be ranked (or rated) according to how *like mother in character* they are, or else "mother" can be one of the elements ranked according to certain constructs. Figures are often used as constructs and this can prove rewarding but there are problems. A discussion of available studies as well as speculations about this type of construct and its inherent problems can be found in Chapter 8 (p. 107).

COMMENT

There are some rules about the elements and constructs to be used in any grid. As one develops new methods and forms of grid, new questions are bound to arise. Provided one goes back to the theory when in doubt, these problems should be soluble. However, if no reference is made to the theory, it is possible to paint oneself into a corner. This has happened to some extent already. There are those who assume that there are such things as elements that are nothing but elements (a piece of pre-emptive construing) and constructs that are only constructs. There are also those who have been involved in measuring cognitive complexity, until so many measures have been introduced without recourse to the theory that no one is now sure what the measures measure (see Chapter 4).

3

Varieties of Grid in Use Today

But we can look beyond words. We can study contexts. For example, does the client use the word "affectionate" only when talking about persons of the opposite sex? Does he apply the term "sympathetic" only to members of his own family or only to persons who have also been described as "intimate"? The answers to questions such as these may give us an understanding of the interweaving of the client's terminology and provide us with an understanding of his outlook which no dictionary could offer. (Kelly, 1955, p. 267).

GRID FORM OF THE ROLE CONSTRUCT REPERTORY TEST

In this long and occasionally long-winded chapter, it is our intention to take you by the hand and lead you through the complexities of actually getting down to doing a grid. The repertory grid, as we know it today, is an extension of the Role Construct Repertory Test (Rep Test) which Kelly developed for "looking beyond the words". The Rep Test was concerned solely with the elicitation of constructs (see Chapter 2).

We are now concerned with the basic methodology Kelly offered for deriving a mathematical description of part of a person's psychological space; a basic assumption being that a mathematical relationship between a person's judgments reflects psychological assumptions underlying those judgments.

The grid form of the role construct repertory test has been elaborated in many ways, some of which will be described in detail. First we describe Kelly's original grid form.

The figure list

The first job for the individual completing this form of grid is to fill in the relevant names for the Figure List given to the subject in the form shown in Fig. 2.

The instructions are:

"Beginning with your own name, write the first names of the persons described. Write their names in the blanks provided. If you cannot remember a person's first name, write his last name or something about him which will clearly bring to your mind the person's identity" (Kelly, 1955, p. 272).

22	21	20	19	18	17	16	15	14	13	12	11	10	9	8	7	6	5	4	3	2	1	FIG. NO	CONSTRUCT		
O		O			O																	1		Se	1
		O				O									O	O						2		Mo	2
		O					O								O		O					3		Fa	3
				O					O		O			O			O					4		Br	4
				O							O	O					O					5		Si	5
O					O	O	O							O								6		Sp	6
	O				O	O								O								7		XF	7
O				O							O			O								8		Pa	8
				O					O		O											9		Xp	9
																						10	MF	Mi	10
																						11	MF	MD	11
																						12	MF	Ne	12
	O									O	O					O						13	MF	RP	13
	O	O							O							O						14	MF	PP	14
			O						O	O												15	MF	UP	15
		O				O										O						16	MF	AP	16
											O	O					O					17	MF	AT	17
									O	O						O						18	MF	RT	18
		O											O			O						19	MF	Bo	19
		O											O								O	20	MF	SP	20
								O								O					O	21	MF	HP	21
		O							O												O	22	MF	EP	22
22	21	20	19	18	17	16	15	14	13	12	11	10	9	8	7	6	5	4	3	2	1	SORT NO.			

Name

Date

CONSTRUCT

CONTRAST

Fig. 1. The format of Kelly's Role Construct Repertory Test (from Kelly, 1955, p. 270).

FIGURE LIST SHEET

1. Write your own name in the first blank here.
2. Write your mother's first name here. If you grew up with a stepmother, write her name instead.
3. Write your father's first name here. If you grew up with a stepfather, write his name instead.
4. Write the name of your brother who is nearest your own age. If you had no brother, write the name of a boy near your own age who was most like a brother to you during your early teens.
5. Write the name of your sister who is nearest your own age. If you had no sister, write the name of a girl near your own age who was most like a sister to you during your early teens.

FROM THIS POINT ON DO NOT REPEAT ANY NAMES IF A PERSON HAS ALREADY BEEN LISTED, SIMPLY MAKE A SECOND CHOICE.

6. Your wife (or husband) or, if you are not married, your closest present girl (boy) friend.
7. Your closest girl (boy) friend immediately preceding the person mentioned above.
8. Your closest present friend of the same sex as yourself.
9. A person of the same sex as yourself whom you once thought was a close friend but in whom you were badly disappointed later.
10. The minister, priest, or rabbi with whom you would be most willing to talk over your personal feelings about religion.
11. Your physician.
12. The present neighbour whom you know best.
13. A person with whom you have been associated who, for some unexplained reason, appeared to dislike you.
14. A person whom you would most like to help or for whom you feel sorry.
15. A person with whom you usually feel most uncomfortable.
16. A person whom you have recently met whom you would like to know better.
17. The teacher who influenced you most when you were in your teens.
18. The teacher whose point of view you have found most objectionable.
19. An employer, supervisor, or officer under whom you served during a period of great stress.
20. The most successful person whom you know personally.
21. The happiest person whom you know personally.
22. The person known to you personally who appears to meet the highest ethical standards.

Fig. 2. Figure List for Kelly's Role Construct Repertory Test (from Kelly, 1955, p. 270).

The person is told that the examiner is not interested in the names themselves. The grid is presented to the person as shown in Figs 1 and 2.

Kelly offered a rationale for each of the triads (or sorts) which the person being examined is asked to compare and they are grouped under seven headings:

SELF
1. Self

FAMILY
2. Mother
3. Father
4. Brother
5. Sister

INTIMATES
6. Spouse
7. Ex-flame
8. Pal
9. Ex-pal

SITUATIONALS
10. Minister
11. Physician
12. Neighbour

VALENCIES
13. Rejecting Person
14. Pitied Person
15. Threatening Person
15. Attractive Person

AUTHORITIES
17. Accepted Teacher
18. Rejected Teacher
19. Boss

VALUES
20. Successful Person
21. Happy Person
22. Ethical Person

The rationale for each of the triads is given as follows:

1. *Value Sort.* The client is asked to compare and contrast representatives of success, happiness, and ethics.

2. *Authority Sort.* The client is asked to compare and contrast a person whose ideas he accepted, a person whose ideas he rejected, even though he was expected to accept them, and a person whose support was badly needed at some period in his life.

3. *Valency Sort.* The client is asked to compare and contrast a person whose rejection of him he cannot quite understand, a person whom he thinks needs him, and a person whom he does not really know well but whom he thinks he would like to know better. All three of these are somewhat phantom figures and one may expect that in interpreting them the client relies heavily upon projected attitudes.

4. *Intimacy Sort.* This is a more difficult sort involving the Spouse, the Ex-flame, and the Pal. It tends to bring out features of personal conflict, both between the client's attitude toward two intimate figures of the opposite sex and also between an intimate figure of the opposite sex and an intimate figure of the same sex.

5. *Family Sort.* This sort involves the Father, Mother, and Brother figures. It is an invitation to form a construct which governs the client's relationship within his family.

6. *Sister Sort.* This is an invitation to construe a Sister figure. It provides an opportunity to see the Sister as like the Accepted Teacher and in contrast to

the Happy Person, like the Happy Person and in contrast to the Accepted Teacher or in contrast to both of them.

7. *Mother Sort.* Here the comparison figures are the person in whom the client was once disillusioned and the person whose teaching was highly acceptable.

8. *Father Sort.* Here the comparison figures are the Boss and the Successful Person.

9. *Brother Sort.* The comparison figures are the person who appeared to reject the client and the teacher whom the client himself rejected.

10. *Sister Sort.* The comparison figures are the same as for the Brother sort.

11. *Kindliness Sort.* The Sister, Pitied Person, and Ethical Person are thrown into context.

12. *Threat Sort.* The client has an opportunity to construe threat in the context of the Brother, Ex-pal, and Threatening Person.

13. *Spouse Sort.* The Spouse figure is compared and contrasted with the Threatening Person and the Happy Person.

14. *Mating Sort I.* The Mother is placed in context with the Spouse and the Ex-flame.

15. *Mating Sort II.* The Father is placed in a similar context.

16. *Companionship Sort.* The Pal, Ex-pal, and Attractive Person are placed in context.

17. *Sibling Sort.* The Self, Brother, and Sister are compared and contrasted.

18. *Achievement Sort.* The Boss, Successful Person, and Ethical Person are placed in context.

19. *Parental Preference Sort.* The Mother and Father are placed in context with the Threatening Person.

20. *Need Sort.* The Self is compared and contrasted with the Pitied Person and the Attractive Person. This gives the clinician an opportunity to study the relatively subjective and objective reference which the client gives to his personal needs.

21. *Compensatory Sort.* By placing the Ex-flame, the Rejecting Person, and the Pitied Person in the same context the clinician can sometimes get some understanding of how the client reacts to the loss of relationship.

22. *Identification Sort.* This is a crucial sort. It involves the Self, the Spouse, and the Pal. From it one sometimes gains an understanding of the client's domestic difficulties. (Kelly, 1955, pp. 275-277).

The grid

Constructs are elicited by asking whether two of the three people indicated by circles (see grid in Fig. 1) in the first row are "alike in some important way that distinguishes them from the third person". When a decision has been made, the person is told to put an "X" in the two circles corresponding to the two people who are alike and to place no mark in the third circle. The person is then asked to write a word or short phrase description under "construct" indicating in what way the two are alike. The opposite of the characteristic is then written under "contrast". The next step is to place a " $\sqrt{}$ " under the name of every other person who has this important characteristic.

The second row is now considered, with people 17, 18 and 19 forming the triad. Again an "X" is placed under those two who are alike in some important way and this characteristic is written under "construct" and its opposite under "contrast". Other people in line 2 who have this characteristic are given a " $\sqrt{}$ " also. The rest of the grid is completed in this way.

The output

Kelly's example grid can be seen in Fig. 3. We have selected this as the example so that we can show some of the ways he thought it might be analysed and the sort of information it offered.

He suggested that grids should first be looked at without their statistical nightshirts to see something of what the person is actually telling one directly. Quite clearly, whenever we look at a grid in its naked form or at the statistical outputs, we look through our own system of constructs. We select what we shall look at and determine what we shall consider important.

Kelly pointed out that in this grid (Fig. 3) some of the constructs are situational rather than social or psychological in nature. But even though they appear situational, it is possible that they are applied in an abstract manner. It is also possible that constructs seeming to be repetitions may be applied differently. Although 14 and 15 have the same verbal labels, they are not applied in the same way. Mother in 14 is one of the "Not girls"—perhaps she is not young—whereas in 15 she is one of the "Both girls"—perhaps she is feminine. It is also necessary to bear in mind that the person named as the Sister was a male. The subject did not have a sister and so selected a person who had played the part of a sister in his life.

But to go one step further, without resorting to a computer for assistance, it is possible to obtain matching scores between any pair of rows. If you take a piece of paper and place it below the first row of ticks and blanks and mark each tick or cross on your piece of paper, then move this paper one row down, you can count up the number of times blanks and ticks/crosses correspond in rows 1 and 2. Taking chance matching to be half the total possible (19 in this case) the probability of actual matching scores or lack of them can be calculated. This is done by expanding the binomial $(p + q)^n$. Just as the rows can be inspected for degree of matching ticks and blanks to find out how the constructs relate to each other, so the same method can be used for the columns to find out how the person sees the people in his life compared with each other. Kelly describes a method of non-parametric factor analysis for extracting the major dimensions the person uses to order his social world. But many people may want to stop at matching scores and simply "eye-ball" the matrix of matching scores to find out, say, which construct is most highly matched with all other constructs and which element most highly matched

FAMILY — INTIMATES — VALENCES — AUTHORITIES — VALUES

1	self	FAMILY
2	mother	
3	father	
4	brother	
5	sister	
6	spouse	INTIMATES
7	ex-flame	
8	pal	
9	ex-pal	
10	rejecting person	VALENCES
11	pitied person	
12	threatening person	
13	attractive person	
14	accepted teacher	AUTHORITIES
15	rejected teacher	
16	boss	
17	successful person	VALUES
18	happy person	
19	ethical person	

— CONSTRUCTS —

SORT NO.	EMERGENT POLE	IMPLICIT POLE
1	Don't believe in God	Very religious
2	Same sort of education	Completely different education
3	Not athletic	Athletic
4	Both girls	A boy
5	Parents	Ideas different
6	Understand me better	Don't understand at all
7	Teach the right thing	Teach the wrong thing
8	Achieved a lot	Hasn't achieved a lot
9	Higher education	No education
10	Don't like other people	Like other people
11	More religious	Not religious
12	Believe in higher education	Not believing in too much education
13	More sociable	Not sociable
14	Both girls	Not girls
15	Both girls	Not girls
16	Both have high morals	Low morals
17	Think alike	Think differently
18	Same age	Different ages
19	Believe the same about me	Believe differently about me
20	Both friends	Not friends
21	More understanding	Less understanding
22	Both appreciate music	Don't understand music

Fig. 3. An example of a completed Role Construct Repertory Test (from Kelly, 1955, p. 270).

with all other elements. A great deal of information can be got by simple arithmetic, but if you want to go into, say, the factor structure of the grid or analyse a large number of grids, it may be best to resort to a friendly computer (see Chapter 5 for some programme suggestions).

One problem experienced by Kelly with this grid was the fact that sometimes a person would see hardly any other people as being characterised by one pole of a construct. Construct 12 (Fig. 3) is lopsided in showing only three people *not believing in too much education.* Kelly suggested that these rows should be eliminated from grid calculations, but Bannister (1959) suggested an alternative method. The subject could be asked to allocate the elements equally to the emergent and implicit poles of each construct. While this does away with the necessity of eliminating those rows with few ticks or blanks, it imposes considerable constraint on the subject.

A RANK ORDER GRID

This method was suggested by Phillida Salmon and first described in Bannister (1963). It arose out of an attempt to deal with the lopsidedness problem and has stayed as the method of choice for many since that time, particularly in Europe. Perhaps one of its attractions is the range of scoring procedures possible, particularly scores that can be obtained without recourse to Aldous, the Personable Computer (Kelly, 1963). The basic task facing the subject is to rank in order those elements most readily subsumed under the emergent pole of the construct to those most readily subsumed under the contrast pole (e.g. from most *generous* to most *mean*).

As the grid has been used more extensively there has been a tendency to abandon the use of a role title list. Clearly a role title list as such is not sacred and Kelly's orginal offered certain problems, such as the fact that "a minister" is not such a common figure in the personal experience of Europeans as it is for Americans. However, the purpose of the role title list—to ensure that the elements are *representative* of the area of construing under consideration—still needs to be served. This applies whatever the elements. If we are interested in people's attitudes to different types of bread then the elements can reasonably be different types of bread, just as when we are interested in ideas about people or relationships, then the elements need to be people or relationships between people as in the dyad grid. But again we always face the problem of whether the elements are a reasonably representative sample for the person who is completing the grid. There is no reason why the subject cannot be directly questioned as to the representative-ness of the sample, just as he can be questioned about whether each element is properly within the range of convenience of the constructs which are being applied. But what does seem essential is that we do not discard the role title list procedure for reasons of convenience and then neglect any kind of check on the appropriateness and representative qualities of the elements in the grid. grid.

The elements and constructs

Suppose you want to find out how a person views particular situations; maybe situations which are related to some annoying or undesirable behaviour, such as stuttering. Then the elements could conveniently be those specific situations. In the following rank order grid, the elements are situations known to be related to the severity of this particular man's stuttering. The constructs were either elicited by the triadic method or else supplied because they were known from interviews to be important.

Each element (E) is written on a separate card and given a number ranging from 1 to 11, written on the *back*. The reason why the element number should be on the back is because the person might find himself ranking by learning the order of the numbers rather than by construing the elements. The elements in this case are:

E1   Talking into the microphone of a tape recorder
E2   Talking to friends or people I know
E3   Talking to strangers
E4   Talking to one person
E5   Talking to a few people
E6   Talking to a large group
E7   Talking to older men
E8   Talking to young men
E9   Talking to older women
E10 Talking into the telephone
E11 Talking to young women

Each construct is also written on a small card and given a number, written on the *front*. The constructs in this example are:

C1   *Situation likely to involve someone in authority over you or senior to you*
C2   *Situation in which you would find it difficult to see or interpret the person's reactions*
C3   *Situation in which you would be most likely to stammer*
C4   *Situation in which you would be most likely to feel confident*
C5   *Situation in which you would be most likely to resent your stammer*
C6   *Situation in which you would be likely to feel anxious or uneasy*
C7   *Situation in which the person would be likely to be critical of you*
C8   *Situation likely to involve your wanting to make a good impression*
C9   *Situation in which the person or people would be likely to think the worse of you if you stammer*

The grid

The rank order grid is compiled in the following manner. All 11 element cards for the grid shown in Fig. 4 are laid out on the table in front of the person. Construct card 1 is placed before him. He is asked to name or point to that element which is best described by the construct. In this case he is asked which of the 11 elements is most likely *to involve someone in authority over you, or senior to you.* He pointed to element 10 "when talking to people on the telephone". That element card is removed from the table and he is asked to point to the card, among the remaining ten, that describes the situation most likely *to involve someone in authority over you, or senior to you.* He points to element 7 "when talking to older men". This card is now removed leaving nine on the table. He is now asked to point to that card from the remaining nine that is most related to construct 1 and so on until there is only one card left on the table.

Constructs

		1	2	3	4	5	6	7	8	9
	1st	10	10	10	2	11	10	10	11	10
	2nd	7	1	1	5	6	3	3	10	6
	3rd	3	3	6	4	10	6	6	6	5
	4th	9	7	5	11	9	5	9	7	3
Elements	5th	1	9	3	9	3	1	7	3	11
	6th	8	8	7	7	7	9	5	5	9
	7th	6	4	9	8	8	11	11	9	8
	8th	11	11	8	3	4	8	8	8	7
	9th	5	5	2	1	5	7	4	4	4
	10th	4	6	11	6	1	4	2	1	2
	11th	2	2	4	10	2	2	1	2	1

Fig. 4. Rankings of 11 elements in a rank order grid by one person (matrix consists of *element numbers*).

When all 11 cards have been ranked on construct 1, they are returned to the table but in altered positions (so that the person does not obtain spurious correlations by simply pointing to cards moving from left to right and so forth). Thus, the grid in Fig. 4 is made up of the 11 elements which have been ranked in relation to each of the 9 constructs.

Now that we have a matrix of rankings, they can be transcribed into rank orders for each element so that the relationships between the rankings can be statistically analysed. The matrix of transcribed rankings shown in Fig. 5 is constructed as follows: under construct 1, look for the rank that element 1 is given. It is placed 5th. Thus, in the new matrix, in the intersect for element 1 and construct 1 the figure 5 is written. Element 2 on construct 1 is given the rank of 11 and so on. Thus constructs are along the top, elements down the side and the body of the matrix gives the rank position of the elements on the constructs.

The output

The rank order grid lends itself to several forms of analysis, both by hand and computer methods. For instance, one hand method described by Bannister (1965a) was designed to give a visual display of construct relationships. Rank order correlations are run by hand between each pair of rankings. The two constructs accounting for most of the variance are extracted to form the main dimensions. The second axis is taken to be that accounting for most of the common variance after the first has been taken out, but which is statistically independent of it. What follows is a detailed analysis by this method of the matrix in Fig. 5.

		Constructs							
		1	2	3	4	5	6	7	8	9
	1	5	2	2	9	10	5	11	10	11
	2	11	11	9	1	11	11	10	11	10
	3	3	3	5	8	5	2	2	5	4
	4	10	7	11	3	8	10	9	9	9
Elements	5	9	9	4	2	9	4	6	6	3
	6	7	10	3	10	2	3	3	3	2
	7	2	4	6	6	6	9	5	4	8
	8	6	6	8	7	7	8	8	8	7
	9	4	5	7	5	4	6	4	7	6
	10	1	1	1	11	3	1	1	2	1
	11	8	8	10	4	1	7	7	1	5

Fig. 5. Eleven elements ranked in a rank order grid by one person (matrix consists of *ranks*).

Rank order correlations are calculated by the formula $1 - \dfrac{6\Sigma d^2}{n^3 - n}$ (Spearman's rho). Table I sets out the calculations for running a correlation between construct ranks 1 and 2 from the grid in Fig. 5. Take the difference between each pair of elements, square it and sum the squared differences ($\Sigma d^2 = 32$). This sum of squared differences is then multiplied by 6 (192) and divided by the cube of the number of elements ($n = 11$) minus the number of elements (1320). This figure is then subtracted from 1.0 (rho = 0.855).

Correlations cannot be directly added in that form, but they can be if squared. If you then multiply each by 100 to remove the decimal point you have a "relationship score". However, although this squaring removes the sign, making all such scores positive, since the score has psychological significance, the sign must be retained. For example, *kindness* and *selfishness* may correlate —0.90 and so have a relationship score of 81. But when it comes to plotting these, or to considering their psychological significance, the fact that their relationship is a negative and not a positive one is important. Table II gives the rho correlations between each pair of constructs forming the situation grid in Fig. 5 plus the relationship score of each.

Table I

The steps in the computation of Spearman's rho rank order correlation.

Constructs		d	d²
1	2	(differences)	(differences squared)
5	2	3	9
11	11	0	0
3	3	0	0
10	7	3	9
9	9	0	0
7	10	3	9
2	4	2	4
6	6	0	0
4	5	1	1
1	1	0	0
8	8	0	0
			$\Sigma\,d^2 = 32$

$$\text{rho} = 1 - \frac{6\,\Sigma\,d^2}{n^3 - n} = 1 - \frac{6 \times 32}{1331 - 11} = 1 - \frac{192}{1320} = 1 - 0.145$$

$$\text{rho} = 0.855$$

The relationship scores for each construct can now be summed to give the total variance accounted for by that construct. The rho's and relationship scores for constructs 1 to 3 have been laid out in full in Table II. You will see that 2-1 is given under construct 1 and again for construct 2 and 3-1 and 3-2 are repeated for construct 3, for it is easy to forget that the sum of relationship scores for construct 8 also includes its relationship with preceding constructs.

It is now possible to plot these constructs along two axes. The construct yielding the highest sum of relationship scores forms the first axis. It is the construct that is most closely related to all other constructs. The second axis is that construct accounting for the next highest amount of variance (having the next highest sum of relationship scores) but which is not significantly correlated with the first construct. From Table II it can be seen that

Table II
Rhos, relationship scores and sums of relationship scores for each pair of element
rankings in the rank order grid in Fig. 5. The full sets of correlations are given for
constructs 1, 2 and 3 only.

Constructs	rho	rho² × 100	Constructs	rho	rho² × 100
1—2	0.86	74	2—1	0.86	74
1—3	0.58	34	2—3	0.48	23
1—4	−0.74	−55	2—4	−0.64	−41
1—5	0.42	18	2—5	0.13	2
1—6	0.54	29	2—6	0.44	19
1—7	0.64	41	2—7	0.31	10
1—8	0.44	19	2—8	0.14	2
1—9	0.32	10	2—9	0.03	0
		280			171
3—1	0.58	34	4—5	−0.46	−21
3—2	0.48	23	4—6	−0.70	−49
3—4	−0.73	−53	4—7	−0.52	−27
3—5	0.10	1	4—8	−0.41	−17
3—6	0.81	66	4—9	−0.40	−16
3—7	0.46	21			
3—8	0.26	7			279
3—9	0.45	20			
		225			
5—6	0.46	21	6—7	0.72	52
5—7	0.71	50	6—8	0.54	29
5—8	0.88	77	6—9	0.77	59
5—9	0.69	48			
		238			324
7—8	0.74	55	8—9	0.78	61
7—9	0.85	72			
		328			267

9 = 286

construct 7 accounts for the most variance and so forms the first axis in Fig.
6, and construct 3 has the next highest total relationship score which is not
significantly (e.g. p<.05) correlated with construct 7. Constructs 6, 9, 1, 4
and 8 were not used to form the second axis, although contruct 4 could have
been; but 3 was favoured because of its central psychological importance.
    This simple form of cluster analysis gives virtually identical results to that

obtained by, for example, a principal components analysis. A comparison between this hand method and Slater's INGRID principal components analysis programme (1964) showed the first axis and first component to correlate 0.95 and the second axis and component 0.77 (Fransella, 1965). So the only substantial difference between the hand and computer methods is that, with the latter, scores and relationships between elements can be easily obtained.

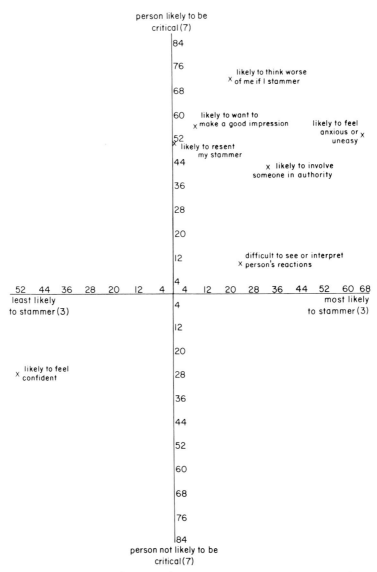

Fig. 6. Constructs plotted along the two main construct axes in terms of "relationship scores".

Another type of hand scoring enables one to quantify the distance between each element in relation to a particular construct (Fransella, 1972). If one is, as in this example, concerned with situations that are likely to provoke stuttering in an individual, then it may be useful to get an idea as to the size of the perceived difference between each situation before proceeding with, say, treatment by graduated desensitisation. The steps in the procedure to derive a measure of perceived distance between elements (a stutter-provoking score in this instance) are as follows:

1. Note the correlations of all constructs with the construct *likely to make me stammer* (construct 3 in this case). Note that construct 3 will correlate 1.00 with itself.
2. Change correlations to relationship scores (rho^2 $\times$ 100).
3. Note the ranked position of element 1 on construct 1. Figure 5 shows this to be 5th.
4. Divide the relationship score for constructs 1 to 3 by 5 (34 ÷ 5 = 6.8).
5. Now note the ranked position for element 1 on construct 2. It is ranked 2nd.
6. Divide the relationship score for constructs 2 to 3 by 2 (23 ÷ 2 = 11.5).
7. Continue in this way until element 1 has a score on all constructs. Now add up all these scores. This gives the stutter-provoking score which, for element 1, is 80.1.

Scores for all elements can be seen in Table III.

What is being done here is to take as a central construct that which most completely expresses the "perception" being investigated. Since in this case we are interested in what situations provoke stuttering then construct 3 *likely to make me stammer* has been chosen. Each situation (element) is then given a score which is the sum of its position on construct 3 plus its position on all other constructs when they have been given a weighting which exactly reflects their relationship to construct 3. Thus the method aims to assess the "stutter-provoking" potential of each situation in terms of the whole network. The results show clearly that talking into a telephone is seen as far and away the most likely situation to provoke severe stuttering. And the gap between that and the next in line, talking to strangers is very great. We would like to stress that this score has not to date been validated.
been validated.

A last example of the type of score one can obtain by hand from a rank order grid is in the so-called "group" grid (see for example Fransella, 1970; Watson, 1970a; Fransella and Joyston-Bechal, 1971). The subjects completing the grids are members of a group and the essential feature is that the elements are the members of the group and include the member completing the grid. Thus, in a patient group of eight, the elements will be the seven other group members and "me". Watson (1970a) used the therapist as one of the elements, but Fransella and Joyston-Bechal (1971) argued that it was more than possible that the therapist was seen as such a different being from

Table III

Stutter-provoking scores calculated from the rank order grid of a stutterer given in Fig. 5.

Constructs	rho² × 100	Elements										
		1	2	3	4	5	6	7	8	9	10	11
1—3	34	6.8	3.1	11.3	3.4	3.8	4.9	17.0	5.7	8.5	34.0	4.3
2—3	23	11.5	2.1	7.7	3.3	2.6	2.3	5.8	3.8	4.6	23.0	2.9
3—3	100	50.0	11.1	20.0	9.1	25.0	33.3	16.7	12.5	14.3	100.0	10.0
4—3	−53	−5.9	−53.0	−6.6	−17.7	−26.5	−5.3	−8.8	−7.6	−10.6	−4.8	−13.3
5—3	1	0.1	0.0	0.2	0.1	0.1	0.5	0.2	0.1	0.3	0.3	1.0
6—3	66	13.2	6.0	33.0	6.6	16.5	22.0	7.3	8.3	11.0	66.0	9.4
7—3	21	1.9	2.1	10.5	2.3	3.5	7.0	4.2	2.6	5.3	21.0	3.0
8—3	7	0.7	0.6	1.4	0.8	1.2	2.3	1.8	0.9	1.0	3.5	7.0
9—3	20	1.8	2.0	5.0	2.2	6.7	10.0	2.5	2.9	3.3	20.0	4.0
Stutter-provoking scores		80.1	−26.0	82.5	10.1	32.9	77.0	46.7	29.2	37.7	263.0	28.3
Rank order of stutter-provoking scores		3	11	2	10	7	4	5	8	6	1	9

the patients that they would not be able to construe him along the same dimensions as themselves (the therapist might be outside the range of convenience of some of the constructs). Not only does the "group" grid method provide a wealth of information about how construing changes over time (when the grid is administered on a number of occasions), but it is possible to derive a score that gives some idea as to how each sees the other. Such a "person perception score" (Fransella, 1970) can be derived because each group member has ranked all other group members on each of the constructs. Thus, if you want to find out whether a particular person sees herself as others see her, you simply look at her ranking of herself and compare this with others' ranking of her (see also Wijesinghe and Wood, 1976).

Figure 7 shows the rankings of group members 1 to 8 using elements A to H on the construct *likely to be a leader*. For each person one of the elements to be ranked will be "me", and this is indicated by an asterisk. Thus person 5 (element A) sees himself as the leader of the group and is seen as such by virtually everyone else. Similarly there is not much confusion about person 6 (element G). But person 2 is interesting in seeing himself as the bottom of the leadership list yet, by person 7, he is seen as the leader. An interesting question to ask is how does this affect behaviour within the group? A global score can be derived by taking the mean of the element ranks (1.1 in the case of element A) and deducting from it the person's own placement of himself (1.1 minus 1 = 0.1).

Group Members

		1	2	3	4	5	6	7	8
	A	1	1	1	1	1*	1	2	1
	B	2	6	8	6	6	8	7	8*
Elements (group members)	C	3	8*	7	7	5	6	1	6
	D	8*	3	3	5	7	4	5	5
	E	4	4	4*	3	4	3	6	3
	F	6	2	2	2	3	5	3*	2
	G	5	7	6	8	8	7*	8	7
	H	7	5	5	4*	2	2	4	4

Fig. 7. Rankings of themselves and the other members of a group on the construct *likely to be a leader*.

Ranked data lend themselves to many methods of analysis other than those examples given and, to be sure, many more will yet be devised. Some computer methods are discussed in Chapter 5. But, no matter what the method of analysis, it cannot be taken for granted that the ranked elements are stretched out evenly from pole to pole. The contrast pole can be only speculatively named.

A RATING GRID

There is increasing interest in the rating grid. Here, instead of ranking elements in terms of constructs, each element is *rated* on a scale defined by the two construct poles. This method allows the person greater flexibility of response than does the rank grid. This format is similar to the semantic differential devised by Osgood and his colleagues (1957). But this superficial similarity of format should not be taken as indicating similarity of underlying theory and assumptions. The differences between repertory grid and semantic differential techniques are great and are discussed in Chapter 9, p. 111 and in Bannister and Mair (1968).

One way of administering this form of grid is to have pages on which the scales (constructs) are typed and have each element rated on one page as in the example shown in Fig. 8.

KELLY

Freedom	___ ___ ___ ___ ___ X ___ ___ ___ ___ ___	Determinism
Rationality	X ___ ___ ___ ___ ___ ___ ___ ___ ___ ___	Irrationality
Holism	___ ___ X ___ ___ ___ ___ ___ ___ ___ ___	Elementalism
Constitutionalism	___ ___ ___ ___ ___ ___ ___ X ___ ___	Environmentalism
Subjectivity	X ___ ___ ___ ___ ___ ___ ___ ___ ___ ___	Objectivity
Proactivity	___ ___ ___ ___ not applicable ___ ___ ___	Reactivity
Homeostasis	___ ___ ___ ___ not applicable ___ ___ ___	Heterostasis
Knowability	___ ___ ___ ___ ___ ___ ___ ___ ___ X	Unknowability

Fig. 8. A rating grid format. The element "Kelly" is rated on eight 11-point construct scales (from "Personality Theories" by Hjelle and Ziegler, p. 231. Copyright McGraw-Hill Book Company, 1976. Used with permission of McGraw-Hill Book Company).

Having done this for each of the elements, the data can be collated into one matrix as in Fig. 9. These data were, in fact, taken from Hjelle and Ziegler's book on personality theories (1976). Each of the eight theorists discussed was rated on eight assumptions thought by these authors to be the basic assumptions underlying personality theories. Each theorist thus becomes an element which is rated along each of the eight constructs (assumptions).

Such a matrix is not as easy to deal with by hand as is a ranked matrix. There are, however, many computer programmes that can deal with these data, and several are discussed in Chapter 5. For this example we used the PA1 programme from the Statistical Package for the Social Sciences (Nie *et al.*, 1975). This takes each pair of scale ratings (rows) and treats them as scores that can be correlated. It plots the constructs and elements along the major components in terms of their loadings, as well as providing inter-construct correlations and other measures.

Elements

	Freud	Erikson	Murray	Skinner	Allport	Kelly	Maslow	Rogers
Freedom	11	8	10	11	5	6	2	1
Rationality	10	3	2	6	1	1	2	1
Holism	3	1	3	11	3	3	1	1
Constitutionalism	3	10	6	11	6	9	5	4
Subjectivity	5	8	4	11	5	1	2	1
Proactivity	4	3	4	11	1	6	1	1
Homeostasis	1	9	2	6	10	6	10	11
Knowability	1	4	6	1	4	11	11	11

(left margin label: Constructs)

Fig. 9. A matrix of ratings of 8 elements on 8 constructs (data from "Personality Theories" by Hjelle and Ziegler. Copyright McGraw-Hill Book Company, 1976. Used with permission of McGraw-Hill Book Company).

The plot of constructs and elements on the two main components derived from the grid matrix in Fig. 9 can be seen below (Fig. 10).

Although the plots of constructs and elements provide a general visual overview of how they relate one to the other, much more information can be gleaned from the intercorrelations. This equally applies to ranked grids when dimensional analysis is used. Those for constructs can be seen in Table IV and those for elements in Table V.

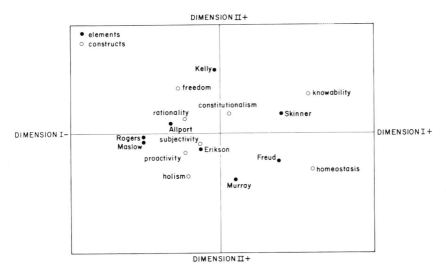

Fig. 10. Constructs and elements from Fig. 9 plotted along the two major dimensions from a principal components analysis in terms of their loadings.

Table IV
Matrix of construct intercorrelations based on ratings matrix in Fig. 9.

					Construct intercorrelations			
		1	2	3	4	5	6	7	8
Freedom/									
Determinism	1	X	0.69	0.58	0.34	0.69	0.68	0.8̄2	0.8̄2
Rationality/									
Irrationality	2	0.69	X	0.40	0.1̄3	049	0.42	0.6̄4	0.7̄3
Holism/									
Elementalism	3	0.58	0.40	X	0.54	0.70	0.90	0.3̄0	0.5̄6
Constitutionalism/									
Environmentalism	4	0.34	0.1̄3	0.54	X	0.61	0.67	0.10	0.2̄1
Subjectivity/									
Objectivity	5	0.69	0.49	0.70	0.61	X	0.62	0.1̄8	0.8̄5
Proactivity/									
Reactivity	6	0.68	0.42	0.90	0.67	0.62	X	0.4̄6	0.4̄5
Homeostasis/									
Heterostasis	7	0.8̄2	0.6̄4	0.3̄0	0.10	0.1̄8	0.4̄6	X	0.48
Knowability/									
Unknowability	8	0.8̄2	0.7̄3	0.5̄6	0.2̄1	0.8̄5	0.4̄5	0.48	X

These show that, for example, in Hjelle and Ziegler's view, theorists who stress that human beings are free as opposed to determined are not "knowable" (—0.82) and not "homeostatic" (—0.82) whereas they are "rational" (0.69), "subjective" (0.69) and "proactive" (0.68) in that causes of action come from within.

Table V
Matrix of element intercorrelations based on ratings matrix in Fig. 9.

					Element intercorrelations			
		1	2	3	4	5	6	7	8
Freud	1	X	0.0̄3	0.35	0.30	0.4̄0	0.3̄7	0.6̄1	0.6̄7
Erikson	2	0.0̄3	X	0.35	0.17	0.78	0.1̄2	0.31	0.26
Murray	3	0.35	0.35	X	0.18	0.06	0.6̄9	0.0̄3	0.1̄0
Skinner	4	0.30	0.17	0.18	X	0.0̄1	0.21	0.7̄9	0.7̄7
Allport	5	0.4̄0	0.78	0.06	0.1̄0	X	0.30	0.61	0.62
Kelly	6	0.3̄7	0.1̄2	0.6̄9	0.21	0.30	X	0.06	0.05
Maslow	7	0.6̄1	0.31	0.0̄3	0.7̄9	0.61	0.06	X	0.99
Rogers	8	0.6̄7	0.26	0.1̄0	0.7̄7	0.62	0.05	0.99	X

IMPLICATIONS GRIDS

Hinkle's Impgrid

The implications grid differs from the rank or rating grid in having no *elements* in the traditional sense. In fact, there is probably one implicit element—the self. Hinkle (1965; also detailed in Bannister and Mair, 1968, and Fransella, 1972) set out to see what meaning each construct had for the individual in terms of other constructs and did so by asking the person to indicate what went with what.

His instructions for the completion of the Impgrid in Fig. 11 were:

Consider this construct for a moment (Construct 1). Now, if you were to be changed back and forth from one side to the other—that is, if you woke up one morning and realized that you were best described by one side of this construct while the day before you had been best described by the opposite side—if you realized that you were changed in this *one* respect—what other constructs of these nineteen remaining ones would be *likely* to be changed by a change in yourself on this one construct alone? Changing back and forth on just this one construct will *probably cause* you to predictably change back and forth on which other constructs? Remember a change on just this one construct is the cause, while the changes on these other constructs are the effects, implied by the changes from one side to the other on this construct alone. What I'd like to find out, then, is on which of these constructs do you probably expect a change to occur as the *result of knowing* that you have changed from one side to the other of this one construct alone. A knowledge of your location on this one construct could probably be used to determine your location on which of these remaining constructs? (Hinkle, 1965, pp. 37-38).

Each construct is in effect paired twice with every other since construct 1 is first paired with 2 and later on, 2 is paired with 1.

As with other forms of grid, each construct is written on a separate card and duly numbered (on either the back or the front). It should perhaps be mentioned that there is no great mystery about using cards and numbering them. No doubt there are many other and better ways of doing things, but we are just giving you our experience of what has been found to be a satisfactory procedure.

Thus, in Fig. 11, the person said that changing on construct 1 would produce related change on constructs 2, 5, 6, 11, 12, 13, 14, 15 and 20. An "R" indicates a reciprocal relationship—when construct 2 implies construct 5, and 5 also implies 2. Some ways of analysing these completed Impgrids will be discussed after the resistance-to-change grid has been described. But some information can be obtained by scanning the grid, for instance, for overall number of implications. If it is replete with ticks, the person is operating a system dominated by one superordinate construct—everything is either black or white. If there are hardly any ticks, one can speculate that the person has difficulty in keeping his system together because few things imply other things. The grid in Fig. 11 is about middle-range. This is a "clinical estimate" statement as there are no formal normative data.

RESISTANCE-TO-CHANGE GRID

This is a grid that Hinkle developed along with the implications grid to test, among other things, the hypothesis that superordinate constructs would be

Constructs

1 Sympathetic — Hard
2 Considerate of others' feelings — Inconsiderate
3 Sincere — Insincere
4 Clear-thinker — Muddled
5 Forthright — Reticent
6 Prejudiced — Tolerant
7 Neurotic — Balanced
8 Reliable — Unreliable
9 Intelligent — A fool
10 Sure of themselves — Insecure
11 Understanding — Self-centred
12 Kind — Unkind
13 Learn more about people — Every man is an island
14 Understand things intellectually — Do not understand intellectually
15 Human society develops — Society stagnates or is in conflict
16 Honest with oneself — Kid oneself
17 Thinking is easier — Thinking is difficult
18 Can communicate better — Communicate poorly
19 They understand what you are conveying — They think you are a fool
20 Assume the right to give an opinion regardless of the effect — Do not assume this (superior) right

Construct	Total Implications
1	9
2	11
3	3
4	3
5	5
6	7
7	1
8	2
9	3
10	4
11	13
12	9
13	10
14	10
15	9
16	3
17	4
18	4
19	3
20	7

Total implications: 4 9 6 3 7 10 5 4 5 3 9 8 7 8 12 2 3 3 3 9

Implications rank orders: 13·5 4 10 17 8·5 2 11·5 13·5 11·5 17 4 6·5 8·5 6·5 1 20 17 17 17 4

Fig. 11. A completed implications grid (Hinkle, 1965).

more resistant to change than subordinate ones and that resistance-to-change would be directly related to the superordinate range of implications of the constructs. For Hinkle, the superordinate range of implication of a construct comprises a simple count of the number of implications in each *column,* rows carry subordinate implications.

The resistance-to-change grid in Fig. 12 was made up by comparing each construct with every other, but only once. As soon as construct 1 has been paired with all other 19, it is removed and not used again. Thus, construct 19 is compared only with construct 20. This yields a half matrix. The instructions Hinkle gave to his subjects, having first found out which side of each construct the person preferred to see themselves on, were:

Look at these two constructs. The check marks indicate the sides you said you would prefer to be on. Now, let's assume for the moment that you had to change from the preferred side to the unpreferred side on one of these constructs, but would remain the same on the other. Which of these two constructs would you prefer to remain the same on? Remember, you will have to change on the other. What we are trying to find out here is if you had to change, which of these two changes would be the more undesirable, as you see it? We would prefer you to make a choice whenever possible, but there are two circumstances in which you will find it impossible to make a choice. The first is when the two changes both appear to be undesirable to exactly the same degree. In most cases, however, you will be able to detect some difference between the two which will enable you to make a decision. The second instance is when it is not logically possible to change on one construct and at the same time remain the same on the other. This is the case when changing on one construct logically implies that you must also have changed on the other construct. Let me know when either of these two circumstances occur. Any questions? (Hinkle, 1965, p. 36).

In the resistance-to-change grid in Fig. 12, an "X" indicates that the column construct resists change; a blank indicates that the row construct resists change; an "I" means that independent change is not possible and an "e" means that both changes would be equally undesirable.

The straightforward scoring of this matrix involves counting all the blanks on the rows and the corresponding "X's" in the columns since these are indications of the construct's resistance-to-change. Thus, for construct 1, there are 8 row blanks, so the score for resistance is 8; for construct 2, there are 14 blanks and no "X's", so the score is 14; construct 3 has 10 blanks in the row and 1 "X" in the column giving a score of 11 and so on. All these scores are given at the bottom of the resistance-to-change matrix in Fig. 12. If these now ranked in order of size, it is immediately discernible which constructs are the relatively more resistant to change. These ranks are given below the scores at the bottom of the columns in Fig. 12.

We can test out some of Hinkle's ideas on the Impgrid and resistance-to-change grids in Figs 11 and 12 respectively. For instance, the hypothesis that was supported in his original study is also supported here—that "The rank order of the constructs as derived from the resistance-to-change grid would be highly positively correlated with the rank order derived from the

Table header: **Constructs** (columns 1–20); rows 1–19; resistance-to-change scores and rank orders below.

	1	2	3	4	5	6	7	8	9	10	11	12	13	14	15	16	17	18	19	20
1			x			x		x	x		x	x	x	x	x			x		x
2						e		e				–								–
3	x					x		x	x			x								x
4					x	x	x	x	x	x	x	x	x	x	x	x	x	x	x	x
5						x		x	x		x	x	x	x	x	x			x	x
6						x		x				x								x
7								x	x		x	x				x		x	x	x
8												x								x
9												x								x
10											x	x	x	x	x	x	x	x	–	x
11												x	x	x	x				x	x
12												x	x	x	x				x	–
13														–	x					x
14																				x
15																				x
16																		x		x
17																		x	x	x
18																			x	x
19																				x
resistance-to-change scores	8	14	11	0	5	12	3	16	11	19	8	17	11	12	13	6	2	6	7	17
rank orders	11.5	4	9	20	16	6.5	17	3	9	1	11.5	1.5	9	6.5	5	14.5	18	14.5	13	1.5

Fig. 12. A completed resistance-to-change grid (Hinkle, 1965).

implications grid". Thus we have the rank order for the 20 constructs in terms of their superordinate implications (column totals) and their resistance-to-change scores as shown below in Table VI.

The Spearman rho rank order correlation between the number of implications and degree of resistance-to-change is 0.70. With an n of 20, this is a highly significant correlation (rho = 0.534 is significant at the 1 per cent level). If it were not for the very large difference between number of implications and the resistance score for construct 8, the correlation between these two measures would be 0.75. Hinkle is arguing that we are more loath to change in any way that entails many related changes. The prospect of massive linked changes is too daunting.

Hinkle also argued and showed that the sum of the implications for the columns 1 to 10 (which are held to be more subordinate constructs as they were directly elicited) will be less than the sum for columns 11 to 20 (which are held to be superordinate constructs as they were derived by the laddering procedure). That is, the superordinate constructs will have more superordinate implications than will the subordinate constructs. In this case the figure for the subordinate constructs (1-10) is 56 and that for the superordinate constructs (11-20) is 64.

Similarly, there are likely to be fewer implications for rows 1 to 10 (subordinate implications for superordinate constructs). In this grid there were 48 and 72 respectively.

Each of these hypotheses about the structure of construct systems and the relative resistance-to-change of subordinate and superordinate constructs that Hinkle tested is borne out on this single grid. Kelsall and Strongman (1977) also found this.

Another aspect of this type of grid is the number of implications for constructs on which people see themselves on the non-preferred side. For this person (Fig. 11), the average number of superordinate implications for the constructs with the self on the non-preferred side (4, 7, 10, 17, 18) is 3.4 compared with 6.9 for constructs where the self is seen as being on the preferred side.

The difference is even more striking when we look at the resistance-to-change scores for the self/preferred and the self/not preferred constructs. The mean score for the former is 11.2 and for the latter 2.4. This, of course, seems eminently reasonable. If we want to be something we are not, then we are not very readily going to resist change in that direction.

But grids are devices in which, once we know some of the ground rules, we can look at some of the inconsistencies. One such anomaly is construct 8 (*reliable-unreliable*). It does not obey the rule stating that resistance-to-change scores and superordinate implications are positively related. It is one of the constructs most highly resistant to change (ranked third) and yet has only 4 implications (shared rank thirteen). It will also be seen that none of the 4 superordinate and only 2 of the subordinate implications is reciprocal. When in doubt, the usual procedure is to ask the person for an explanation

Table VI
Rank orders of resistance-to-change scores (Fig. 12) and total column implications (Fig. 11).

Rankings of	Constructs									
	1	2	3	4	5	6	7	8	9	10
(a) total column implications	13.5	4	10	17	8.5	2	11.5	13.5	11.5	17
(b) resistance-to-change scores	11.5	4	9	20	16	6.5	17	3	9	19
	11	12	13	14	15	16	17	18	19	20
(a) total column implication	4	6.5	8.5	6.5	1	20	17	17	17	4
(b) resistance-to-change scores	11.5	1.5	9	6.5	5	14.5	18	14.5	13	1.5

of such a discrepancy. In this case it transpired that he was constantly having problems with this construct. People being late or not doing things they said they would do, would throw him into a quite unreasonable state of annoyance (unreasonable in others' view, of course). This was apparently a construct that was part of the family pattern—everything was done to order, and time-keeping was much emphasised. But it may never have been "updated" in Kelly's sense. That is, the question "is it as personally important now as it was in childhood?" has never been asked.

The bi-polar implications grid

Another aspect of the implications grid that can be examined is what Hinkle termed "implicative dilemmas". The different types of relationship between the poles of two constructs are:

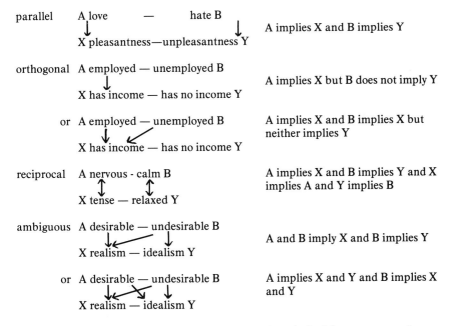

realism and idealism have both desirable and undesirable aspects to them.

The simple act of considering how many patterns of relationships there can be between two bi-polar constructs underlines the degree to which we over-simplify when we express such a relationship as a matching score or a correlation. But the identification of orthogonal and ambiguous "dilemmas" can only be carried out if the implications of both poles of a construct are noted. One way of doing this has been described and used by Fransella (1972) in her research relating speech change to construct change during the treatment of stutterers. An example of a bi-polar implications grid is given in Fig. 13.

Fig. 13. A completed bi-polar implications grid.

	No. implications
1a sensitive to people's feelings	7
b insensitive	8
2a overweight	4
b thin	8
3a impatient	7
b stop to think	9
4a like I'd like to be in character	6
b like I wouldn't like to be in character	6
5a take advantage of people	6
b don't take advantage of people	6
6a able to sit down and relax	6
b always on the move	7
7a like me in character as I am now	5
b not like me in character as I am now	9
8a more likely to be liked	8
b less likely to be liked	6
9a like I will be when a normal weight	8
b as I will not be when a normal weight	7
10a less likely to be taken for a ride	6
b more likely to be taken for a ride	7
11a heedless	6
b careful	9

The constructs in this grid were elicited from triads consisting of people known to the person, but always containing the person herself (Kelly's self identification method). This grid was the second in a series completed by an obese woman designed to map the implications she had about herself as an obese person. When the constructs had been elicited, they were laddered in the manner already described (pp. 16-17).

Instructions for the bi-polar Impgrid as well as the method of presentation differ. Fransella had found with her sample of stutterers that the task Hinkle set the person was too complex. This might be due to cultural differences as well as individual differences in ability to perform the conceptual task. Hinkle's subjects were American college students, while Fransella's were people of wide ranging abilities from several countries.

The task set for the person in this bi-polar implications grid is as follows: each construct is written on a card with the construct pole labelled "a" and the contrast pole "b". The resulting 11 cards in this example are then all laid out on the table. A second set of identical cards is also prepared and each card cut in half so that there is one pole of a construct on each of the half-cards. These half-cards are shuffled so that there is no consistent order of presentation.

The person is then presented with one half-card and asked to consider the item, for instance *insensitive,* and to imagine to herself "all you know about a person is that she is *insensitive.* What, from all these other characteristics on these cards in front of you would you expect to find in an *insensitive* person?". The cards are scanned and when she comes to a construct pole that describes a characteristic she would expect to find in an *insensitive* person, she is asked to call out the construct number and the letter "a" or "b". In this case she called out 3a, 4b, 5a, 7b, 8b, 9b, 10a and 11a. A very similar procedure has been adopted by Honess (1977a) for use with children.

Scoring

There is, at present, no entirely satisfactory method for scoring such a grid. A straightforward correlational procedure cannot be used because there are certain constraints on the data. For instance, a person is not allowed to say that both "a" and "b" of a construct would be expected in the designated person. One computer programme has been written that yields the binomial probabilities for the ticks matching or mismatching in any two lines. It was argued that only a definite statement of a relationship existing between two construct poles should be taken into account as a blank might indicate either "this construct is irrelevant to this particular characteristic" or "this construct is definitely *not* related".

A new format and scoring method are now being developed which overcome this problem. Instead of the construct cards indicating one pole as "a" and the other as "b", the two poles will define a scale, probably of an analogue type. The person will simply mark each comparison construct according to the degree to which it is related to, for example, *insensitive*. But until such time as this method has been developed, analysis is based on matching and mismatching ticks.

But with all grids, a great deal of information can be gathered from the grid itself by looking at the dispersion of ticks or simply adding them. For instance, Fransella (1972) gave a grid focused on "self as stutterer". She found that a simple count of implications in relation to total number possible significantly discriminated between the stutterers who improved to a certain level and those who did not so improve or who opted out of treatment prematurely. That is, those who had a higher ratio of ticks were less likely to improve—they had a more tightly-knit system about themselves as stutterers.

It is to be expected that the "self" side of a construct will have more meaning and therefore implications than the "non-self" side. Exceptions may therefore be of interest. In one grid of a stutterer, there were 3 implications on the "self" side (defined by *speaks his mind and means it*) and 13 on the "non-self" side (defined by *crawlers and snides*) (Fransella, 1969). He saw himself as someone who speaks his mind and many of his constructs had to do with honesty and sincerity. But as a stutterer he was unable to speak his mind and so, presumably, knew a good deal about dishonesty in interpersonal relations.

The implications and resistance-to-change grids have not been widely used until recently. Those interested in some of the ways in which they have been used might refer, in the case of the implications grid, to Morse (1966); Mair and Crisp (1968); Bender (1969); Fransella and Crisp (1970); Wright (1970); Coleman (1975); Fransella (1977); and, in the case of the resistance-to-change grid, to Bender (1969); Honikman (1976); Kelsall and Strongman (1977).

DEPENDENCY GRID

A little used but potentially valuable type of grid is that described by Kelly as the Situational Resources Repertory Test. As that is a rather cumbersome title, it is often referred to as the Dependency Grid. In this grid form, the person relates situations and people. The situations are those which are essentially stressful which any of us might meet. The people are those upon whom we may call for help or on whom we may lean. Naturally enough, being Kelly, this grid does not set out to enable the psychologist to assess the degree of dependence or independence an individual possesses relative to the general multitude. "Everyone is dependent; the problem is to make appropriate allocations of one's dependencies" (Kelly, 1955, p. 312).

Kelly described this grid approach thus: "You might list only the catastrophies in your life and then ask yourself which of the persons you had named could, if they had been available at the time, have been helpful to you in meeting each emergency. Such a matrix provides information about one's allocation of his interpersonal dependencies—whether he has faced difficulties in which he feels no one could be of help, whether he turns to one or two persons only for all kinds of help, or whether he is indiscriminate in his selection of persons upon whom to depend" (Kelly, 1961).

In concrete terms, the person is presented with a list of role titles and a number of situations which are likely to be relevant. He supplies names for the role titles where appropriate and notes date and place against a troublesome situation. He then places a cross in those intersects showing to whom he turned for help in that situation. An actual example given by Kelly (1955, p. 316) can be seen in Fig. 14.

Trouble with	Date, place	1 Mate	2 Father	3 Mother	4 Sister	5 Brother	6 Boss	7 Noncomm. Officer	8 Com. Officer	9 Minister	10 Relative	11 Neighbour	12 Buddy	13 Confidant	14 Physician	15 Advisor	16 Self
A. Finances		·	X	X	·	·	·	·	·	·	X	·	·	X	·	X	·
B. Mate		·	·	X	X	·	·	·	·	·	·	·	·	X	·	X	·
C. Police	OMITTED																
D. Neighbour	OMITTED																
E. Jealousy	OMITTED																
F. Parents		X	·	·	X	·	X	·	·	·	·	·	·	X	·	X	·
G. Sibling	OMITTED																
H. Loneliness		X	·	·	X	·	X	·	·	·	·	·	·	X	·	X	·
I. Anger		X	X	X	X	·	·	·	·	·	X	·	·	X	·	X	·
J. Fear of death	OMITTED																
K. Shame		·	·	X	·	·	X	·	·	·	·	·	·	X	·	X	·
L. Persecution		·	X	X	·	·	X	·	·	·	·	·	·	X	·	X	·
M. Discouragement		X	X	X	·	·	X	·	·	·	·	·	·	X	·	X	·
N. Sickness	OMITTED																
O. Suicidal thoughts	OMITTED																
P. Misunderstood		·	·	·	·	·	X	·	·	·	·	·	·	X	·	X	·
Q. Effeminacy		·	·	·	·	·	X	·	·	·	·	·	·	X	·	X	·
R. Cowardliness	OMITTED																
S. Stupidity		X	·	X	·	·	X	·	·	·	·	·	·	X	·	X	·
T. Hurting someone		·	X	·	X	·	X	·	·	·	·	·	·	X	·	X	·
U. Gullibility		·	X	·	X	·	X	·	·	·	·	·	·	X	·	X	·
V. Confusion		X	·	·	·	·	X	·	·	·	·	·	·	X	·	X	·
W. Failure		·	·	·	X	·	X	·	·	·	·	·	·	X	·	X	·
X. Women	OMITTED																
Y. Passivity		·	·	·	X	·	X	·	·	·	·	·	·	X	·	X	·
Z. Needed help	OMITTED																

Fig. 14. Kelly's Situational Resources Repertory Test (Kelly, 1955, p. 316).

Face inspection of such a grid yields information as to whether the person calls on everyone for every kind of help or turns always to one or two people. Both of these strategies are taken by Kelly to indicate "undistributed dependency" and to be less hopeful signs than the distribution of ticks which suggest that the person has "specialised" his different needs among a number of people.

It has been suggested by Hinkle that this grid can be turned on its ear by asking the question "Who turns to you for help or leans on you in what sorts of situation?". In the psychotherapeutic or counselling setting it can be useful to know whether a person has only one or even no person to whom he turns for help yet seems to be submerging under a sea of people leaning (or perceived as leaning) on him. It is psychologically of interest to see whether "I turn to" and "turn to me" are reciprocals within the two types of grid.

This form of grid needs working on. It is not particularly easy for example, to think whether you would have turned to X if he had been around at the time of the trouble. People change. A person on whom you leaned when you were 18 years old may have changed so that you would not lean on them 20 years later, because *you* have changed. In this case it may be necessary to develop a grid for important life stages for an individual—say, up to marriage and during marriage. Another difficulty is that you may be lucky enough to have had 10 years of relative calm in life so that no "leaning" was really needed. An "if" dependency grid might be useful here. "If" such and such a disaster happened, to whom would you turn amongst those around you at the moment?

GROUPS REQUIRING SPECIAL PROCEDURES

Very slowly variations of elicitation and grid procedures are being described so that they can be of use to more and more people. These modifications have emerged mainly from work with children and the mentally handicapped but we also include here one recent development of the technique for use with the deaf.

Elicitation of constructs

Kelly's triadic method of elicitation has been found too complex for children under 10 to 12 years-of-age; the mentally handicapped; the deaf; and those who do not have command of the examiner's language. Where the triadic method has been used with any of these groups, some limitation on the constructs elicited seems to be imposed. For example, Ravenette (1964) found that the triadic method elicited constructs such as *old—young*, and *girl—boy*, whereas a much wider range of constructs emerged when the same children were asked to write short essays about children and adults they liked and disliked.

Many have since used the essay approach to elicit constructs. Others, however, find a simple conversation about the elements gives more scope to the child and is often less demanding for someone who lacks full command of language. For yet others, both essay writing and conversation is difficult. For example, Salmon (1976) suggests asking the very shy child to group the elements together in some way and then to try and give some word or phrase to each grouping. Salmon also sounds a cautionary note about range of convenience problems. She cites Ravenette (1964) who found that many constructs used in essays by secondary school children were applied to children whereas the number applied to adults was small. Generality of usage cannot be assumed.

In a study of 26 mentally handicapped people with ages ranging from 15 to 55, Barton, Walton and Rowe (1976) used the "talking about the elements" technique and noted down the constructs used (see also Salmon, 1976). But they point out the necessity for checking on the meaning these constructs have. Some pick up words or phrases and use them without really having any clear idea of their meaning. This study confirms the impression that people of below average intelligence tend to use behaviours as ways of describing people instead of more abstract personality characteristics. So one reply to the question "what sort of person is this" (element), may be "he is the sort that bumps into you when you pass him". He can then be "laddered" up by asking what sort of person is likely to do that.

Baillie-Grohman (1975) elicited constructs from deaf children in a highly imaginative way—she used mime. She first argued that deaf people with little or no language, nevertheless have complex construct systems. However, the discriminations between events in their lives are much finer than those they can express verbally. Since many deaf people communicate quite satisfactorily through facial expression, mime, gesture and signs, these were the media she used.

Her approach and method are given in some detail as an example of how, with imagination, grid method can be modified to break new ground with those who cannot communicate verbally with ease.

First, the 14 children were given details of what they were going to be required to do on the following day. Everything was explained until all appeared to understand. The next morning, when all 14 children were present, 4 constructs were elicited with their opposites from each child in the following way. After a preamble about the task in hand, each child was asked to write down the name of ONE person he/she knew. They were then asked to think about the sort of person this was and then to tell the person next to them what this person was like.

The children were next asked to write down the names of TWO people they knew and to think about how these people differed. When they had been able to find one way in which these two people differed they had to tell the person next to them what this difference was. Two further people were then thought of and differences elicited.

After the elicitation of the constructs, each child in turn mimed their own construct. So as to capture the non-verbal moment, an artist was present whose job it was to sketch the "meaning" of the mime. With each mime, all the children were asked to think of a person who showed that behaviour. There was thus a pool of elicited constructs and each person had provided someone they knew who shared the characteristic of the person mimed. This example highlights the point, often made, that it is repertory grid TECHNIQUE. This means there is not a rigid set of rules but that it is a highly flexible device to enable one to elicit constructs and quantify them in some way. Without the use of construct theory, the technique tends to become rigid. But when we start off with the premise that all living creatures derive meaning from their world by seeing similarities and differences between events and construing their replications, then we have a truly flexible measuring instrument at our disposal.

Supplying the constructs

The same ground-rules apply here as for all other groups of people. Basically, one must be careful to ensure that the construct supplied means what you think it means to the other person or, more basically, ensure that it is comprehensible. One restriction suggested by Salmon (1976) is that whole-figure constructs (*like mother, like me* and so forth) should be restricted to those over 7 years-of-age at least. Above that age there are indications that whole figure constructs can be used. For instance, Salmon (1967) found that children between seven-and-a-half and nine-and-a-half years could use the ideal self construct with photographs of children of a similar age as well as such supplied constructs as *probably does as he's told—probably gets into trouble with grown-ups.*

Choosing the elements

The elements must be within the range of convenience of the constructs. Having said that, the choice is basically determined by the reason for the investigation. With the particular groups under discussion here, the individuals will probably have a relatively narrow world of experience. For those in institutions the world may well be peopled by those like oneself, and the staff. Barton and her colleagues (1976) emphasise the importance of this. It is often the case that people "like oneself"—that is, "patients"—are of no importance in life, whereas "staff" are the staff of life. But even if this is so, elements may include the flowers in the garden, the meals of the day or other aspects of life that are important to the person. Elements do not have to be people. Ravenette (1968, 1975) for instance, uses pictures depicting situations in which a child is alone, with other children, with members of the family and so forth. Some children find this easier than having as elements the names of people. However, names of people are widely used in work with children.

Little (1967) found them suitable for children between 10 and 18 years-of-age; Brierley (1967) studied children as young as 7 years and Allison (1972) as young as 4 years. However, Salmon (1976) says that Allison's study was exploratory and that it is best to stick to the principle that names of people should only be used with older children for the present.

Presentation of the elements

Barton, Walton and Rowe (1976) found no problem in administering the grid with mentally handicapped people down to an IQ level of 50, providing the person could read. They point out that many who do not score on a formal reading test can recognise names when printed in large capital letters, especially if these are supplemented by symbols or drawings. If no letters can be recognised then drawings or non-verbal symbols alone can be used. They found that those with the lower IQ levels could manage to deal with at least 8 or 9 elements.

Salmon (1976) suggests the use of brightly coloured stand-up models of people of both sexes, various ages, wearing different types of clothing and so forth. Having first elicited the constructs by encouraging the child to talk about them, the child looks at the first model in terms of the first construct and is asked "Is he a . . . person or is he a . . . (opposite pole) person?". This procedure is repeated until all elements have been placed at one pole or the other on all constructs.

Rating methods appear to be comparatively easy for children. Salmon (1976) suggests that children over 6 years can usually manage this task. The categories for rating should be defined by such words as "very", "a little bit" and so forth rather than by numbers. She also suggests that the number of ratings be limited to 5 or even 3 for those under 12 years old. A more physical approach to rating is often preferable to a verbal one, especially for the younger children. For example, the elements can be placed into 3 or 5 piles, or the table can be marked to indicate the two poles of a construct and the child instructed to place the elements between these two as for ranking.

Barton and her colleagues (1976) apparently often found it difficult to convince their subjects that there was no "right answer". Most could rank using the general method described earlier. But one event that can disrupt the procedure, reported with all types of people on occasion, is when the person says that none of the remaining elements is, say, *snobbish*. The easy way round this is to start the ranking from the other pole and ask who, among the remaining elements, is *least snobbish*, or who is definitely *not snobbish*. They suggest also that with mentally handicapped people, tied ranks should be allowed. Another problem reported in this study is that sometimes the mentally handicapped person refused to rank staff members on "bad" constructs. They needed reassurance that staff would not be told. One suspects that this is a common difficulty with all those who spend a long time in institutions. It could of course be that staff are no longer construed as people and so cannot be "bad" and consequently the range of convenience rule has become a problem.

When there is some insuperable difficulty with ranking, the paired comparison method may be used. Orley (1976) employed this method in his study of how Ganda villagers viewed 6 classes of spirits. With 6 elements, there are 15 possible pairs. Each of these 15 were presented to the villagers who were asked which member of the pair was best described by the construct. When all 15 elements had been presented and compared on one construct, the examiner went on to the next construct. A score of "1" was given for the spirit chosen on each pairing. This method has also been used with those mentally handicapped people who find it impossible to rank the elements (Barton et al., 1976). They also suggest a means of overcoming the difficulty experienced by some people in using the "ideal self" as an element. When all elements have been ranked, the person is asked whether "you would really like to be more or less *kind* than "X" starting at the median rank. In this way the correct rank placement or rating for the element can be found on each construct.

Baillie-Grohman's deaf children completed both an individual grid based on personally elicited constructs plus *easy to talk to* and *difficult to talk to*, and a "common" grid consisting of the 9 most frequently occurring constructs plus *the same as me*. To complete the personal grid, each child was presented with their first sketch and asked if they remembered who they were thinking about at the time and the characteristic they were portraying in mime. The child was asked next to think of the person who was the first element (these were role titles, e.g. mother, teacher I dislike and so forth); and to indicate, by placing the element card in the appropriate box on the table, whether they were a little bit, fairly much or very much like the construct. The group grid was repeated in the same manner.

There are inherent difficulties in this procedure, as Baillie-Grohman points out. The main one being the problem of attaching a verbal label to the sketched mime. However, if we are ever going to get beyond our verbal screen and find out how non-verbal human beings think about their world, we are going to have to experiment in this way.

But not all grids have elements to present. Implications grids are one such (see pp. 42-52). Honess (1977a) used the bi-polar method with 203 children at four age levels. The youngest children were asked to suppose that there was a new child coming to the school the following week of the same age as himself. All he knows about this child is that he (for instance) likes doing gym. A card with *"likes doing gym"* written on it is placed on the table and another construct pole card is placed before the child with, say, *bully* written on it. "Remember, the only one thing we know about the new boy is that he likes doing gym, do you think he will be a bully?". If the child indicates that he will, he is told to put the *bully* card by the card with YES on it. There are two other alternatives open to the child—to put the *bully* card in a MAY OR

MAY NOT pile or a VERY UNLIKELY pile. The procedure is repeated with all construct cards. Honess had found in a pilot study that this method produced meaningful results with children as young as 6 to 7 years old.

COMMENT

The reader should not become mesmerised by the particular examples of grid forms that have been included here. The grid is truly a technique and one which is only limited by the user's lack of imagination. It needs to be borne in mind that the grid evolved in the context of psychotherapy and formed part of the process of making sense of a person's life problem. For Kelly "the primary purpose of psychological measurement in a clinical setting is to survey the pathways along which the subject is free to move, and the primary purpose of clinical diagnosis is the plotting of the most feasible course of movement. As a whole, diagnosis may be described as the planning stage of therapy" (1955, p. 203). Because of this therapeutic focus of convenience, the emphasis in grid technique was very much on interpersonal relationships. But, as can be seen from the annotated bibliography (Appendix 3), many have used it imaginatively in other contexts.

All forms of grid are sorting tasks which enable the person to tell us something of the way in which he sees and orders his world. We need not rely on normative data for an understanding of the construct patterning revealed. There is no fixed content and no one particular form that is the only right one for a particular context. Last, and perhaps most important of all, is that inferences are based on the assumption that statistical relationships within the grid reflect psychological relationships within the person's construing system. These psychological relationships represent something relatively stable and permanent in a person's construct system. Because of this, it is important to obey the rules of statistics when interpreting grid results. If all correlations in a rank grid with 8 elements are no higher than 0.4, no meaningful interpretation of construct relationships should be made, though this fact itself is a state of affairs of psychological interest. The examiner must be content with some general statement concerning this lack of structure—perhaps that the person seems confused about life, was saying she refused to do the grid or was trying to convey a message that help was required. One of the important areas for future research is to find out the level of *statistical* significance that is of *psychological* significance. At what level of significance will a person *act*? If construct A (which describes a situation) implies/relates to construct B (which implies an action) what level of statistical relationship (query 0.5 query 0.7 query 0.9) predicts that a particular person will *act* B in situation A.

4

Some Measures of Construct Relationships and Construing

> ... We can arrange those events according to some issue—or construct—placing those to which one pole of the issue is more appropriately applied on the one side and those to which the other pole is more applicable on the other. Having done that, we can scramble the events and rearrange them in terms of another construct. As this rearranging proceeds, each event becomes locked into psychological space in greater depth. That is to say, an event seen only in terms of its placement on one dimension is scarcely more than a mere datum. And about all you can do with a datum is just let it sit on its own continuum. But as the event finds its place in terms of many dimensions of consideration it develops psychological character and uniqueness. (Kelly, 1969, p. 118).

The overlap and confusion between grid measures in common use is enormous. Some problems stem from the lack of theoretical underpinning. All we aim to do here is to describe some of these measures not already covered in previous chapters and indicate where they overlap with other measures. Other problems arise from the sheer magic of grid data. It is easy to become mesmerised by the figures confronting one. We assume they relate to something meaningful for the individual who produced them, they mean something to us, so it is well-nigh impossible to resist the temptation to invent more and more complex methods of analysis and derive scores that we hope will indicate some *underlying* relationships and structures and processes.

MEASURES OF COGNITIVE DIFFERENTIATION

Intensity

For Kelly, a construct used in a "tight" way is one that leads to unvarying predictions whereas a "loose" one leads to varying predictions. Bannister (1960) developed this idea in his study of thought disorder. He argued that there is a relationship between the size of correlations obtained on a rank grid and the notion of tightness-looseness. This operational definition he called the *Intensity* score. The Intensity score is simply the sum of all relationship scores ($rho^2 \times 100$) for all constructs (ignoring sign). The score for the grid in Fig. 5 (p. 33) is thus 1199.

Intensity is one of the measures that has been shown to discriminate between thought disordered schizophrenics (when they are construing people) on the one hand and both other psychiatric and normal groups on the other. The lower the Intensity score (that is the lower the correlations), the more disordered (loose) is one's thinking (Bannister and Fransella, 1965).

Kelly was not arguing that loose construing (i.e. using constructs in a propositional way) is itself pathological and indeed he pointed out that in some contexts the person who can deal with social relationships in a relatively differentiated way may be more successful. The essence of Kelly's argument is that we loosen and then tighten and then loosen our thinking in a cyclic manner. Our aim is first of all to gain a perspective and then become concrete enough to define our themes operationally and so regain a new perspective. Bannister is arguing that thought disordered persons have become exclusively loose in their construing (certainly where thinking about people is concerned) and are unable to tighten their thinking into plans for action.

Cognitive complexity

But Bannister's Intensity measure looked mighty like a measure of complexity as defined by Bieri (1955). Cognitive complexity is defined as

". . . the capacity to construe social behaviour in a multidimensional way. A more cognitively complex person has available a more differentiated system of dimensions for perceiving others' behaviour than does a less cognitively complex individual" (Bieri *et al.,* 1966, p. 185).

The more loosely knit the constructs (the lower the correlations), the more complex is the person's construct system. In these terms it might seem that the thought disordered schizophrenic is the most cognitively complex person there is. This is due to the fact that the thought disordered person is completing the grid in a largely random manner, and randomness is the most complex possible mathematical state of affairs. This paradox can be resolved by reference to Bannister's additional measure of Consistency (see Chapter 5, pp. 79-80). While it can be assumed that Bieri's "complex" normals would repeat the pattern of their structure when tested on a second occasion (Bannister's normals certainly did), thought disordered persons do not. Unfortunately, for those who like a quiet, ordered life, Honess (1976) reports finding no relation between Intensity and Bieri's measure.

It is outside the scope of this book to review the entire literature on cognitive complexity which is now virtually an independent area of research. The most recent discussions will be found in Bonarius (1965), Crockett (1965) and Adams-Webber (1969, 1970a). We are here limiting ourselves to a brief overview of measures available and some of the inherent confusions.

Bieri's original method of scoring is by far the most commonly used and is as follows. The ratings in a grid are compared element by element for each pair of rows. Whenever there is exact agreement between ratings, a score of "1" is given. The more agreement, the higher the score, and the *lower* the degree of cognitive complexity. The score for the rated grid in Fig. 9 (p. 41) is 28. But there are many other measures. As long ago as 1965, Bonarius listed ten. These include those based on variability in number and content of constructs, parametric and non-parametric factor analyses; and multidimensional scaling methods. One of the most recent is Landfield's Functionally Independent Construction Score (1971).

In an attempt to clarify the position, Vannoy (1965) produced evidence suggesting that the concept of cognitive complexity was multidimensional and that the different indices measured different aspects of it. Adams-Webber (1970a) looked at the discriminant validity of some grid measures, including cognitive complexity, and found a degree of functional similarity. But Kuusinen and Nystedt (1975a) assessed the convergent validity of four measures of cognitive complexity, including Bieri's, and found it to be low. They added another dimension to the problem by finding that whether the constructs in the grid were provided or elicited affected the intermeasure correlation. Honess (1976) found that measures only correspond when there is similarity in their computation.

Crockett (1965) pointed out that Bieri's cognitive complexity was a measure of differentiation as opposed to integration. Smith and Leach (1972) took this up and distinguished between the two in measurement terms. Their hierarchical measure was found to be unrelated to Bieri's measure. Metcalfe (1974) reports similar findings and concludes ". . . cognitive differentiation is a measure only of how much S's constructs distinguish between elements, whereas cognitive complexity additionally reflects the hierarchical arrangement of the constructs" (Metcalfe, 1974, p. 1306).

It is important not to get bogged down in semantics here. It seems clear that Bieri's measure, called "cognitive complexity", is not measuring anything that is yet clearly defined in theoretical terms. There are at least two easily recognisable aspects—measures that describe something about how closely knit the constructs are and measures that describe something about how they are integrated.

MEASURES OF COGNITIVE INTEGRATION

Hinkle and the organisation corollary

A major attempt to deal with the hierarchical aspect of a construct system (derived from the organisation corollary) for people in general was Hinkle's (1965). His development of the implications grid and resistance-to-change grid has been discussed in detail (pp. 42-49). He showed that superordinate constructs have more implications (hence meaning) than subordinate constructs and that the former are the more resistant to change. Unlike other forms, the implications grid enables one to determine not only overall levels of integration, but exactly which constructs are superordinate to which others; for instance, where A implies B but B does not imply A.

Saturation scores

Fransella (1972) used a modification of Hinkle's Implications grid to look at integration within a sub-system of constructs.

The basis of the saturation measure was Hinkle's statement that "The total number of implications in the range of implications of a construct could be used as a measure of the meaningfulness of that construct". The only difference was that she looked at construct sub-systems and not single constructs (for example, the sub-system of constructs focused around "me as a stutterer"). Using a bi-polar implications grid (see p. 49), the score is a simple arithmetic count of actual numbers of implications between constructs stated to exist by that person. This is then given as a percentage of the total number that it is possible to obtain in a grid of a particular size.

The saturation score has been shown to be related to whether or not stutterers improved. Stutterers who improved in speech 50 per cent or more had significantly lower saturation scores (p<.001) on the grid to do with being a stutterer than did those who did not improve so much or who left treatment prematurely. Honess (1977b) found this score to have a test-retest correlation of 0.79 (N=24).

Fransella speculated about the meaning of such a score in construct theory terms and suggested it is perhaps a measure of constellatoriness. This Hinkle defines as *the relation between a given construct and others such that a polar position on the given construct implies polar positions on the other constructs.* The opposite pole to constellatoriness is propositionality. Propositional thinking *implies a suspension of judgment (i.e. a superordinate construction) as to the implicative gain of each of the alternative patterns of construction under consideration.*

These definitions make a statement about the way a system or sub-system works as well as about single constructs. But such sub-systems are not *either* constellatory *or* propositional on their structure, they are *relatively* so. Thinking along these lines makes it more and more obvious that implications grids should allow the person to make a *probability* statement about the extent to which two constructs (or construct poles) relate to each other. This is a more time-consuming procedure but seems to be capable of producing more meaningful results.

Extremity ratings

Interest in the extent to which people tend to use the extreme points on bi-polar scales as opposed to the more central points has lead to another relatively discrete area of research. One explanation of the tendency to use extreme points on a scale is that it indicates pathology or maladjustment (e.g. O'Donovan, 1965; Arthur, 1966; Hamilton, 1968). Others have seen it as a measure of personal meaningfulness of the scales. This is related to the fact that more extreme ratings are usually found on constructs elicited from the person than on constructs supplied to him (e.g. Mitsos, 1961; Landfield, 1965, 1968; Bender, 1969, 1974; Warr and Coffman, 1970).

Bonarius (1971) offers the most sophisticated approach to the problem of explaining why people rate more extremely on some constructs than on others by suggesting an Interaction Model. The interaction that will deter-mine how extreme a rating will be is between object (element) rated, the person who does the rating, and the poles of the construct defining the scale. Bonarius traces its line of descent to Cronbach (1946). Rising above the then prevalent stimulus-response Sargassa Sea he pointed out to psychologists that a person's responses on a questionnaire may not be totally determined by the content.

Ordination

Landfield and Barr (1976) describe a measure they call *ordination*. The subject rates elements (people) on 13-point scales defined by bi-polar constructs. The central point is given the score of zero and the other scores range from 1 to 6 on either side. Assuming (and this is arguable) that the more extremely an element is rated the more meaningful it is, then the more extreme scores a construct receives the more superordinate that construct is. Landfield's score of ordination for a construct is obtained by first noting the number of different levels of extremeness, e.g. if elements have been rated 0, 2, 4 and 5 on the construct *rigid—flexible,* the score is 4. This is multiplied by the difference between the highest and lowest rating, i.e. 5 in this case, to give the construct an ordination score of 20. Scores for the elements can be obtained in the same way.

Leitner, Landfield and Barr (1975) discuss how such ordination scores can be combined with the Functionally Independent Construction scores (Landfield, 1971) to yield predictions about individuals' behaviour in groups.

Superordinacy

This derives from the theoretical proposition that constructs are organised into systems.

"Not only are the constructs personal, but the hierarchical system into which they are arranged is personal too . . . One construct may subsume another as one of its elements . . . When one construct subsumes another its ordinal relationship may be termed *superordinal* and the ordinal relationship of the other becomes subordinal." (Kelly, 1955, pp. 56-58).

But just as there is nothing that is *only* an element and nothing that is *only* a construct, no construct is *either* superordinal *or* subordinal. For

". . . the ordinal relationship between the constructs may reverse itself from time to time. For example, "intelligent" may embrace all things "good" together with all things "evaluative" and "stupid" would be the term for "bad" and "descriptive" things; or, if the other kind of subsuming is involved, "intelligent" might embrace the construct *evaluative vs. descriptive* while "stupid" would be the term for the *good vs. bad* dichotomy. Thus man systemizes his constructs by concretely arranging them in hierarchies and by abstracting them further. But whether he pyramids his ideas or penetrates them with insights, he builds a system embracing ordinal relationships between constructs for his personal convenience in anticipating events." (Kelly, 1955, pp. 57-58).

Superordinacy is then a relative term. A construct is seen as being more or less superordinate more or less of the time. Several attempts have been made to quantify this theoretical construct in grid terms. Some are logical deductions from the theory while others, like cognitive complexity, have emerged more from grid technique.

In 1967, Bannister and Salmon reported an experiment which investigated 10 measures. These were:

(i) number of extreme ratings subjects made when using a 6-point scale.

They argued that research suggests that the degree to which people use extremity ratings indicates the importance of that category to them.

(ii) range of convenience.

Subjects rated their elements on a 6-point scale for each construct and were given the opportunity to say "doesn't apply" if the element for them lay outside the range of convenience of the construct so that neither pole of the construct was relevant. The range of convenience score for each construct was the number of times elements were rated on it and the "doesn't apply" category not used.

(iii) degree of relationship with the most important construct.

This was derived as described on p. 35. It is essentially that construct which is most closely related to all other constructs.

(iv) relative variance accounted for.

This was also derived by the method described on p. 35. Constructs were rank ordered in terms of the closeness of relationship to all other constructs.

(v) resistance-to-change.

Hinkle's measure of the degree to which a person is prepared to change from his preferred pole to his non-preferred pole on each construct, relative to each other construct, as described on p. 45.

(vi) laddering.

This procedure of Hinkle's is described on pp. 16-17.

(vii) size of loadings on the first factor determined by principal components analysis.

The rationale for this measure was that it seemed to be another, mathematically more sophisticated, way of showing relative number and strength of inter-construct relationships. Since the first factor normally accounts for a considerable amount of the total variance, it was argued that loading on this factor alone would give a fair impression of the importance of the construct. It was suggested that this measure would be closely related to measure (iii) "the degree of relationship with the most important construct".

(viii) size of loadings on all components extracted by principal components analysis.

This measure is similar to (vii) except that, in this case, loadings on *all* significant components are added for each construct. It was argued that this measure would show the relative importance of each construct in a more general sense.

(ix) lopsidedness in using constructs on a 6-point scale.

In their previous work, it had been noticed that, given freedom to use the two poles of a construct as much or as little as they wished, subjects tended to mal-distribute elements onto the poles more for some constructs than for others. Bannister and Salmon felt that degree of lopsidedness might be relevant to superordinacy, but there were arguments both for expecting a positive and a negative relationship.

(x) subjective estimate of importance.

Subjects were asked to give their own view as to the degree of superordinacy of their constructs.

To obtain these measures 14 constructs were elicited from 10 subjects. Each subject then rated the 20 elements on the 14 constructs. The elements were written on 20 small cards—one element per card. For the rating task, the subject was presented with 7 large cards laid out in front of him. These were $+++$, $++$, $+$, $-$, $--$, $---$, and "doesn't apply". The positive pole of the construct was written on a piece of paper and placed beside the $+++$ card and the negative pole by the $---$ card. The subject was asked to place his small element cards on the appropriate large card. Measures of superordinacy (i), (ii) and (ix) were obtained from this grid.

The subjects then completed a rank grid with the same 14 constructs and the 8 elements ranked highest on the range of convenience measure. Measures (iii), (iv), (vii) and (viii) were obtained from this grid.

The resistance-to-change measure was calculated as described by Hinkle (see p. 45). The person was presented with each pair of the 14 constructs and asked to state which out of each pair of non-favoured poles he would choose to be described by if he were forced to change to one of them.

Instructions for laddering were modified so the subject was simply asked why he had chosen a particular pole rather than the other. The questioning continued until the person could produce no further constructs. This was repeated with each of the 14 constructs. The measure was the total number of additional constructs elicited in this way. But Bannister and Salmon state that they regard this as the weakest of their measures (see pp. 16-17 for a discussion of the difficulties implicit in the laddering procedure).

The intercorrelations resulting from these 10 measures of superordinacy can be seen in Table VII.

For each individual subject the 14 constructs had 10 different superordinacy scores or ranks. It was therefore possible to calculate the correlations between the different measures of superordinacy for each individual. Bannister and Salmon comment that the most outstanding feature of these individual matrices is the very great variability in both the size and direction of intercorrelations between superordinacy measures. The effect of this individual variability is, of course, to flatten out the correlations when they are averaged. Some of the near-zero mean correlations in Table VII do reflect near-zero correlations for all individual subjects, e.g. number of extremity

Table VII

Intercorrelations for 10 different measures of superordinacy. From Bannister and Salmon, 1967.

Measures		1	2	3	4	5	6	7	8	9	10
Extremity Ratings (%)	1	X	0.01	0.07	0.10	0.04	0.15	0.04	0.03	0.10	0.07
Range of Convenience	2		X	0.22*	0.19	0.26**	0.16	0.22**	0.16	0.04	0.31**
Anchor Method	3			X	0.77**	0.08	0.01	0.81**	0.15	0.13	0.02
Total Variance	4				X	0.11	0.04	0.95**	0.15	0.08	0.16
Resistance to Change	5					X	0.11	0.03	0.06	0.09	0.52**
Laddering	6						X	0.00	0.01	0.08	0.10
P.C. 1st Factor	7							X	0.17	0.07	0.14
P.C. Total Loadings	8								X	0.12	0.12
Lopsidedness	9									X	0.01
Own Rating	10										X

* = $p < 0.05$
** = $p < 0.01$

ratings (i) and size of loadings on all components (viii). But this is not so in other cases. From an inspection of the averaged correlation matrix, it appears that the only *consistent* tendencies towards positive relationships are between (a) those measures concerned with quantifying the total amount of relationship of a construct with other constructs; (b) those measures which concern the subjects' more or less conscious ordering of priorities. The situation seems to be that "statistical"-type measures of superordinacy inter-correlate; "ask the subject"-type measures intercorrelate. The only measure that seems to link these two types of measure is range of convenience.

In commenting on this study, Bannister and Mair (1968) argued that "Until the various operational definitions of major constructs of the theory are more carefully derived from an examination of the logic of the theory, confusion is likely to increase" (p. 206).

Articulation

Makhlouf-Norris, Jones and Norris (1970) describe a measure of integration within a construct system based on inter-construct correlations. Those constructs correlating significantly with each other at beyond the 5 per cent level are regarded as primary clusters. For the remainder, (i) a construct significantly correlated with one or more constructs in one primary cluster is termed a "related off-shoot" construct; (ii) a construct significantly correlated with one or more constructs in two or more clusters is a "linkage" construct and (iii) a construct not significantly correlated with any other construct is an "isolate".

Grids of obsessionally neurotic patients were compared with those of a group of people with no psychiatric disorder. A difference was found between the two groups.

"The normal conceptual structure is articulated. It contains at least two different clusters which are joined together by linkage constructs. The obsessional conceptual structure is non-articulated, it is monolithic consisting of one dominant cluster with secondaries, or segmented consisting of more than one cluster but with no linkage constructs" (Makhlouf-Norris, Jones and Norris, 1970, p. 271).

While this measure is of potential interest, much more needs to be known about what difference it makes to live with a system that is articulated as opposed to non-articulated. Also, what happens if a level of significance other than the 5 per cent is taken? It might well be useful to know what clusters together at the 0.01 per cent level and how the system appears more integrated as the level of significance is reduced.

Integration between self and others

Makhlouf-Norris and Norris (1972) extended their analysis of structure to focus on the relationship between self, ideal self and others. Their measure is based on element distances given in Slater's INGRID principal components analysis programme (1964). It can equally well be derived from inter-element correlations obtained by hand or from a standard principal components analysis.

Their procedure is to plot all elements on two axes defined by "ideal self" and "actual self" in terms of their correlations or distances. Figure 15 shows the plot of elements (people) as they relate to "actual self" and "ideal self". The "actual self" is isolated, all people are seen as more or less like the "ideal self" with some also unlike the "actual self". The person could be said to know what he would like to be and not like to be, also he knows what he is not. What he appears to be in a quandry about is who he is actually like at present. The authors give examples of other ways of defining the self in grid terms and also of how to interpret these element alignments (Norris and Makhlouf-Norris, 1976). It is important to remember that the self and ideal self may well not be orthogonal although they are plotted as such.

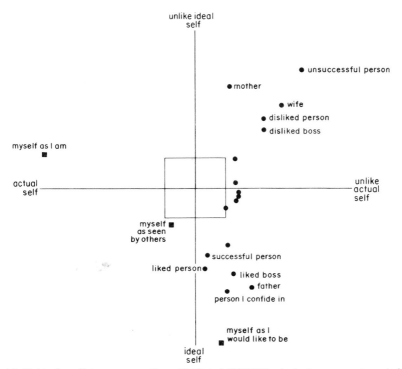

Fig. 15. Plot to show distances on a rating grid (Slater's INGRID principal components analysis) of all elements from the elements "actual self" and "ideal self" for one subject indicating actual self isolation. Redrawn from Norris and Makhlouf-Norris in "The Measurement of Intrapersonal space by Grid Technique", Vol. 1, edited by Slater, John Wiley & Sons Limited, 1976.

CONFLICT

Hinkle (1965) suggests how "implicative dilemmas" (see pp. 49-50) can be related to conflict theory. For instance, an *ambiguous* relationship between constructs is evident when either both poles of a construct imply one pole of another or when both poles of two constructs imply each other, as below:

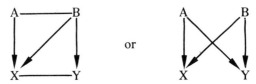

Bannister and Mair (1968) speculate that in the implications grid

"lines of implication may be indexed by the subject (in a series of descrete paired comparison judgments) which eventually cross over and run into the "wrong" poles of a later construct, e.g. construct A+ — A— may imply B+ — B— and C+ — C—, but it later transpires that C+ implies Z— while A+ implies Z+. Psychological concepts such as "conflict" might be examined in terms of manifest implicative contradictions." (p. 96).

Logical inconsistencies within a resistance-to-change grid, for example (see p. 43), can be examined without recourse to computer analysis. Bannister and Salmon (1966b) devised a method for scoring what they termed "intransitivity". If a subject says he would rather change on construct B than on construct A and he would rather change on construct C than on construct B then, logically, he should be more prepared to change on construct C rather than on construct A. The following is a scoring system designed to examine every case where X is more resistant to change than Y, in terms of whether X is then more resistant to change than all constructs to which Y is more resistant to change—the obvious logical requirement.

When the subject has indicated relative resistance-to-change on every possible pair of constructs, a matrix should be constructed in which a cross indicates that the subject would rather move on the construct on the horizontal intersect and stay put on the construct perpendicular to the cell. That is to say a blank in a column equals a construct on which the subject would prefer to change and a blank in a row indicates a construct on which the subject would prefer *not* to change.
1. Take row 1 and copy it so that you leave blanks where crosses are in the original row 1 and put crosses where blanks are in the original row and write the column numbers in the blanks on the copy.
2. Apply this copy line to every row beneath the number of which there is a cross in the original row (i.e. to every row in which there is a column number written in the copy).
3. Count the number of crosses in the line which you are examining which coincides with crosses on your copy line. Enter this figure on prepared matrix at the appropriate intersect. This matrix will be referred to as the results matrix. This figure represents the numbers of intransitive triads for that construct. It should be noted that unlike scanning in ordinary grids, you do not continually work downwards so that 1 to 2 is considered equal to 2 to 1. Thus on reaching, say, row 12 the copy made of it in the manner described will be taken back up the line and all relevant rows examined and their number of intransitivities counted. This is because a particular construct may be involved with another construct twice in an intransitive relationship first as a major premise or secondly as a minor premise in the syllogism.

4. When the above process is completed and all the relevant intersects in the results matrix have been entered with the number of intransitivities counted, turn your attention towards this results matrix. Total the entries along and down for each construct and write this total at the row end for the construct. This total is the raw total of intransitivity for that construct.

5. For each row multiply the number of blanks in the row by the number of crosses in the row (omitting entirely the "construct with itself" cell) and add on the number of blanks for each row that was compared with that construct. This total will be the total possible intransitivity score for each construct in turn. The final relative intransitivity score for each construct will be its raw intransitivity score over its possible intransitivity score expressed as a percentage. The relative intransitivity score for the grid as a whole will be simply the mean of the percentage relative intransitivity scores of the constructs in the grid. (Bannister and Salmon, 1966a).

Slade and Kjeldsen (1976) have taken this a step further. They were struck by the similarity between the data generated by Lauterbach's technique for assessing psychological conflict (1975a) and that obtained from the rank and rating forms of grids. Lauterbach's technique, based on Heider's cognitive balance theory (1946), involves the rating of the dynamic relationships between personal concepts, taken three at a time. These concepts are elicited from the subject or patient in the form of the personal problems that are most important or have led to a request for professional help. The concept "myself" is always included. The dynamic relationships between these concepts are rated by the patient on a 7-point scale and are either positive (e.g. liking, increasing, helping, strengthening, and so forth) or negative (e.g. disliking, decreasing, hindering, weakening, and so forth).

The method of conflict assessment is based on the social-psychological concept of "imbalanced triads". A triad consists of three concepts and the relationship between them. It can be either "balanced" or "imbalanced". The example of an imbalanced triad given by Lauterbach (1975b) is presented diagrammatically below:

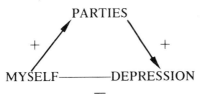

These relationships would be expressed verbally as: (1) "I like going to parties", (2) "Parties increase my depression" and (3) "I don't like being depressed". A "balanced" triad is one in which all three relationships are positive (i.e. +, +, +) or one is positive and two negative (i.e. +, —, —). An 'imbalanced' triad is one in which all three relationships are negative (i.e. —, —, —) or two are positive and one negative (i.e. +, +, —). Lauterbach has developed a computer programme for determining a total balance score, a total imbalance score and a percentage imbalance/conflict score with this procedure (Lauterbach, 1972).

Slade and Kjeldsen have developed a computer programme for assessing the ratio of imbalanced and balanced triads of constructs based on inter-construct correlations. They are at present investigating the practical implications of this potentially important method of identifying conflicts within a grid. For example, in the grid in which two psychologists construed two personality theorists, the Slade and Kjeldsen measure showed that by far the greatest amount of imbalance (ambiguity) surrounded the element "Kelly". What this seems to be saying, assuming the validity of the conflict measure, is that they find Kelly difficult to construe. (See Fig. 9.)

Another measure of conflict or ambivalence was suggested by Fransella and Crisp (1971). Using Slater's INGRID analysis, it was noted that on a measure of "distance", element and construct pairs (the same verbal labels) varied according to type of label. For example, "my ideal self" as construct and as element were seen in very similar terms whereas there were often very large distances between the construct and the element "me at a normal weight" for anorectic patients It was suggested that the extent of the distance could be related to ambivalence. The person was ranking the elements on the *construct* "me at a normal weight" somehow diffently from the way she was using the *element* in the rankings on other constructs. This idea was examined further as part of a larger study (Fransella and Crisp, 1977).

All that can be said at the moment about measures of conflict or ambivalence derived from different types of grid is that the search is interesting and, it seems to us, worthwhile, but speculative.

COMMENT

Faced with the danger that measures derived from repertory grids will become more and more complex and involve more and more levels of abstraction, how can we avoid reaching a stage approaching statistical gibberish? Perhaps the best way is to apply a simple test in the form of the following question. If you are deriving a measure from the grid can you trace out the links between the operations carried out by the subject who completed the grid and your measure? In other words, if you are going to call your measure something like "the self ideal creativity conflict measure", can you trace out an argument from the kind of judgments made by your subject, on through your mathematical processing of the grid, to the title which you are now giving to the measure? Can you show that there is reasonable justification for such a title?

There can be little doubt that as grids are used more and more the variety of grid measures and scores will increase. It is therefore important that users of grids should tighten up their thinking as to the theoretical assumptions underlying what they believe themselves to be measuring. In our view, they can do not better than to turn to the theory from whence the grid came.

5

Methods of Computer Analysis and Grid Comparisons

Neither abstraction nor generalization has ever been computerized, nor can either be realized by any unimaginative obedience to the canons of rationality, or by performing the symbolic transformations of mathematics, useful as these procedures may otherwise be. What can be computerized, for example, is the elimination of redundancy in a construction matrix. The resultant shrinkage in the matrix is sometimes mistaken for abstraction, for it appears to result in the expression of a great deal in relatively few terms. But the contribution the computer makes is to economy of the language employed, not to conceptualization; albeit one must grant that linguistic parsimony may serve to clear away the clutter that stands in the way of fresh thinking. But housecleaning is not abstraction and economizing does not constitute theoretical thinking. Occam's razor is a surgical instrument, not a creative tool. (Kelly, 1969, p. 290).

COMPUTER ANALYSIS

Statistical games with grids have captured the interest of many a psychologist-statistician manqué. Programmes have become more and more complex until it is virtually impossible to see how the print-out bears any relationship to what the person actually did when she filled out the grid. This is not a plea for the primitive and the pure, rather it is a reminder to those in danger of being caught up in the number game, that there are many interesting things that can be done working directly with the grid's raw data. Some of these methods are described in Chapter 4.

George Kelly, himself, bears some responsibility for fostering the idea that complex statistical procedures should be applied to grid data. In his Psychology of Personal Constructs (Vol. 1), Kelly outlined a non-parametric method of factor analysis. The first computer programme for this was written by Fager (1962) which was later elaborated by J. V. Kelly (1963). The next major assault on the subject was by Slater who, in 1964, described his method of analysing ranked grids into their principal components. Slater then went on to develop methods for comparing grids, both with the same elements and constructs and with different elements or constructs. By conceptualising psychological space as a hypersphere, he was able to quantify the extent to which elements and constructs on a rank or rating grid interacted. For a number of years the availability of these programmes under the sponsorship of the Medical Research Council, prevented people looking further afield. There were exceptions, of course. Bannister developed a programme that separately clustered constructs and elements. Others, particularly Thomas at Brunel University, use modifications of McQuitty's (1966) cluster analysis. Ravenette (1975) mentions that this can very simply be done by hand and that he has developed a "two-way" analysis which isolates the influence of specific elements within each cluster of constructs.

Wilson (1976) sets out the problem as follows:

"The ideal way to investigate construct-element relationships would require the simultaneous standardization of rows and columns. So, although Slater's programme attempts to reveal the relations between constructs and elements, these relations are distorted because only construct columns are normalized while element rows are not. In order to reveal undistorted relationships, it would be necessary to standardize both. Cattell (1966) however has reported that a method for obtaining a unique solution for simultaneous standardization of both rows and columns has not yet been found. This is a very interesting statistical problem, as well as being of importance for grid analysis."

For implications grids there is very little by way of computer analysis. Hinkle's original Impgrid can be analysed by a modification of J. V. Kelly's factor analytic method but this faces one with the eternal problem of correlating tick-blank data. That is, equal importance is given to the blanks as to the ticks and there exists the whole problem of lopsidedness (see p. 30).

In an attempt to avoid these difficulties, a programme calculating the binomial probabilities of matching and mismatching ticks between pairs of rows and columns has been developed for the bi-polar implications grid (Fransella, 1972). But it is now clear that this is not the most appropriate statistic. At the present time an entirely new approach to the analysis of implications grid data is being developed. This is based on a subjective probability model which would result in a matrix of similarities between constructs. The similarity matrix could then be subjected to some form of cluster analysis.

For those who are statistically inclined and who feel they would like to investigate the computer analysis of grids further, we are including here a general discussion on the subject for which we are greatly indebted to Paula Wilson (1976). In her paper, Wilson points out that there are two main categories of analysis open to those wishing to analyse ranked or rating grid data.

Metric factor analyses

The advantage of these methods over any other is their availability in Britain and America in the form of commercial statistical packages (e.g. the SPSS or Statistical Package for the Social Sciences, Nie *et al.,* 1975). The SPSS includes options for five different methods of factor analysis.

A principal components analysis (PA1) requires no assumptions about the data being analysed (this is not so for the other four methods). It is essentially an analysis of the total variance of the data and can be done by row and column, but not the two together. The final solution can be rotated to one of three criteria (Varimax, Equimax and Oblimax) and the outcome plotted as part of the computer output.

The remaining methods are based on the common factor model which assumes that the variables being factored are composed of both common and specific parts and that it is only the common variance whose dimensionality is of interest.

Principal factor analysis (*PA2*) is the most frequently used of the four methods. But Wilson points out that it is a special case of the more general Image factor analysis (Rummell, 1970), and it is this method that Rummell recommends. Image factor analysis does not have the implicit assumptions underlying common factor analysis and it has the additional advantage of providing a way of testing the explicit assumption of the common factor model, that is, that the variance of interest is that portion which is shared by all constructs. As part of the output, the anti-image covariance matrix is printed. The presence, in this matrix, of off-diagonal values which tend toward zero, allows the investigator to have increased confidence in the validity of the final solution because this indicates that a substantial portion of the variance is indeed shared by all constructs. Wilson says that it is important to note that Image factor analytic solutions are generally of $m/2$ dimensionality. That is, there are roughly half as many factors as there are variables. She comments that this number of factors may be too large to provide a parsimonious description of the data and that it is possible to reduce the number of factors in the final solution and then to rotate this solution.

The two remaining methods make assumptions in addition to that inherent in the common factor model.

Rao analysis assumes that the variables being factored (constructs) comprise the universe of variables and the cases (elements) are a sample from the population of elements.

Alpha analysis, on the other hand, assumes that the elements included are the population and that the variables are a sample from the universe of variables. In this case, the solution is generalisable to the universe of constructs. Wilson says that the choice between these techniques must be determined by the purpose of the research. All these five methods are discussed by Nie and his colleagues (1975).

Wilson goes on to make two further points about the forms of factor analysis contained in the SPSS package. The first is that factor analysis can be carried out on either a correlation matrix or a covariance matrix both of which are derivable from the raw data. But the factor solutions for principal components analysis or principal factors analysis are different. For Rao and Alpha analysis and for the Harris version of Image factor analysis (Harris, 1962) this is not the case. For these three methods, the solutions obtained for the correlations and covariance matrices are proportional and therefore perfectly correlated. So, as Wilson points out, this removes the dilemma posed by both principal component and principal factor analysis—that is, choosing which matrix to factor.

Wilson's second point concerns the number of elements relative to the number of constructs being factored and the related issues concerning the representative nature of the constructs. Generally, it is a correlation matrix which is factored and the reliability of the solution depends, to some extent, on the stability of the correlation coefficients. This stability is enhanced when the number of elements on which the correlation is calculated is increased. Wilson therefore suggests that, wherever possible, there should be three times the number of elements to the number of constructs. Also, the dimensionality of the final solution may be artificially restricted by a poor choice of constructs, that is, by an unrepresentative sampling of constructs. If only two kinds of constructs are supplied or elicited, it is reasonable to expect a two dimensional solution.

Wilson is arguing about what is desirable statistically but this leaves aside what is desirable and useful psychologically. Bannister and Mair (1968) found, certainly with rank grids using people as elements, that increasing the number of elements from 10 to 15 markedly reduced the amount of structure the subject was able to impose.

Non-metric methods

This group includes multidimensional scaling (Shepard, Romney and Nerlove, 1972). Whereas the previous group of metric methods assumed linear relationships between the variables and the factors, the multi-dimensional scaling techniques assume only monotonicity between the final solution and the matrix being analysed. For example, in ranked and rating grids, the ordinal relations among constructs, with respect to an element (i.e. which construct the element is rated highest on, rated second highest on and so on) will be retained in the final solution, but the distance between the constructs (i.e. how *much* higher the element is rated on one construct than another) is not retained. Wilson rightly points out that, in a discipline where much of the data are measured on ordinal or even nominal scales, the decreased emphasis on linear relationships is proving to be a boon to dimensional analysis. But there are a number of disadvantages to this method. The most important is a practical one—there are few programmes available in the form of commercial packages. Although there is a long history of non-metric investigations (Coombs, 1954), these techniques are not as widely accepted as are the metric methods.

The most comprehensive taxonomy of non-metric models, computer programmes and data suitability has been published by Shepard (1972). Wilson says that Shepard's list is not exhaustive and that developments are progressing "at an alarming rate". She discusses one development which she sees as directly relevant to implications grids. Hays (1958) proposed an implications model which uses conditional probabilities as raw data and calculates a distance matrix which can subsequently be analysed using one of the non-metric methods. She sees the characteristic of Hay's model as being its ability to handle asymetric conditional probabilities. His model also allows for the determination of weights or saliences of construct poles. These combined characteristics mean that the constructs which are the most closely related to the dimensions are the most central constructs. These are the most heavily weighted constructs which imply the largest number of constructs while being implied by the least number of constructs. She points out that this definition of centrality is very close to Hinkle's (1965) conception of superordinacy. Wilson sees Hay's distance measure, in combination with a non-metric multidimensional scaling technique, as possibly providing the first valid means of determining the dimensionality of implications grids.

Other computer programmes and methods of statistical analyses can be found in Landfield (1971), Fransella (1972), Wilcox (1972), Guertin (1975).

GRID COMPARISONS

Between different grid forms

With all the activity in the repertory grid world, with people designing grids for a multitude of imaginative purposes, it comes as something of a surprise to find so little work on the comparison of different grid methods. Are the different forms of grid asking the same questions and, if so, does one get the same answers?

One of the first attempts to do just this suggested that the answers might not be the same (Fransella, 1965). She compared ranked with rating grid formats for one person. The plots of the constructs along the two main principal components showed little similarity.

But a more recent report (Fransella, 1976) gives a correlation of 0.76 between these two methods, again on a single case. As there was one construct that had a test-retest correlation of —0.47, it is clear that the remaining constructs had very high test-retest correlations indeed, in spite of the different methods of administration.

In 1967, Mair and Boyd reported the results of a comparison between the rank order and split half forms. There was already some evidence that these two methods had some comparability in terms of the kinds of group discrimination they yielded. Bannister's original findings concerning thought disorder using a split half method (1960) were confirmed using the rank order form (Bannister and Fransella, 1966).

In their study, Mair and Boyd gave 24 delinquent boys the two types of grid, one immediately after the other and then repeated this two weeks later. The elements were photographs, 20 for the split half method and 10 for the rank order form. The constructs *like I am, like father* and *like mother* were compared with the remaining 15 constructs on each grid and the construct relationships compared between grids. The mean correlation for the three constructs on the two types of grid was 0.50 for *like I am* (range —0.76 to

0.82), 0.57 for *like father* (range —0.64 to 0.91) and 0.48 for *like mother* (range —0.36 to 0.84). These means, with an N of 19, all are significant at least at the 5 per cent level. But what is interesting is the wide range of correlations. Does it mean that, for some subjects, *like I am* as presented on the split half method is somehow opposite when presented in rank order form? If so, what is the difference perceived between the two methods by the subject? If it could be shown that people scoring —0.76 for *like I am* between the two methods were also likely to obtain high negative correlations on the other construct comparisons and those obtaining high positive correlations on one also obtained high correlations on the others, then we would be a step closer to discovering exactly what the perceived differences are. This would be especially so if the test-retest correlations on both types of grid were high for these individuals. Mair and Boyd conclude that the split half and rank order methods cannot be considered as interchangeable.

The rank order grid has recently been compared with the bi-polar implications grid, using children as subjects. Honess (1977) supplied these children (average age 12.8 years) with 8 constructs which he had obtained from an analysis of some of their essays. Once again, the elements were photographs. One group of children completed the rank grid followed one week later by the Impgrid and then 4 weeks later by a repeat of the rank grid, the other group had the order Impgrid, rank grid, Impgrid. The correlation between the two techniques for the same group of children was 0.50. This is very similar to that found by Mair and Boyd, but with an N of 41, it is much more highly significant statistically.

Honess also gave some other comparison data. For instance, the test-retest correlation was considerably higher for the Impgrid (0.82 compared with 0.66) and, when the least stable construct was eliminated, the correlations rose to 0.89 and 0.75 respectively. The Impgrid also seemed superior to the rank grid in establishing more truly bi-polar constructs. Honess' criterion for bi-polarity was reached by 28.8 per cent of the constructs in the rank order grid reached compared with 56.9 per cent on the Impgrid.

The implications grid has also been compared with a grid using tick/blank data (Kelsall and Strongman, 1977). It was found the overall patterning of constructs was very similar (p<.001) for the two forms but there was again considerable individual variability.

The picture emerging from these few studies is that grids of various forms cannot be considered identical either in terms of the perceived task or in terms of results. The answer to the question why do different forms not always give the same results will only be found by studying the task the person is being required to carry out in each case. In doing this, we will no doubt find out something more about psychological measurement generally.

Between identical grid forms

There is little difficulty in estimating the degree of stability between identical grid forms administered to different people or to the same people on different occasions when the focus of interest is the pattern of relations between constructs.

As part of his investigation into the disordered thinking often found in those diagnosed as schizophrenic, Bannister derived a method for obtaining a statistical statement concerning the degree of construct pattern stability when identical grids are used. If construct 2 is highly positively related to constructs 3, 4 and 5 on the first test occasion, does the same pattern occur on the second occasion? Figure 16 shows how this can be done.

The correlations between each pair of constructs are ranked, from highest positive, through zero to highest negative. This has been done for the construct correlations from the ranked grid in Table II (p. 35). The same is done for the correlations obtained on the second test occasion and a Spearman rank order correlation coefficient obtained between these two sets of rankings.

The same can be done with matching scores or rating data. They can be ranked from pairs with highest positive degrees of association through zero to those with highest negative associations.

But there is another type of consistency which can be calculated for ranked or rating grids. This is the extent to which the allocation of elements remains stable. Constructs can remain similarly related to each other (e.g. high Bannister Consistency) while elements are construed differently. A person can continue to think that certain qualities are desirable and others undesirable, but the people seen as having these qualities can change. Element consistency can be calculated simply by correlating their ranks on construct 1 on the first test occasion with their ranks on the second occasion. The differences between element consistency and construct pattern consistency can be seen in Table VIII.

Between the two test occasions, this person has retained the essential meaning of the constructs as measured by their relationship to each other but has sometimes radically changed her mind about the people (elements) being construed in terms of these constructs.

Faced with the task of comparing a set of grids, perhaps to find evidence of conceptual change during treatment, one can use Bannister's Consistency method or resort to the computer and use Slater's COIN programme which "In the conditions where Bannister's measure can be applied (it) gives almost exactly equivalent results" (Slater, 1972, p. 45).

Alternatively, one can focus on element placements and correlate the rankings on first and second test occasions for each construct. A more complex analysis along these lines can be carried out by compiling a matrix of element differences. That is, each element rank or rating in grid 1 is subtracted from its rank or rating in grid 2. The dimensions of change can be obtained by applying a standard form of principal components or factor analysis to the matrix. Slater's DELTA programme (1968) was designed for this purpose. In addition to the usual output provided by standard procedures, DELTA gives element change as well as construct change and yields a correlation between grid 1 and grid 2 as a whole.

Slater has developed other computer methods for analysing the relationships between more than two grids, two grids with different elements or two grids with different constructs (see Slater, 1977).

| | FIRST TEST OCCASION | | SECOND TEST OCCASION | | | |
Constructs	rho	rank	rho	rank	d	d²
1−2	0.86	2	0.80	6	4	16
1−3	0.58	12	0.61	11	1	1
1−4	−0.74	36	−0.73	36	0	0
1−5	0.42	21	0.44	18	3	9
1−6	0.54	13.5	0.59	12	1.5	2.25
1−7	0.64	11	0.70	8.5	2.5	6.25
1−8	0.44	19.5	0.42	19.5	0	0
1−9	0.32	22	0.40	21.5	0.5	0.25
2−3	0.48	15	0.52	14	1	1
2−4	−0.64	33	−0.63	33	0	0
2−5	0.13	26	0.20	25	1	1
2−6	0.44	19.5	0.42	19.5	0	0
2−7	0.31	23	0.35	24	1	1
2−8	0.14	25	0.17	27	2	4
2−9	0.03	28	0.05	28	0	0
3−4	−0.73	35	−0.70	35	0	0
3−5	0.10	27	0.18	26	1	1
3−6	0.81	4	0.85	4	0	0
3−7	0.46	16.5	0.49	17	0.5	0.25
3−8	0.26	24	0.37	23	1	1
3−9	0.45	18	0.40	21.5	3.5	12.25
4−5	−0.46	31	−0.50	31	0	0
4−6	−0.70	34	−0.68	34	0	0
4−7	−0.52	32	−0.49	30	2	4
4−8	−0.41	30	−0.52	32	2	4
4−9	−0.40	29	−0.39	29	0	0
5−6	0.46	16.5	0.51	15.5	1	1
5−7	0.71	9	0.81	5	4	16
5−8	0.88	1	0.92	1.5	0.5	0.25
5−9	0.69	10	0.67	10	0	0
6−7	0.72	8	0.51	15.5	7.5	56.25
6−8	0.54	13.5	0.58	13	0.5	0.25
6−9	0.77	6	0.92	1.5	4.5	20.25
7−8	0.74	7	0.86	3	4	16
7−9	0.85	3	0.70	8.5	5.5	30.25
8−9	0.78	5	0.79	7	2	4

$$\Sigma d^2 = 208.50$$

$$\frac{6\,\Sigma d^2}{n^3-n} = \frac{1251}{46620} = 0.03 \qquad\qquad rho = \underline{0.97}$$

Fig. 16. The calculation of a Consistency score between inter-construct correlations obtained from one rank grid completed by one subject on two test occasions.

Table VIII

Consistency of (a) element rankings on each construct and (b) overall interconstruct patterning between two administrations of identical grids for one person participating in group psychotherapy. From Fransella, 1970.

Constructs	Element Consistency	Construct Pattern Consistency
1	—0.52	0.96
2	—0.43	0.83
3	0.29	0.63
4	—0.31	0.79
5	—0.24	0.86
6	—0.69	0.96
7	—0.36	0.39
8	0.81	0.48
9	0.55	0.61
10	0.02	0.82
11	0.29	0.78
12	—0.71	0.91
13	—0.57	0.60
14	—0.52	0.70
15	—0.24	0.80
16	—0.07	0.91

COMMENT

In one sense, the development of computer methods of analysis has had an unfortunate effect on the development of grid method. They have inclined some to see grids as a scientific procedure not because of their value in helping us understand another's outlook but simply because of the reams of paper output. This pseudo-precision has made some people forget the basic rules of statistics; for example, that a correlation of 0.2 is likely to have occurred by chance unless the N is sufficiently large. Even if the N is sufficiently great to make the correlation significant at the glorious 5 per cent level, in most cases there will be little of psychological significance in a relationship that only accounts for 4 per cent of variance.

In case we are now being seen as purists, we hasten to add that we are all for multidimensional methods of analysis for, as Kelly himself said

"The conceptual grid . . . . . is (therefore) a premathematical representation of an individual's psychological space, and it is designed to set the stage for a mathematical analysis of that space. As we see it, it is essentially multidimensional in character" (1955, p. 304).

Our plea is that the grid user should have at least some intuitive grasp of the procedures being so competently carried out by the computer.

6

Reliability

Reliability is that characteristic of a test which makes it insensitive to change.
G. A. Kelly

THE MEANING OF THE TERM

When psychologists talk about the reliability of a measure, they often seem to hover between various definitions of the term. Sometimes they seem to be talking very generally of the capacity of a measure "reliably" to assess a characteristic, whether or not the "amount" of the characteristic is changing in the subject. At other times they seem to mean by reliability, the tendency of a test to produce exactly the same result for the same subject at different times. One can imagine circumstances under which the second definition could be looked on as a reasonable operational form of the first definition. As, for example, when it is assumed that the characteristic is relatively stable and unchanging for a given subject, e.g. the height of an adult person. However, since much of life is about change, the second definition stated as a requirement of a measure becomes fatuous when it is universally applied. A thermometer which steadily recorded the temperature of a given subject as 98.4 degrees Fahrenheit would not be much of an asset to medicine. The overall aim is surely not to produce stable *measures*—stability or instability exist in what is measured, not in the measure. Our concern is, as Mair (1964) put it, to assess *predictable* stability and *predictable* change.

The above paragraph labours the obvious yet psychologists have so worshipped "reliability" that the obvious needs labouring. Stability is often assumed to be "the normal state of affairs". Thus, we are taught to expect for adults stability of intelligence test scores for a single person over time unless some unusual event such as damage to the person's brain has taken place. Equally that most intellectually disastrous form of personality theory, trait psychology, has strengthened the myth of unchanging man. Change is of the essence. Man, in Kelly terms, is "a form of motion" not a static object that is occasionally kicked into movement.

If we consider forms of grid to be attempts to enquire into a person's construct system then under what circumstances would we expect stability or change? If we were to investigate your notions of the rules of arithmetic from time to time, we might expect to find a very great degree of stability. Regularly it might turn out that you considered odd numbers indivisible by even numbers and that you held steadily to the expectation that fractions multiplied by fractions result in a smaller amount than either fraction. On the other hand if we were periodically to measure your view of films, we might find that as time went on you found musicals "more enchanting" or the work of Ford "less accurate from a documentary point of view". More important, the relationship between "enchanting" and "documentary accuracy" might well change. If we were to examine and re-examine any part of your viewpoint when you were drunk we might expect more variation in outlook than a series of such examinations when you were sober. If we were to examine any part of the views of children we might find that (children being more adventurous and experimental) they changed their views more than adults. If you thought that our investigation was designed to test your constancy then you might give more stable responses than if you thought our investigation was a challenge to see if you could grow, learn and diversify. If we were (in, say, chess) to examine your *superordinate* constructs we might find you clung to strong centre theory while *subordinately* changing merrily from a period when you favoured King's court gambits to one in which you favoured Queen's court gambits and so *ad infinitum*.

The idea of a static mind is a contradiction in terms. We should look to the grid not to repeat the same result but to see, when it shows change, what it is signifying. In short, reliability is perhaps best seen as merely one aspect of validity.

Apart from the general debate about the meaningfulness of particular concepts of reliability, there are specific problems where the grid is concerned simply because there is no such thing as *The* Grid. Given the multiplicity of form, content and analysis for extant grids (and envisaging the many kinds of grid which have not yet been invented) it is clearly nonsense to talk of *the* reliability of *the* grid. It is even less sensible than say talking of *the* reliability of *the* questionnaire. We would be bound to ask of any question about *the* reliability of questionnaires, *what* questionnaires in *what* area administered to *what* kind of subjects under *what* kind of conditions and analysed in *what* kind of manner.

We can best illustrate the problem by considering a few of the obtained variations in reliability coefficient where grid methods have been used.

THE RELIABILITY OF DIFFERENT MEASURES
WITHIN THE GRID

The grid is a data form open to many kinds of analysis. If we briefly consider only eight kinds of measure which at one time or another have been derived from grid data, we can compare and contrast the test re-test reliability for each measure.

Mal-distribution

This is a measure of what Kelly referred to as lopsidedness in constructs. If you are asked to divide 20 of your acquaintances into those you consider *radical* and those you consider *conservative,* then one characteristic of your judgement which immediately becomes apparent is the relative number of elements allotted to each pole of the construct—your world apparently may be largely inhabited by *radical* characters or by *conservative* ones, or the distribution may be approximately equal. Bannister (1959) reported a study in which subjects allotted 19 of their acquaintances to the two poles of 22 constructs and then immediately afterwards allotted a different set of 19 of their acquaintances to the two poles of the same constructs. The proportion allotted to each pole of the constructs was examined from first to second set of elements and the reliability coefficient was 0.70. A repeat (Bannister, 1962a) using photographs as elements with 30 subjects gave a reliability coefficient for the mal-distribution score of 0.76.

It should be noted here that our prime question should be, under what conditions and with what implications does the degree of lopsidedness a person shows change, rather than focus on whether the measure as such is "reliable". For example, in an unreported study, Bannister found that anxious people (i.e. high scorers on the Taylor Manifest Anxiety Scale) tended to put most of their elements into one pole of each construct and leave the other fairly empty ($p<.05$).

Intensity

This is a global measure of the amount of correlation or relationship between constructs in a grid so that a high Intensity (see p. 60) score indicates that most of the constructs are seen as implying each other and are not used independently. Intensity correlates very highly with other global measures of structure such as the amount of variance accounted for by the first factor when the grid is factor analysed. Intensity tends to have low reliability from test to re-test. For example in one study (Bannister, 1962a) the test re-test correlation was 0.35. Exactly the same correlation was reported recently by Honess (1977) for Intensity in a rank order grid. Honess' subjects were children and the test re-test interval was four weeks. In the same study Honess reported a much higher test re-test correlation for a measure of Intensity in a bi-polar implications grid ($r=0.62$). A point to note here is that Intensity scores tend much more often than not, to increase when a person completes a second grid a short time after the first, so that some sort of *process* is inherent in the actual completion of the grid (Bannister, Fransella and Agnew, 1971).

In a number of studies to be reported later in this chapter, it can be shown that Intensity increases or decreases under specifiable conditions and that the degree of Intensity is significantly different for groups of subjects variously identified in terms of their psychopathology. So here we have a measure of relatively proven validity (in that it predictably relates to characteristics of subject and situation) but of low reliability. This might lead us to speculate that it is not that the measure itself has unwelcome "error variance" but that it perhaps very sensitively reflects rapid changes in the structure of construing and that it should be used with this in mind. Its lack of "reliability" might denote its most significant theoretical implication.

Pattern of construct relationships

Basic analysis of grid data tends to yield a matrix of measures of interelationship between constructs, though the form in which the relationship is expressed may be matching scores or Spearman rhos or other forms of relationship index. Obviously, the similarity of one pattern of construct relationships to another can be measured in a number of ways. Perhaps the most simple is to use what used to be called an index of factorial similarity. This is calculated by rank ordering the relationship scores of each matrix from the highest positive through zero down to the highest negative and then running a Spearman rho between the two (see p. 80). This measure has been used in a large number of studies on repeat grids using either the same or different elements with the same constructs. Studies tend to yield coefficients of reliability which fall largely within the range of 0.60 to 0.80. Lansdown (1975) found there was a decrease in correlation from immediate retest to a retest interval of more than eight days for 59 children (9—11 years). The correlation between construct pattern consistency and time interval was —0.35 (p<.01). Watson, Gunn and Gristwood (1976) also used rank grids in their study of prisoners. Thirty-two prisoners repeated the grids over intervals of seven to ten days. Slater's measure of overall similarity of element placement between pairs of grids averaged 0.74 with a range of 0.30 to 1.00 for individual subjects.

A prime question then is under what conditions would we expect to have more stable patterns of interrelationship between constructs and under what conditions would we expect less stable patterns. Equally, for what particular constructs or what subsystems of constructs with the person's total system would we expect to have high stability and low stability respectively.

Specific relationships between constructs

In any grid study, whether it focuses on the investigation of an individual's construct system in clinical work or is part of a more general experiment, it may be the relationship between specific constructs within the total matrix which is of particular interest e.g. the relationship say between self constructs (*like I am, like I'd like to be* and so forth) and particular value constructs. A very noticeable feature of grid results is the difference in the reliability (consistency of matrix relationship position on re-test) of the same pair of constructs for the same person. This is clearly demonstrated in Table IX and applies whether the same or different elements are used.

In the study reported in Appendix I it was noted that for one subject the two "problem" constructs had very different fates so that as between first and second testing the relationships with all other constructs for one remained relatively stable (0.63) whereas the other had changed its pattern of implications substantially and its consistency from first to second testing was 0.31 (see Table XII). On a more general basis there is clear evidence that certain kinds of construct seem to be generally more consistently and stably used than others. Thus a re-analysis of the data from Bannister (1962a) shows that for 30 subjects the average reliability coefficient for the construct *good—bad* (relationships with all other constructs) was 0.80 where the average reliability coefficient for the construct *usual—unusual* was 0.50.

Table IX

Correlations of the construct *like me* with other constructs in four rank grids completed by an arsonist on four separate occasions over one month. The elements were people known personally to the subject on occasions 1 and 4 and photographs of men unknown to the subject on occasions 2 and 3. From Fransella and Adams, 1966.

LIKE ME correlated with:	People	Photos	Photos	People
Like I'd like to be	+0.88	+0.92	+0.93	+0.84
Enjoy power	—	+0.78	+0.89	+0.87
Upright	+0.88	—	+0.94	+1.0
Feelings *re* fire	+0.87	+0.88	+0.93	+0.89
Pleasure in being sexually aroused	+0.05	—0.77	—0.39	—0.39
Likely to commit arson	—0.59	—0.75	—	—0.90

Stability of elicited constructs

A basic question to be asked in relation to grid method is whether constructs elicited from subjects are likely to be a representative and stable sample or whether, in fact, there is an almost infinite pool from which (more or less randomly) constructs appear from one occasion of inquiry to another. This issue was early investigated by Hunt (1951) who elicited constructs to fit 41 role titles by the triadic method. He found that over an interval of a week about 70 per cent of the constructs elicited on the first occasion were repeated on the second. Fjeld and Landfield (1961) repeated Hunt's experiment in a more elaborate form and showed that, given the same elements, there was over a two week interval a correlation of 0.80 between first and second sets of elicited constructs.

Stability of elements

A similar question could be asked about the elements that a subject supplies and Pedersen (1958) found that when his subjects were twice asked to fit role titles for a grid, with an interval of one week, there was a 77 per cent reproduction of the same elements. Fjeld and Landfield (1961) also checked on this feature and found an average 72 per cent agreement for elements supplied to fit a role title list.

Insight measures

Clearly the grid can be used as a measure of Insight, meaning by this the degree to which a person can predict or postdict the grid relationships between his constructs. Bannister (1962a) tested the stability of this measure on immediate retest and found a correlation of 0.53. Obviously, nothing would be more foolish than to begin to say that *the* reliability of *the* Insight measure is 0.53. A whole series of questions arise as to whether or not very different reliabilities might be found depending on which part of the person's construct system has been subjected to "insight" test.

Social dictionary measures

One use of the grid could be to establish a kind of dictionary of average relationships between constructs for populations. For a given group of constructs a large number of grids could be averaged and the resulting matrix of relationships between constructs looked on as a kind of normative map. This, of course, raises the question of how reliable that normative map would be. Bannister (1962a) constructed such a table of norms (using photos of unknown people as elements) for eight constructs and the matrix of matching scores on first testing is shown in Table X. A normative table using the same constructs but this time using people known to the subjects as elements was obtained. The correlation between the two normative tables was 0.98. This very high equivalent form reliability suggests that, though there are considerable variations in *individual* construct relationship pattern, it may be that from samples of a relatively limited size, reliable *normative* estimates can be established.

Here we have looked at only a few of the possible measures which can be derived from repertory grids and briefly examined their reliability. The reliabilities quoted range from around 0.30 to 0.98. Clearly, therefore, any statement about the reliability of a grid must be cast in the form of a particular grid. As will be shown later, even this will have to be hedged around with all kinds of specifications of condition and provisos as to the theoretical meanings to be attached to the term reliability. To underline this, we now consider not merely the question of different measures which can be derived from a grid but issues of variations in construction of grids, the varying populations with which grids might be used and the conditions under which they might be applied. All of these are factors which produce considerable variation in "reliability".

POPULATION VARIANCE

A common finding with grids is that different individuals will show widely varying degrees of stability when they are given repeat grids. Additionally, it has been established (e.g. Bannister, 1960 and Bannister and Fransella,

Table X

Average matching scores for 9 constructs from 30 normal subjects using 20 photographs as elements.

	Mean	Good	Unusual	Narrow minded	Sincere	Selfish	Unreliable	Kind
Likeable	−10	+9	−2	−7	+8	−7	−5	+8
Mean		−9	+3	+8	−8	+10	+4	−8
Good			−4	−6	+10	−8	−6	+8
Unusual				+2	−3	+3	+2	−3
Narrow minded					−7	+7	+4	−7
Sincere						−9	−7	+9
Selfish							+5	−9
Unreliable								−7

1966) that clinically different populations may have very different reliabilities. This second point is of particular interest because it shows the way in which reliability can itself be used as a measure of *populations* rather than as an assessment of "The Test". In a long series of studies, grids were applied on an immediate test-retest basis to populations of thought disordered schizophrenics and to normal and other psychiatric populations. The stability of the pattern of relationships between constructs on the first and second grid (Consistency—see p. 80) was itself used to measure a characteristic of each subject. However, it can also serve as a test retest reliability coefficient for the particular grid in use. Repeatedly it was found that normal and psychiatric populations in general have Consistency scores of between 0.6 and 0.8 whereas thought disordered populations have Consistency scores of the order of 0.2.

ELEMENT VARIANCE

If we accept that different subsystems within a person's construct system may have different degrees of stability, then clearly we would expect to find, for both individuals and groups, that different elements (which represent different subsystems of constructs) will yield different retest correlation coefficients. Experimentally this is very clearly the case for the pattern of construct relationships. For example in Bannister and Mair (1968) subjects rank ordering photographs on supplied constructs had, over an interval of six weeks, a correlation coefficient of 0.86 across time and 0.73 if the actual photographs were changed. The names of real objects rank ordered on appropriate constructs over six weeks, yielded a reliability coefficient of 0.92 over time and 0.91 with different objects supplied on the second testing occasion. Mitsos (1958) found much lower test-retest correlations when "friends" were used as elements rather than people to fit role titles (possibly because the latter are a more representative sample).

Even a multiplicity of statements about relative reliabilities for different types of element would not cover the case since there is evidence that the formal structure of the grid has to be taken into account. Thus, in one study (Bannister and Mair, 1968) when subjects were asked to rank order *ten* photographs on six constructs their mean reliability coefficient over six weeks was 0.86 whereas when they were asked to rank order *fifteen* people the mean reliability coefficient over six weeks was 0.56. Again, it cannot simply be stated that a higher number of elements in a rank order grid tends to reduce reliability because very high reliabilities were achieved with a 15 element rank order grid using real objects as elements (0.92).

THE EFFECT OF VARYING VALIDATIONAL FORTUNES

In Bannister (1965b) subjects were asked to rank order photographs on "personality" constructs for a total of twenty trials. In each case the pattern of interrelationship between constructs was correlated with the pattern of interrelationships for the following trial. One group of subjects had been validated, that is told that their judgements were largely accurate through all trials. This group had a grand mean reliability coefficient (from a total of 19 comparisons for each of the ten people in the group) of 0.74. For an invalidated group (who had been told that their judgements were largely inaccurate after each trial) the grand mean was 0.56. Clearly, it would be nonsense here to talk about these very different reliability coefficients as indicating different reliabilities of *the test*. What they show is that reliability (or "consistency" since we wish to indicate that we are talking about a psychological characteristic of people and not a characteristic of the test) is a function of the psychological processes of individuals and perhaps in particular varies with their conviction that they are doing well or badly in the task they are undertaking.

CONCLUSIONS

Clearly it would be possible to cite almost an infinity of further reliability coefficients for different grid measures. One study alone (Sperlinger, 1976) yielded, over a seven month test retest, a variety of stability coefficients. The degree of perceived similarity between self and the eleven other figures in the grid correlated 0.95. The percentage variance accounted for by the first factor was not significantly correlated test to retest. The two sets of elicited constructs, in terms of percentage of each type of construct on a modification of Landfield's (1971) categorisation system, were 58 per cent in agreement. Again, wide individual variance was reported for all types of reliability coefficient.

Our vision of the possible number of reliability coefficients increases enormously when we reflect that the varying conditions briefly discussed here are additive. Thus not only are there many different measures to be derived from the grid but each measure can almost invariably be derived from grids which themselves have varying elements and constructs and which might be applied not only to varying individuals but to varying populations of individuals with varying modes of administration and with varying validational fortunes.

It seems sensible, therefore, to regard "reliability" as the name for an area of inquiry into the way in which people maintain or alter their construing and to estimate the value of the grid not in terms of whether it has "high" or "low" reliability but whether or not it is an instrument which enables us effectively to inquire into precisely this problem.

7

Validity

Validity refers to the capacity of a test to tell us what we already know.
G. A. Kelly

THE MEANING OF THE TERM

It is reasonable to talk about the validity of the grid only in the way that it is reasonable to talk about the validity of say, the, chi-square. We readily recognise that the chi-square, like any other statistic, is a format in which data can be placed, which will reveal if there is pattern or meaning to the data. This is exactly what a grid is. It is not a test. It has no specific content and its validity can only be talked about in the sense that we can question whether or not it will effectively reveal patterns and relationships in certain kinds of data.

This means that we have to talk about the validity of the grid in a very different way from that which we use to talk about the validity of, say, a questionnaire. If we have a thirty-item questionnaire which is alleged to measure a person's "submissiveness" then we are necessarily involved in the meaning we attach to the term "submissiveness" and the question of what, in turn, we would expect "submissiveness" to relate to and predict. Grids do not measure a trait or characteristic in this sense. Basically they are ways of looking at the relationships between a person's constructs. We can argue about whether "submissiveness" or any other kind of named characteristic is conceptually useful in psychology but it is difficult to set up the argument that people's constructs do not relate or that it is unimportant whether or not they relate.

The fact that we attach meaning to the world around us is itself a way of stating that our constructs relate. A dictionary is simply a catalogue of how constructs represented by linguistic symbols relate formally for a particular population. The whole structure of logic, both formal and informal, is based on the notion of one construct *implying* another (if p then q). Therefore the basic contention that constructs relate is not disputable since the very act of disputing it would involve organised argument which can only be contrived if constructs relate. Nor is it reasonable to argue that grids do not measure relationships between constructs, although we can argue about the ways in which they measure such relationships and the kinds of prediction we can derive from such measurements.

If we take any common form of grid, say a grid in which ten elements of any kind have been rank ordered on a number of constructs, then we will observe that there are a series of significant Spearman rho correlations between those constructs, many more than would have been expected by chance. Clearly the grid has revealed a pattern of relationships between the constructs by revealing a pattern in the way in which the person has ranked his elements. Thus it can be argued that the grid has, in one sense of the term, *intrinsic* validity. For any given grid the meaningfulness of the operations carried out by the subject can be demonstrated (see Draffan, 1973). This is because the kinds of statistic, such as significance level of correlations, binomial expansion, cluster analysis and so on, which we normally apply to data resulting from a population of subjects, can be applied to the performance of one subject in a single grid. The "population" is the population of the subject's responses and it can be explored by many of the group statistics which traditionally have been used primarily for groups of subjects. Our first contention then, is that the grid is essentially a format for data and that while it is eminently reasonable to question the validity of a *particular* grid format constructed to try and yield particular information, it is not sensible to dispute the validity of *the grid* as such.

The second aspect of grid validity which needs particular note rests on the argument that was used in relation to reliability, namely that the grid has an infinity of forms and therefore cannot be talked about as an entity in the sense that we normally talk about particular tests as entities. If we found that a particular form of grid had no predictive value and was not yielding information we would look for flaws in that format rather than make any general statement about the validity or non-validity of *the grid*. Examples are ready to hand. Almost certainly if we provide a subject with elements with which he is entirely unfamiliar we may find that, on analysis, we are faced with a grid in which there is very little in the way of relationship between constructs. However, even this is in a sense a valid picture. What the grid is here telling us is that the subject has no constructs with which they can make sense out of these particular elements. In construct theory terms they are outside the range of convenience of the person's construct system. The grid has very properly produced a random picture.

If we provide a subject with verbal labels which are relatively unfamiliar to her, she may arbitrarily attach meanings to these verbal labels and produce a pattern of relationships which misleads us. Alternatively, she may react by sorting the elements in a random manner thus reflecting her bewilderment at this strange array of verbal labels. Either way we shall be deprived of really useful information and left with perhaps no more than the fact that these verbal labels are truly unfamiliar to the subject.

If we were to try laddering a subject from her subordinate constructions to more superordinate constructions and our questioning was badly formulated and if we failed to notice the comments of the subject, she might ladder downwards, giving more subordinate constructions rather than superordinate constructions. This would be misleading in terms of any predictions we wish to base on the presumption that we had correctly ascertained something of this construct hierarchy.

Just as there are vast numbers of ways of constructing grids so there are vast numbers of ways of constructing grids badly. Each grid format is essentially an experiment within itself involving us in all the problems which we normally expect to find in designing an experiment. Thus the decision to administer a grid to one subject or a group of subjects involves us in questions such as what kind of elements do we provide or elicit, what kind of construct labels do we provide or elicit or do we mix provided and elicited, what kind of format do we ask the subject to work in (rank order, rating, dichotomous allotment), what overall format do we use (a multi-celled grid, implication grid, laddering and so forth), what aspects of structure or content in the construing system are we investigating (lopsidedness, degree of structure, relationship between particular constructs such as self and ideal, degree of insight of the subject into his own construing, degree of commonality between the subject's construing and some given standard or average and so forth). We are equally involved in the question of forms of analysis (some form of cluster analysis, direct measurement of matching between particular constructs, overall measures of structure, measures of lopsidedness and so forth).

Already the grid seems to have become a problem and a burden for many psychologists because they have looked on it as a ready-made device for their purposes rather than a broad methodology which involves them in solving a series of experimental problems, if it is to be of any value.

Before examining the validity of particular uses of the grid, we specifically reject one kind of estimate of validity. There is a tradition in psychology whereby the validity of a test is arbitrarily equated with its degree of correlation with another test or with its capacity to predict some arbitrarily chosen and relatively trivial aspect of human behaviour. Kelly was very prepared, in terms of a construct theory approach, to equate validity with usefulness and to see understanding as the most useful of enterprises.

VALIDITY IN TERMS OF USEFULNESS

The *usefulness* of a test or measure is clearly a difficult thing to assess and to start on such a venture is to deprive oneself of the opportunity of producing a quick series of journal papers and a ready claim to have shown "validity". It involves many people trying to use grid method as a mode of exploration and finding by direct experience, whether or not it is of value to them. They then have to devise ways of communicating their experience in such a way that other people can grasp it and make yet further use of the strategy that grid method provides.

Faced with the ever-growing literature of work using repertory grid technique perhaps all that can be done is to present an assortment of studies which will show something of its range and usefulness.

In the clinical setting

Perhaps because George Kelly was primarily a clinical psychologist or perhaps because so-called abnormal subjects will not psychologically sit still for standard tests and experimental procedures, the grid has been widely used in areas of so-called psychopathology. Much of its use has been with individual patients as a way of trying to increase the psychologist's understanding of the way in which the person views their world and their situation. The grid draws attention to those aspects of life which are problematic for the individual as opposed to the ways in which the individual is problematic for society. Obviously the vast majority of such investigations are never formally published but enough are available to indicate the richness of interpretable material which the grid can provide in the field.

An early published study is that of Fransella and Adams (1966) in which it was shown that a man who has committed a number of acts of arson did not in fact see himself as an "arsonist" in terms of his own view of his motives and purposes. Such a finding suggests reasons why the man would not necessarily be subject to remorse or consider himself in need of treatment, whatever the view of those around him. Rowe (1971b) similarly showed that a depressed woman was unlikely to improve under treatment in terms of *her* view of the nature of her depression, while Wright (1970) explored in detail the uniqueness of one person's "common" complaints.

Other authors have sought to show, *via* the grid, some hypothesised general differences between normal and clinically defined construing. Makhlouf, Jones and Norris (1970) showed that if a grid sample of normal construing is analysed into its principle components it will essentially consist of a number of clusters which are linked together by "bridging" constructs. This kind of system they referred to as "articulated". One would expect such a system to be effective in enabling a person to differentiate aspects of his life and deal with them in terms of varied sub-systems while at the same time possessing superordinate constructs which allow him to take an overview and, in a sense, hold his life together. The obsessional patients who were included in the same study showed different types of pattern when their grids were analysed and in particular they showed two patterns which would seem to present problems at that time. Some of them manifested what the authors termed "monolithic" construing, that is there was a single major cluster which dominated the grid. One might argue that such a mode of construing would lead to rigidity, to over-simplification of issues and to an inability to adapt to varying personal circumstances because they would not be seen as "varying". Other obsessionals showed a "segmented" pattern in which there were indeed different clusters of constructs but there were few or no bridging constructs to allow inferences to be made from one cluster to another. This might mean, in practice, that the person could deal with different aspects of their life, say "home life" and "work life" and "political life", but at the same time they would be unable very effectively to conceptualise the self who lived these separate lives. They might find themselves compartmentalised. There is evidence, since this paper, that these differences may be general differences between so-called neurotics and normals rather than restricted to obsessionals. Additionally, the generality of the categories is subject to the kinds of cricicisms made in Chapter 8 (p. 109).

Smail (1970) showed that neurotics have a tendency to produce fewer constructs which deal with psychological aspects of human behaviour, tending to be more concretistic in their construing. Similarly quite sharp differences in patterns of construing were found between people differentially characterised on the Middlesex Hospital Questionnaire by Ryle and Breen (1972a) although further work would be needed to enable us to understand the basis of the differences found.

Changes in construing in a marital therapy setting have been studied. Ryle and Lipshitz (1975) studied a married couple where the grid elements were the relationship of husband to wife and wife to husband, rated in terms of eighteen "behaviour" and fifteen "feeling" constructs and with progressive changes shown on the eleven occasions of testing which preceded marital therapy sessions. A further study of a married couple and their relationship, particularly in sexual terms, is presented in Bannister and Bott (1974).

Psychotherapy groups have also been studied. Smail (1972) used the grid as a measure of empathy in a small therapy group and showed that there were positive relationships between the grid empathy measures and therapists' and patients' ratings. Caplan *et al.* (1975) showed that repeated grid measures of self-esteem and patterns of identification with parents were significantly associated with aspects of mutual interaction within the group. A long term study of individuals suffering from the same disorder (stuttering) is reported in Fransella (1972). She found that a form of implications grid effectively monitored changes in construing which in turn related to changes in speech pattern. More importantly, perhaps, the grid operationally defined the theoretical argument on which the therapy was based.

These and other related investigations suggest that the virtue of the grid (its validity) does not rest simply in its capacity to discriminate between one diagnostically defined group and another or between before and after treatment groups and so forth. More significantly it distinguishes between groups in such a way as to test hypotheses concerning psychological process. Such hypotheses may be framed in construct theory terms or in other psychological languages but they can be logically related to the explicit rationale of repertory grid technique.

Social relationships

The general area of acquaintanceship, relationship, friendship, mutual understanding, has begun to be explored in grid terms and two studies will exemplify modes of attack. Adams-Webber, Schwenker and Barbeau (1972) faced people with the task of guessing which constructs had been derived from which of two new acquaintances to whom they had talked. They found that if the person doing the guessing had the kind of interpersonal viewpoint which saw other people as very similar to himself or herself, then they were less accurate in allotting constructs to their new acquaintances. If they were able to differentiate between their own viewpoint and that of others then they would be more accurate in the practical test situation. The study indicates that grid measures can be readily related to and predictive of people's capacities in formalised life situations. Duck (1973) published a related finding in a study which revealed that friendship pairs did possess construct systems which are more similar to each other than non-friendship pairs but that even so subjects tended to over-estimate the similarities between themselves and their chosen friends. Bender (1976) has used the grid with similar aims.

The sociality corollary of personal construct theory states that "to the extent that one person construes the construction processes of another he may play a role in a social process involving the other person". Clearly it is vital that grid technique enable us to construe the construction processes of others who are construing the construction processes of yet others. There is the beginnings of evidence that this may be possible.

Language

Linguistic meaning can be theoretically defined as the relationship between personal constructs and operationally defined in grid terms. Three studies have explored this contention. Mair (1966) found that the relationship between constructs averaged from the subjects' grids and the relationship that would have been predicted between the verbal labels used in terms of dictionary meaning were closely associated, that is, synonyms were highly positively related, antonyms were highly negatively related and so forth. Equally of note is the fact that the relationships for an *individual*, between their constructs were not *precisely* those which a dictionary would have predicted. This is an expected finding in that both common sense and construct theory (the commonality corollary) would predict that a substantial part of the relationship between our constructs reflects cultural teaching, but also that each of us develops idiosyncratic meanings (the Individuality corollary) for words, derived from our unique personal experience.

Agnew and Bannister (1973) looked at language, in grid terms, in the specific area of the language used by psychiatrists to classify patients. In this study psychiatrists completed grids using their patients as elements and using both formal diagnostic categories and lay descriptive terms, as constructs. Analysis of the grids enabled the authors to show that psychiatric diagnosis is only a pseudo-specialist language and that it is no more stable and has no greater interjudge agreement than everyday language and additionally that it is heavily contaminated by lay language. The significant feature of the experimental design is that it could be used in any study of the degree to which a particular technical or specialist language is an effective, stable and separate sub-system.

A further study which was essentially linguistic in point of attack was that of Warren (1966) which tested out Bernstein's argument concerning class differences in linguistic coding. In terms of the strength of intercorrelations between constructs (Intensity) Warren found that his working class population had more highly inter-related constructs than his middle class group.

One of the puzzling gaps in the use of grids has been, in fact, in the area of psycholinguistics. Language is so dense and rich that it presents extreme problems for anyone attempting a systematic analysis. It is therefore strange that among the many studies in the formal field of psycholinguistics virtually none have made use of what is clearly one of the most flexible forms of systematic attack on the nature of language—the repertory grid. Perhaps the reason is that psychologists suffer from what Kelly called "the dread disease of hardening of the categories" and have seen the grid as a measure of "psychopathology" or "personality" or some such and thereby have not recognised that it can be equally viewed as a tool for investigating language and symbolic processes. Equally they have ignored the degree to which personal construct theory could provide a framework for the study of "language" which did not divorce it from "behaviour" and "perception".

Children

Repertory grid technique involves no particular age restriction on the populations with which it can be used (see Chapter 3). If the elements and constructs are appropriate, even very young children can complete a grid simply by making the kinds of judgment which characterise their everyday choices. In view of this, the lack of grid work in the field of developmental psychology is perhaps surprising.

Some time ago Brierley (1967) and Little (1968) showed that there were marked evolutionary changes in child to adolescent construing but in general relatively little has been done to extend such work. Salmon (1969) conducted an extensive experiment using grid methods with children around the eight-year-old mark, studying the development of conformity. She showed that in rep grid terms, if we use as a measure of value identification constructs such as "ideal self" and "actual self", then there is a significant relationship between "ideal self" and the construct *tough* predicting peer conformity and "ideal self" and the construct *obedient* predicting conformity with adult values.

In a more general study Applebee (1975, 1976) used grids spanning the age range 6 to 17 and showed that there is increasing concensus in construing across the age span. The consensus was substantially higher for the pattern of interrelationships between constructs (the *structure* of the system) than for the ratings of specific elements on specific constructs (the *implications* of the system). He also showed that there is a somewhat more equal elaboration of both poles of each construct (less lopsidedness) with increasing age and that there is a recognition of more "shades of gray".

Politics

Fransella and Bannister (1967) sought to validate a rank order form repertory grid technique as a predictor of declared voting behaviour. Their subjects rank ordered personal acquaintances on evaluative (e.g. *prejudiced*), political party (e.g. *likely to vote conservative*) and political "brand image" constructs (e.g. *patriotic*). It was found that voting behaviour was predictable from the relationship between the evaluative and political party constructs. An interesting feature of the relationship between constructs was that the difference between adherents of the different political parties often emerged at what might be called a second level of implication. Thus both Conservative and Labour voters produced the same grid relationships in so far as there was a high positive correlation between *conservative* and *patriotic*. However, for Labour voters there was in turn a high positive correlation between *patriotic* and *prejudiced*, whereas for Conservative voters there was a negative correlation between *conservative* and *prejudiced*.

Apart from the confirmation of the predictions in this experiment it was interesting that there seemed to be a possibility, in terms of repertory grid measures, of defining notions like "degree of interest in politics", "certainty of voting intention" and "brand image".

Professional training

Just as it seems possible to investigate the way in which construing develops in children, grids can be used to investigate the learning process. For example, Lifshitz (1974) studied the changes that take place in the outlook of social work students as compared with their older and more experienced supervisors during training. Significant differences were found between the two groups. In particular student groups tended to use much more concrete descriptive categories (e.g. age, sex and profession) in construing their clients as compared with the more abstract constructs used by the experienced professionals. Runkel and Damrin (1961) and Ryle and Breen (1974) have explored the same area.

Maps

Stringer (1974) turned to a relatively unusual topic area and grid element in studying the effects of colour and base on laymen's construing of urban planning maps. Since such maps are designed to introduce the general public to planning projects which will affect their future environment then the degree to which they can be understood and the ways in which they are understood needs to be assessed. The maps and plans were used as the elements of a grid and the effect of the use of colour in such plans was particularly clearly demonstrated.

Sex differences

Unsurprisingly, no overall differences in the degree of structure in grids have been manifest as between sexes. Differences have, from time to time, been found in grid content. Thus Carlson (1971) found that in terms of the way in which people differentiated themselves from other people in a grid, males seem to see themselves as having more "agency" and "effect" qualities than females. Additionally one content finding in the study by Bannister, Fransella and Agnew (1971) was that the pattern of construct relationships for a psychiatric sample of females was closer to the general norm than was the pattern for a psychiatric sample of males.

VALIDATION IN TERMS OF THEORY

Since repertory grid technique is intimately bound up with personal construct theory it is important to investigate the validity of the technique in terms of how effectively it can operationally define terms within the theory and provide means for testing hypotheses derived from the theory. So far, psychologists have rarely used the grid for such purposes but an early and classic study well exemplifies this form of investigation. Levy (1956) was concerned with the difference between propositional and constellatory constructs in terms of Kelly's theory. A constellatory construct is one which "defines the other realm membership of its elements". That is to say it takes a form somewhat like a stereotype in asserting that, for example, if we construe someone as *female* then they must necessarily be *sensitive, over-emotional, timid, unpunctual, impractical* and *fond of flowers*. A propositional construct on the other hand does not imply a series of inevitably related constructs. It takes an essentially "as if" form so that we may construe any *she* as if she were, among many other things she might also be, a *female*. Levy argued that because a constellatory construct implies many other constructs a great deal of consequential reconstruction will be required when it is invalidated. The invalidation of a propositional construct will entail relatively little reconstruction. He then used a form of grid to distinguish between the two types of construct assuming that constructs which were grouped in clusters and were highly inter-related could be dubbed constellatory, whereas constructs which had few linkages with others (which were residual in a factor analytic terms) could be assumed to be propositional. He examined the degree to which his subjects changed their views using these two types of constructs and found that indeed there was an inverse relationship between the range of inter-dependancy of a construct and its susceptibility to change following predictive failure.

In Bannister (1963 and 1965b) attention was given to the question of what psychological processes underlie thought disorder and a serial invalidation hypothesis was tested. This argues from construct theory that variation in the structure and content of construct systems is a function of varying validational fortunes. Any construct, because of its position in a system, is intrinsically a prediction—if our constructs of *kinsfolk* and *trustworthiness* are linked, then we expect our cousin to pay us back the money he owes us. It was argued that the thought-disorderd person has so frequently experienced invalidation (events contrary to the expectations generated by his construct system—too many cousins had not repaid the money they owed him) that he eventually loosened the linkages between his constructs so that no very specific expectations were generated. Invalidation was thus avoided at the cost of living subjectively in a fluid and largely meaningless universe.

This hypothesis was tested in the form of a laboratory game in which normal subjects made repeated psychological judgements from photographs of faces and experienced either repeated invalidation or validation or "no information". In summary, results indicated that, if a person is faced with repeated invalidation of part of his construct subsystem for viewing people, he first of all alters the pattern of relationships between his constructs (in effect, repeatedly alters his psychological theory), but eventually begins to loosen the relationship between his constructs (in effect, begins to go out of the theory-holding business). Conversely, repeated validation (confirmation of expectations) leads to an intensification of the linkages between constructs until the system becomes simple and monolithic.

The study by Fransella (1972) was directly concerned with the treatment of stuttering. It validates grid method by linking it to therapeutic methods derived from personal construct theory and demonstrating that this *common conceptual base* provides an adequate ground for effective practice.

If we accept that theory making is the prime strategy of science then we can argue that the usefulness of grid method should ultimately be assessed in terms of its contribution to the elaboration of theory.

One important way of assessing the validity of particular methodologies of psychological investigation is to consider the degree to which they can sustain an extensive and sequential line of research. Repertory grid technique has been used in two areas which themselves have been subjected to extensive study, one being the area of "cognitive complexity" (see Chapter 4) and the other being research around the issue of "thought disorder".

Bannister (1960, 1962a), Bannister and Fransella (1966) and Bannister *et al.* (1971) reported studies in which thought-disordered schizophrenics were discriminated by grid method from normals and other psychiatric groups. The grids of thought-disordered subjects were characterised by low correlations between constructs and low consistency of the pattern of relationships between constructs when grid measures were repeated. Thought disorder was thereby defined as grossly loosened construing (a loose construct being one which leads to varying predictions).

The *simultaneous* lowering of both Intensity and Consistency was seen as inevitable. If you are certain today that *decency* is essentially *British* (high Intensity, tight construing) then you may well be certain of this tomorrow (high Consistency), but if you become vague as to whether *decency* is related at all to *British* (low Intensity, loose construing) then tomorrow you may toy with the notion that *decency* may relate to *foreign* (low Consistency, loose construing). Other studies which elaborated these findings are reported by, for example, Foulds *et al.* (1967), Presley (1969), McPherson *et al.* (1971, 1973), Spelman *et al.* (1971), McFadyen and Foulds (1972) and Kear-Colwell (1973). Studies adversely critical of this line of argument are those of Williams (1971), Frith and Lillie (1972), Slater (1972) and Haynes and Phillips (1973)—for a discussion of these criticisms see Chapter 9.

As previously noted studies by Bannister and Salmon (1966a) and Salmon, Bramley and Presly (1967) indicate that it is people, rather than the physical world, who puzzle the thought-disordered person. Damage is focal to the area of psychological construing. This finding suggests that the origins of thought disorder may be *interpersonal* and relates to the arguments of such workers as Laing and Esterson (1964), Lidz (1964) and Bateson and his co-workers (1956). Indeed, "mystification", "the inculcation of confused and distorted meanings" and "double binding", can be looked on as *particular* interpersonal strategies which all produce the *general* effect of serial invalidation, experimentally illustrated in the Bannister (1963 and 1965) studies already cited.

In the most recent study in this series by Bannister and others (1975) an attempt was made to reverse the process of thought-disorder by serially validating the construing of a selected number of severely thought-disordered patients. In this study the grid was used not only as a way of estimating the degree of thought disorder but as a technique for locating surviving areas of structure within the generally disordered interpersonal construing of the patients.

The various issues arising within this long-term research continue to receive attention in terms of grid investigations. For example, Heather (1976) has investigated the issue of whether thought disorder is specific and focal to the construing of people in "psychological" terms or whether it is more diffuse. McPherson and others (1975) considered the problem of "difficulty level" in construing, both as a general problem of definition and as a problem in the interpretation of grid analyses.

CONCLUSIONS

It is possible to define validity in terms of personal construct theory. The validity of a technique is its capacity to enable us to *elaborate* our construing. Elaborations, from the point of view of a construct theorist, can take one of two forms. We can elaborate our construing by *extension* or by *definition*. If we elaborate by extension then we increase the *range of convenience* of our constructs so that more elements are taken into account. We widen the area to which we can apply a particular "theory" and the "theory" may, as in the case of repertory grid technique, take the form of a measurement instrument. We can elaborate our construing by definition, in which case we do not extend the range of convenience of our construing but we do tighten the construing within a given area so that we have a more precise, exact and detailed grasp of it. Whether we elaborate by extension or by definition, it is in terms of its capacity to enable us to anticipate that we measure the validity of our technique.

The term anticipate is chosen because it carries implications beyond the more limited notion of prediction. It suggests that we seek to understand in order to involve ourselves with our world and to act upon it. Thus validity ultimately refers to the way in which a mode of understanding enables us to take effective action. The "us" who takes action may well be the *subject* of the grid rather than its administrator.

Kelly (1969) succinctly states the relationship between measurement, prediction and action in the following words:

"Accurate prediction, then, can scarcely be taken as evidence that one has pinned down a fragment of ultimate truth, though this is generally how it is regarded in psychological research. The accuracy confirms only the interim utility of today's limited set of constructs. Tomorrow's genius will erect new dimensions, open up unsuspected degrees of freedom, and invite new experimental controls.

And yet, however useful prediction may be in testing the transient utility of one's construction system, the superior test of what he has devised is its capacity to implement imaginative action. It is by his actions that man learns what his capabilities are, and what he achieves is the most tangible psychological measure of his behavior. It is a mistake to always assume that behavior must be the psychologist's dependent variable. For man, it is the independent variable." (Selected Papers, p. 33).

8

Difficulties and Cautions

> Man has difficulty construing along unfamiliar lines, even when they are drawn with mathematical simplicity. His notions are held fast in a network of personal constructs and any ideas or feelings that have not yet found their place in that network are likely to remain exasperatingly elusive. Science, therefore, not only has the task of coming to simple terms with events, but it also has the psychological task of achieving some accomodation between what man believes and what, indeed, confronts him. (Kelly, 1969, p. 326).

Many of the points discussed in this chapter are considered again in the final overview chapter. Here the aim is to look at issues such as bi-polarity or whether to provide or elicit constructs, at the level of practical grid construction, while Chapter 9 discusses these same issues in more super-ordinate terms.

THE DIVORCE OF GRID FROM THEORY

Perhaps the greatest controversy at the present time concerns the relationship of personal construct theory to grid technique. While the technique was developed within the confines of the theory there can be no argument but that it can be used independently of the theory. But because something *can* be done does not carry with it the implication that this is how it *should* be done.

If you intend to use grids for something more than a one-off analysis of the attitudes of a group of people to asparagus, then some theory is going to guide you in what you do—be it implicit or explicit. We therefore suggest that, rather than using grids in the context of learning theory, or notions like cognitive dissonance or your own personal theory, personal construct theory is the theory of choice.

In general, the practical difficulties and dangers in grid method discussed in the following pages derive from the historical tendency to divorce grid methodology from personal construct theory.

BI-POLARITY

You may or may not think it important to know whether you are measuring language usage or construct interrelationships. But it becomes important in grids when only one pole of a construct is used (for example, in ranked grids) and inferences are made about the constructs' polar opposites. It is tempting to infer that because the *ideal self* is related to *kindness, sincerity, honesty* and general wholesomeness that it is definitely undesirable to be *unkind, insincere, dishonest* and generally unwholesome. This inference may be correct, but there are indications that this is not always so.

Mair (1967a), for instance, showed that constructs appearing bi-polar in terms of their verbal labels are not always *used* in grids as if they are. While the ranked grid is the most likely to give rise to unfounded assumptions about bi-polarity, the rating grid can also give rise to misinterpretation. In this form the construct poles are both given, defining as they do either end of a scale. But here again the assumption of bi-polarity is made. Because the construct *kind—unkind* is significantly correlated with *sincere—insincere*, the assumption is that *kind* people are *sincere* and *unkind* people are *insincere*. There is no way in which the person can say that *kind* people are *sincere*, but *unkind* people can be both *sincere* and *insincere*. The only grid that really allows the person freedom to say how each pole of a construct relates to all other construct poles is the bi-polar implications grid (see pp. 49-52).

It also appears to make a difference how the opposite pole is obtained. One way to elicit the contrast pole of a construct is to ask how the element in the elicitation triad is *different from* the two who are stated to be alike. The other approach is to ask what the *opposite* of the stated likeness is. If two people are alike because they are *kind*, you can either ask in what way the third person differs from these *kind* people, or what is the opposite of *kind*. Epting and his colleagues (1971) investigated this and found that the use of the "opposite" method produced more explicit bi-polarity.

No doubt people often give the conventional opposite of the construct rather than the opposite that the person actually "uses". It is possible that Mair was getting more of these conventional as opposed to construct opposites since he supplied the construct poles to which the opposites had to be given. The construct poles might therefore be less easily used by the subjects than if both poles had been elicited. It is, therefore, important that opposites for elicited construct poles as well as for supplied construct poles be obtained since this is part of the definition of the construct.

We may assume that *charitable* to you means the same as *charitable* to me. But for you the opposite pole may be *intolerant* and for me *hold strong opinions*. For you to be *charitable* is good and for me undesirable. It was for this reason that Hinkle used both poles of each construct in his implications grid. He wanted to find out how constructs interacted and not how verbal labels are strung together.

RANGE OF CONVENIENCE

This is not flogging a dead horse but one that is alive and kicking. *The elements in any form of grid must be relevant to the constructs used.*

CONSTRUCTS IN CONTEXT

The context in which constructs may be used is largely ignored by grid technicians at the present time. *Flirtatious* has different implications in the context of a party as opposed to the context of a meeting of a Board of Governors. Hinkle (1965) suggests that it is such contextual confusions that can give rise to implicative dilemmas and conflict. In grid terms it can produce low construct interrelationships or ambiguous implication interactions. He suggests that

"The range of convenience of a construct covers all those contexts in which the user found its application useful. In contrast, the range of implication of a construct is an index of the extensiveness of its subordinate and superordinate network of implications in a given context. It would thus be possible to investigate the ranges (plural) of implication for a given construct in various contexts" (Hinkle, 1965, p. 18).

Grids using situations or different selves as elements are moving in this direction as are grids a person completes from the standpoint of "as I am now", "as I was in the past" and "as I expect to be when . . .".

ELICITED VERSUS PROVIDED CONSTRUCTS

It is not surprising that a person regards his own constructs (in general) as being more important to him than those selected from a pool of constructs (in general) (see Isaacson and Landfield, 1965; Adams-Webber, 1970b). A construct's importance has usually been determined by extremity of ratings on scales (see pp. 63-64). Findings generally support the idea that elicited constructs are more meaningful (have more extreme ratings) than do provided constructs. But this is not always the case as Warr and Coffman (1970) found. Bender (1974) offered an explanation of this anomalous finding. Warr and Coffman changed only one element at a time in the triads for elicitation. This he showed produced less "important" constructs than when two elements at a time are changed. The person has less access to important constructs if there is not sufficient variety in the elements during elicitation.

Apart from their influence on the extremity of ratings on construct scales, the differences between using elicited and provided constructs have been looked at in measures of cognitive complexity (e.g. Kuusinen and Nystedt, 1975a, b; Metcalfe, 1974; Caine and Smail, 1967; Tripodi and Bieri, 1963) and the Intensity and Consistency measures on the Grid Test of Thought Disorder (e.g. McFayden and Foulds, 1972); also in the therapeutic setting (Landfield, 1965); and independent sorting tasks (Stringer, 1972).

From a practical point of view, the providing of constructs can be vital, perhaps particularly in the clinical and educational fields. Here one is most often focusing on individuals' construing of themselves and others. It is quite common, for instance, to supply one or more varieties of the *self* in a grid. Or one may want to include constructs to do with, say, sex or aggression if you have failed to elicit these and you believe they are important for a more complete understanding of that individual.

As with reliability, if you are fussed about the relative importance of constructs you think it necessary to provide for your subject, then it must be determined for those particular constructs in that particular grid for that particular person. You could follow Isaacson's procedure (1966) and ask your subject to rank elicited and provided constructs in order of importance. There is no definite evidence to indicate that you should not provide constructs for a grid. On the contrary, there is some evidence to suggest that results using provided constructs produce meaningful results (Nystedt, Ekehammar and Kuusinen, 1976) and are significantly related to individuals' behaviour (e.g. Fransella and Bannister, 1967).

PEOPLE AS CONSTRUCTS

Mair (1967b) rightly points out that "self" as element may not be used in a grid in the same way as *self* as construct. Mair and Boyd (1967) found that on the ranked grid, the direct rating of "self" as element correlated 0.47 with rankings of *self* as construct, but the range of element/construct correlations for *self, mother* and *father* was from —0.58 to 0.89. It is, for instance, a different task to think of oneself (as construct) in relation to a number of people, as opposed to deciding whether one is more or less like them in terms of some other construct. In the former, person A may be *like me in character* because she is *kind,* person B next most *like me* because she is a *spendthrift* and person X *least like me* because she is *just plain nasty.*

However, the person as construct is widely used and meaningful results are being obtained. It has even been suggested that the difference between person as construct and element may be an indication of conflict or ambiguity surrounding that person (see p. 72). In other words, the discrepancy could be used as a measure just as Bannister used reliability (or lack of it) as a measure of construct system integration.

ELICITATION AND LADDERING PROCEDURES

Anyone involving themselves in these procedures will rapidly come to the conclusion that, as in all psychological experiments, they are involved in a social situation. But these are clearly social, interactive procedures in which the subjective element is of far greater importance than in the experimental situation because of the lack of objective criteria to guide one. Laddering, in particular, is a situation in which two personal construct systems attempt to interlock. The only thing that stops the situation becoming one in which the two people engage in an orgy of introspection is that one person (the examiner) is attempting to subsume the construct system of another (the examined). It is in the attempts to subsume that the distortions can occur.

Judkins (1976) points out that the subjective aspect of "introspective dialogue technique", as he nicely calls it, is hidden by the growth of grid technology and the ever increasing sophistication of methods of statistical analysis. This encourages the impression that grid methods are fairly precise, step-by-step, scientific procedures.

The elicitation and laddering of constructs is an art and not a science. So the examiner must expect to have to gain experience in this art and so learn to minimise his influence in determining the constructs given. Although the social constraints on the constructs elicited are determined by how the subject construes the situation, most distortion occurs as the examiner tries to make sure he understands the construct underlying the verbal labels produced. This is particularly so when a laddered construct is given consisting of far too many words to be of practical use, when you do not quite understand what the person is getting at, or when he has great difficulty in verbalising the construct at all.

Perhaps the most important rule to bear in mind when laddering or eliciting constructs, is that the examiner must LISTEN. He does not have to be silent. He can mutter, nod approval, even rephrase what the person has said and ask whether this was what he meant, but he must never *impose* constructs. This is where the art lies.

But it is also important to allow the person to give you his constructs, both subordinate and superordinate, in spite of the subjective nature of the interaction. For you are only, at best, gathering a small sample of the person's existing constructs. You hope it is an important sample. And if you inadvertently distort one or two of the constructs from their "true" meaning, they are meaningful to that person if he can use them to discriminate between the elements. If you have succeeded in distorting the construct out of all recognition, then it will show no relationship with other constructs.

ELICITATION AND CONSTRUCT REPETITION

Kelly (1955) and Bannister and Mair (1968) recommend encouraging people to provide as many different constructs as possible, but Shubsachs (1975) points out that, maybe, the person is saying something when he repeats constructs. He does so because they are important to him. This was tested in an experiment in which some people were allowed to repeat constructs. The constructs were then rated by their owners in terms of importance and it was found that repeated constructs were rated more highly. What we have here is another measure of superordinacy.

People do repeat constructs during elicitation and particularly so during laddering. In the latter case this is predicted from theory since constructs are hierarchically related and there are relatively few "at the top". If one is only going to elicit and ladder constructs, then repetition could well be a good index of relative superordinacy. However, if the constructs are subsequently going to be used in a grid, then the grid analysis itself will give an indication of superordinacy. In this case, it is as well to encourage variety.

DIFFERENT TYPES OF GRID

The few studies looking at grid comparisons have been discussed in Chapter 5. Here we want to underline the cautionary note that the form of grid you choose matters because not all grids give the same results. You are not just choosing from a grid pool the one you find technically the most convenient. It is not simply that some forms may prove to be valid and others invalid. But it is that different grids may prove to be answering different questions.

THE FASCINATION OF FIGURES

Few who have used grids have not found themselves mesmerised by a matrix. Bannister recounts how, in the search for a score, he once found himself adding up ranks along the diagonals. Where there is cause for caution is when increasingly sophisticated methods of computer analysis take us further and further away from the raw data—from what the person actually told us about the relationship between constructs and elements or constructs and constructs.

Hardly any work has been done on comparing different methods of analysis. Do they all come up with the same answer? The limited information available suggests "yes" and "no". For instance, Fransella (1965) found that the first component in Slater's INGRID programme correlated almost perfectly with Bannister's first axis (see p. 34) but the second component and axis did not correlate significantly. Does this matter? The basic answer is that we do not know. To some extent it must depend on why one is employing grid technique.

MEASURES INTO TRAITS—A SHORT STEP

Is, for example, cognitive complexity—simplicity a dimension along which one can place each thinking creature? Are we to be chained by yet another label? Some writers do seem to suggest that this may be so. Is your system monolithic, articulated or segmented? It would be fatally easy to extend Makhlouf's work (Makhlouf-Norris, Jones and Norris, 1970) with obsessional patients and a non-psychiatric group to all mankind for all time. She showed that systems could be categorised in these ways (see p. 68) by analysing grid correlation matrices into clusters of constructs significant at beyond the 5 per cent level. But let us not tighten our construing too fast and come to the conclusion that that person has a monolithic system and this person a segmented one. An important theoretical problem is to determine what level of statistical significance is psychologically significant. It seems likely that the picture obtained of the construct structure changes as we change the level of significance applied. Maybe this is how systems really do work and this will be important to know. At what level of significance will a person act?

But if we look around there is evidence that such labels apply only temporarily. Both elements being construed and time at which we do the construing have an effect. For instance, Bannister and Salmon (1966a) showed that schizophrenics may be judged thought disordered when construing people, but are similar to the rest of us when construing objects. Fransella (1974) suggests that the obsessional's construct system may be characterised by being very tightly-knit in the area of his symptoms and bordering on the thought disordered when dealing with the rest of his world. Complexity may also be something that varies in the individual over time and across sub-systems (Hall, 1966); so also may Intensity. Fransella and Joyston-Bechal (1971) demonstrated that Intensity scores varied during the course of psychotherapy in a group. May we not also be inclined to think in a loose fashion when in the depths of despair, when drunk, drugged or delirious with happiness and then tighten our construing as we move out of these states?

COMMENT

More and more people are using grid technique in more and more ways, but hand-in-hand with this come more and more questions. Not only questions about the usefulness of the technique or questions about its validity, but questions about construct systems. How do people construe different sorts of grid procedure as they complete the grid? What is the best way of identifying a person's superordinate as opposed to subordinate constructs? At this point in time how integrated is the person's sub-system of constructs in which we are interested?

9

Overview

> A psychology that participates in the human enterprise must perceive that the guidelines channelizing a person's processes are drawn by the person himself— that they are therefore personal constructs, and may be redrawn and revalidated by the user to structure anew his thought and his behavior. They are not the residue of biographical incidents, nor are they projected facsimilies of reality. They are, instead, the axes of reference man contrives to put his psychological space in order and to plot his varying courses of action.
>
> With such personal constructs a man can make his entrance into the world of reality by acting with initiative and ingenuity. Failing to erect them he can only repeat concretely what has been "reinforced", in the circular manner that psychological journals—themselves deliberately acting, I fear, as products of their own concrete satisfactions—describe. It is difficult to see how a psychology so addicted to its reinforcements can ever participate imaginatively in the mounting behavioral ventures of the coming generation. (Kelly, 1969, p. 36).

Despite its formal and mathematical structure, repertory grid technique is much more akin to conversation than it is to standard psychological procedures. Traditionally, a psychological test is based on dimensions proposed by the psychologist, in terms of which the subject will be allotted a position. Thus, whether it be a questionnaire, a laboratory measure or a projective test, the subject's contributions are compounded into categories and scale positions, the subject cannot do what we allow him to do in conversation, *propose his own terms.*

We approach our subjects convinced that they must be either "introvert" or "extrovert" and our test will be arbiter; they necessarily have some quantity of "intelligence" and our test will determine how much; they are either highly conditionable or poorly conditionable and our experimental procedures will settle the issue; the most meaningful thing that can be said about them is whether they are psychotic or neurotic and our test will decide. Always our base and point of departure is the notion of the subject as an element to be allotted a place on our constructs. The subject is seen as an object.

What we are not concerned with in psychological testing is the question of the person's own constructs as such. We are not willing to grant them parity with our professional dimensions.

Because grid method has often been viewed as if it were a standard test it has been asserted that it is close relative to the semantic differential. Yet a detailed examination of the two techniques (Bannister and Mair, 1968) suggests that they are diametrically opposed on the question of whether we should seek to understand the dimensions in terms of which the person makes sense of his world or whether we ought simply to compound his dimensions onto our predetermined dimensions. Thus, despite enormous technical effort and ingenuity, Osgood and his colleagues (1957) were unable to break free of the conviction that they must choose dimensions of meaning within which the subject's individual meanings could be delineated. They settled, on the basis of normative studies, mainly for the dimensions of evaluation, potency and activity.

There is much evidence that in cultural terms (certainly in Western industrial civilisation) these are common superordinate constructions. But inevitably the degree to which the subject has constructions which are truly different from these is ignored within semantic differential technique. Within the grid a person's own superordinate axes as well as his particular judgements may be recognised. But nothing except our own ideology prevents us from acknowledging that the "subject" is a theoriser, an experimenter, a constructor of meanings exactly as "we" are. Grid technique is an attempt to see the person in these terms.

In originating the grid Kelly was striving to find a particular form for his central argument that the person completing your questionnaire or taking part in your experiment is your equal. Psychology is thereby faced with a scientifically unique problem, a problem which cannot be solved by mimicking the natural sciences. It requires a unique solution. Any grid is an attempt to enable the subject to present his own construing of aspects of his world in such a form that they can be understood and communicated. In this sense the grid is a form of communication and, as has been stressed, is thereby nearer to conversation than it is to the standard psychological test. Conversation is between equals, between peers, between people who are striving to understand each other—traditional psychological test procedures are a mimicry of the scientist measuring the object.

However no method is immune from distortion by the ways in which and the purposes for which, it is used. Whatever Kelly's orginal intentions may have been there are clearly ways in which the grid can be used so that, while its formal properties are retained, its essential quality is lost. Thus if the grid is used not to attain any kind of understanding of the other person's construing but serves simply to derive indices in terms of which the person can be manipulated, then its nature changes. The behaviourist, the person who experiments upon rather than with, the market researcher, can and have used the grid to generate simple indices for purely manipulative purposes. If the market researcher finds that X characteristic in a person's grid indicates that he will be responsive to Y type advertising then he can proceed, on a massive scale, to use the grid in this mode and the underlying ethos of the grid is thereby rendered null and void. The thought disorder grid was not only a logical derivative of personal construct theory but was intended to be used for purposes appropriate to the values of the theory. Thus an indication that a person construes in a very loose "thought disordered" way should be the very basis on which his or her ideas might be interpreted, understood and responded to. If the thought disorder grid is used simply to categorise the person as "thought disordered" and thereby to be institutionally disposed of as beyond communication, then the grid is reduced to a standard test. It becomes of the type of the "intelligence" test whereby we decide that a child is "unintelligent" and thereby less effort will be made to communicate with (i.e. educate) him or her.

GRIDS FOR GRIDS' SAKE

Equally the grid can and has been turned into a technology which generates its own problems and then solves these problems. Such problems do not necessarily relate to any attempt to understand the meaning which the person attaches to his universe. an example of such a grid generated problem is the continuing question of "elicited" versus "supplied" constructs, a question which has figured in a number of papers from Isaacson and Landfield (1965) onwards. The general argument has been that elicited constructs can be used more consistently and in a more structured way by a person than can constructs which have been "supplied" to him. Although this question essentially comes out of a face inspection of the technology of grids it has been justified, at times, by a vague reference to construct theory and to the argument that Kelly was essentially interested in personal constructs and personal constructs are equated with "elicited" constructs.

If this question is looked at a little more seriously, in personal construct theory terms, we can readily see why the studies have yielded contradictory results. On some occasions subjects appear to be able to use the "supplied" constructs more adequately than they can the "elicited" constructs and on other occasions they seem to cope more adequately using "elicited" constructs.

The first point to bear in mind is that it is of course impossible to "supply" a construct. A construct is *not* a verbal label. It is the actual discrimination which the subject makes between elements and the verbal label is merely a handy hook for carrying constructs about with. Thus all that can be *supplied* is the verbal label to which people will attach *their own* constructs. The issue of whether they will use constructs they attach to the psychologists' verbal labels as adequately as they used constructs attached to their own verbal labels, can be argued in fairly simple terms. If experimenters try to supply verbal labels which are in the native tongue of the subject and which relate to constructs likely to be important to the subject and the experimenters' guesses are good then there will be no difference in the subjects' ability to use "supplied" as contrasted with "elicited" constructs. If, however, the supplied verbal labels are unfamiliar to the subjects or peripheral from the point of view of their system, then there will be a marked difference in the structural outcome as between "supplying" and "eliciting".

It can be similarly argued that the whole issue of cognitive "complexity—simplicity" from Bieri (1955) onwards is largely *grid generated.* Any consideration of an individual grid throws up the issue of whether it can be mathematically accounted for in simple terms or whether its pattern is complicated and elaborate. Construct theory or common sense or our own personal experience or any number of other theories would suggest that we move from complex to simple and back within one subsystem and that we find that some aspects of our life can be seen in relatively few and ordered terms while others are problematic. Deriving the question from the grid has given it a largely trait psychology flavour so that it becomes the cognitively simple question of "is a person cognitively simple or cognitively complex?"

A further example of the confusions that can arise from combining a concern with grid mechanics with *ad hoc* psychological explanations is provided by the work which followed the development of the grid test of thought disorder (Bannister and Fransella, 1966). Frith and Lillie (1972) argued from their work that the low consistency scores of thought disordered schizophrenics indicated not instability of construing but "element inconsistency". They argued that it was simply a matter of the thought disordered subjects changing their minds on the second occasion as to which photograph was most or least characterised in terms of each construct. It is interesting to note here that the argument is so closely tied to the mechanics of this one particular grid that it could not have arisen at all if earlier forms of thought disorder grid had been maintained. Bannister (1960) presented a first and second grid to his thought disordered subjects, such that each grid had the same constructs but *different* elements. Therefore, the instability in the pattern of construct relationships could *only* be attributed to inconsistency in construing since there were no standard elements about which subjects could be inconsistent.

The essential weakness of the "element inconsistency" way of conceptualising what is going on is that it is so close to the concrete data that it amounts essentially to a re-naming of the process rather than an explanation of it. Certainly thought disordered schizophrenics change their mind about the judgements they make (as do many others of us drunk or sober), but the problem remains—why do we change our minds? Construct theory, in terms of its description of construing processes and arguments from the nature of validation and invalidation, offers an explanation. It is this explanation which is embodied in the notion of loose construing which underlies the grid test of thought disorder. To retreat to a kind of conceptual pointing to the concrete data of grids is literally to make them good for nothing.

Williams (1971) continued this tradition of being "stimulus bound" and also looked to the nature of the elements to explain grid data. He demonstrated the obvious experimentally, namely that people achieve higher degrees of structure and consistency when they are construing photographs of people than when they are construing (in personality terms) addresses. Again he offered a notion which is at so low a level of abstraction as to be a non-explanation, namely that thought disordered schizophrenics are "cue-insensitive". Probably in some sense they are, but what can we further derive from such a labelling? If we view these data in construct theory terms we can readily see that the addresses which were the elements in one of Williams' grids are more distant from the focus of convenience of the "personality" constructs being used by the subjects than are photographs of people. Inevitably, as we construe elements which are moving steadily towards being outside the range of convenience of our constructs then our construing will manifest less and less structure and consistency. If the elements to be judged on personality constructs had been variously sized strips of blotting paper then structure and consistency of contruing might virtually have disappeared altogether.

Haynes and Phillips (1972) faced thought disordered subjects with the task of comparing photographs in terms of personality characteristics and found that their subjects were inconsistent in that they produced illogical triads of comparison (A is stronger than B, B is stronger than C, C is stronger than A.). This is rather in the manner of the Lauterbach (1972) experiments. Their conclusion was that thought disordered schizophrenics are "simply more inconsistent than other groups". Here again there seems to be a morbid fear of theoretical explanation and instead we are faced with a naming of the concrete behaviour of subjects in a formal experiment. The concept of "inconsistency" as Haynes and Phillips are using it is not defined any further than its actual operational definition in their experiment, though its common sense meaning makes it seem explanatory. If we consider these data in terms of construct theory then we are likely to conclude that any general disturbance in the stability and structure of construing will produce all kinds of operationally detectable anomalies of the type explored by Haynes and Phillips.

We gain little from detecting anomalies if we are unwilling to relate our instrumental invention to theoretical inventions, in say the manner demonstrated by Radley (1974).

UNEXPLORED AVENUES

Some possible lines of future development in grid technique have already been tentatively explored. One such is the possibility of investigating the nature of conflict and contradiction. Work with implications grids and with the notion of intransitivity was discussed earlier in this volume but clearly this is very much in embryo. There has been a strong tendency in grid work both to look on construct systems as if they were simple, logical patterns and to use formats which concealed contradiction (such as the rank order format). Thereby we forget that contradiction is both the source of personal disaster and personal growth. Jung in his *Memories, Dreams, Reflections* said, "I am astonished, disappointed, pleased with myself. I am distressed, depressed, rapturous. I am all these things at once, and cannot add up the sum." It is this aspect of human experience that we are but poorly exploring in terms of grid method and thereby limiting the method as a mode of insight. Wright (1970) showed how a form of laddering could be used to explore conflict. Bannister (1960) indicated the discrepancy between our assumed and actual patterns of judgement. Fransella (1972) has explored the paradox of how we privately cherish and elaborate those stances which we publicly wish to be rid of. But there are ample opportunities for the invention of yet more ways in which we can explore the paradoxical in construct systems.

A further limitation of our use of grids to date has been our requirement that the subject present his judgements in handy grid statistical format before we can analyse pattern. Any passage of prose or transcript of conversation is a revelation of aspects of a construct system and though they inevitably contain ambiguities and unstated construings we have not yet begun to examine the extent to which they could be analysed into a pattern of construct relationships, that is essentially into the form of a grid. Rosie (1976) has touched on such a possibility with his analysis of children's conversation to reveal patterns of preemptive, constellatory and propositional construing and Rowe (1977) has explored some of the relationships between the propositions inherent in the personal arguments of psychotherapy patients. But we are still largely limited to demanding that the subject place his constructions into the template of the grid; we have not developed the skill to use the grid as a template which we can place over the free-flowing constructions of the person.

A further problem and possibility for grid work relates to the question of *context*. Kelly pointed out that a construct only has meaning within a context and though psychologists using the grid have varied the subsystems they have explored by varying elements, little attention has been paid to the context within which people construe. Agnew and Bannister (1973) took specific note of context in that their psychiatrist subjects were asked to view their patient elements first as "patients" in diagnostic terms and then as "people" in personal terms and the value of the study lies in what it revealed about the contextual differences of the two subsystems.

Yet it is still customary to ask subjects to make judgements about a variety of people entirely out of context—simply as abstract general statements. It may be that we construe very differently in the context of our family to the way we construe in the context of our work mates, even though the verbal labels of the constructs are identical. Perhaps some of the confusing results which come out of grids from time to time may derive from the fact that the people completing the grids are assuming a context for their judgements (implicitly) but are changing this context during the course of completing a single grid because the later elements are mostly experienced in a different context. Future grid work needs to take context into account both as a source of confusion and as an opportunity to come to a better understanding of how people construe.

One of the misunderstandings of the nature of constructs which derives from excessive use of the grid and underuse of the theory relates to the meaning of the word "personal" in the term personal construct. In theoretical terms *all* constructs are personal. Even constructs drawn from say science or technology which have highly publicly specified relationships and implications and which have had their predictive validity tested and retested are still personal. They are personal in the sense that each person has to acquire them and integrate them into his total system. Grid studies have tended, perhaps because of the "clinical" origins of much grid work, to be concerned with constructs which are likely to be more individually used, to the point where some people seem to think that a construct is essentially a personal prejudice. Yet there might be much of interest to be investigated using grids where the elements and constructs are drawn from areas of high public agreement. Mathematicians completing grids where the elements were numbers and the constructs were mathematical concepts might produce many grids which were identical from one mathematician to the next except in the case of some borderline or novel constructions in mathematics. It might be precisely the relationship between these sources of individual variation and the orthodox and well-established constructs that are of primary interest. An older generation of biologists using biological constructs to sort their elements might differ marginally but significantly from a younger generation of biologists completing the same grids. Work in the Piagetian tradition on children's acquisitionof constructs to do with the physical world might be richly elaborated using the grid as a way of exploring how these constructs fitted into the more total construct system of the child.

It is a cliché of research that "more work needs to be done" but it may be a cliché particularly appropriate where grids are concerned since their very flexibility and as yet unexplored range of convenience, means that they represent a continuing challenge to our inventiveness.

CAVEAT

The history of psychology provides us with fearsome examples of the way in which an exploratory technique, once separated from its theoretical base and cherished in its own right, can proliferate. Thus the Rorschach has become an industry, a club and a self-justifying pastime.

It is a fair guess that it is the mathematical ingenuity of the grid which has attracted psychologists rather than its possibilities as a way of changing the relationship between "psychologist" and "subject". An indication of this is the fact that the grid has received vastly more attention than self characterisation technique, which Kelly offered at the same time as a parallel instrument; the latter has no arithmetic scoring method. Though no way is offered of "scoring" self-characterisations, there are a large number of questions which can be meaningfully asked of such material—what are the major themes of the self-characterisation, is it written historically or "here and now", how often does it refer to other people's views of the person, what are its apparent contradictions, how sympathetic is the friend and so forth. What is clear is that George Kelly regarded self-characterisation and grid method as essentially similar in design, with perhaps a major difference being that self-characterisation seeks out superordinate rather than subordinate constructions. It particularly focuses on what Kelly called core role constructions, ways in which a person understands himself. Essentially self-characterisation and the grid are methods of bringing to the surface for examination both by the person and by others to whom he might wish to offer them, his way of viewing the world.

An essential further similarity between self-characterisation and grid method is that both are methods of self-exploration. In clinical work, as has already been mentioned, the yield of grid analyses can be returned to the person who has completed it, so that he can achieve insight into his own modes of interpreting his situation. Certainly the best way of becoming familiar with and achieving an understanding of the nature of grid method is to apply the grid to oneself and analyse the results. From a construct theory point of view if these results are not meaningful, if they make no sense to the psychologist—the person completing the grid—then he is entitled there and then to dispense further with the services of the grid. Thus to complete a grid on oneself is both a significant way in which one can come to understand the mechanisms of the grid and a vital way of evaluating the method itself.

THE PSYCHOMETRIC FALLACY

Psychologists have taken pride in their ability to create tests, pride in the whole history of psychometrics and indeed have used the development of testing as their most identifying feature and as proof of their dedication to science. Yet a consideration of that twentieth century phenomenon, the development of the psychological test, has dismal aspects.

The urge to quantify and categorise behaviour in test terms has led to a kind of continual over-simplification of our ways of construing people and to a concern with trivia. We have behaved like the drunk who dropped his key in an unlit alley and then crawled off and searched under a distant lamppost because "there was more light there".

Our own public faith in tests and a desire to establish our public usefulness have led us to make them instruments for the disposal of people to an extent which cannot be justified either by their known usefulness or by political morality. We have provided tools for tyranny in pursuit of spurious precision.

Finally, our preoccupation with testing has often led us away from a truly scientific search for explanation—thus our massive development of intelligence testing and our miniscule attack on the problem of "thinking".

If repertory grid technique is completely absorbed into the traditions of psychological testing and used in terms of the assumptions which underly such testing, then it will have little value and may well turn out to be an unfortunate excrescence of the theory.

We owe Kelly a debt for one brilliant mathematical solution to the problem of perceiving pattern in the way in which people see their universe. It would be a singularly poor way to repay that debt to distort his methods away from the values and intents which inspired him.

Appendix I

The Prediction and Measurement of Change in a Psychotherapy Group Using the Repertory Grid

J. BRENDA MORRIS*

Questions being asked about psychotherapy are changing. Instead of asking whether psychotherapy has a good or bad outcome Bergin (1972) suggested we ask what changes if any take place in people as a result of psychotherapy. He assumes that

> "given the process of change is extremely divergent for different people, divergent methods of criterion measurement should be used to match the divergency of human being and the divergency of change processes that occur within them." (p. 257).

This study describes a way in which the role repertory grid is used to answer such questions about members of a psychotherapy group although it could equally be used for the study of individuals. I am assuming that each person in a therapy group starts from a very different place, has different attitudes to relationships and different problems and so will be affected by being a member of a psychotherapy group in different ways. The only way of testing this hypothesis is to use the repertory grid in an individual case study approach which is flexible and sensitive enough not only to allow one to focus on the very different change processes taking place but which also makes it possible to specify different directions of change for each person.

Another theme explored in this study is the nature of prediction in psychotherapy. This research moves away from the earlier rather simplistic hope that one could predict final outcome (good or bad) in psychotherapy, to looking at the way therapists may make a series of extremely complex predictions about desired and actual change taking place in their clients *during* therapy.

BY WAY OF INTRODUCTION

The group studied consisted originally of eight psychiatric outpatients and two therapists. As is in the nature of psychiatric outpatients groups, three people dropped out within the first three months and one dropped out after

*This is based on my clinical dissertation submitted for the Diploma in Clinical Psychology to the British Psychological Society in 1974.

120

six months. Two of the people who dropped out agreed to do the reassessments, so there were eight people (six patients and two therapists) on whom a complete set of data was obtained. The therapists were included as it was hypothesised that they would be affected by the group as well. It was also felt that for the therapists to be assessed by the same methods as their clients would make this research more truly reflexive as Kelly advocated.

The group was a closed one in that no one was allowed to join it once it had started meeting. It met for weekly sessions over a period of a year. The therapists followed Kelly's approach to group psychotherapy (1955, pp. 1155-1178) using also role enactments and some conversational model techniques (Mair, 1970).

Following Kelly's six phases of development of a psychotherapy group was not always straightforward. The therapists found that, despite their attempts to regulate the move from one phase to another, certain members of the group would jump the gun and initiate activities relevant to other phases. In those situations therapists occasionally had to revert to assessing each person's individual needs and encouraging them or not accordingly. On the whole, however, therapists felt satisfied with the progress of the group, and felt that they learned from it too.

METHODS USED

The design has two main parts: (a) assessments based on a repertory grid and an interview structured around the grid, and (b) predictions made by the therapists concerning change in the patients.*

The patients' repertory grid

The rank order form of grid was used. The elements were elicited from the patients in the usual way by supplying them with certain role categories to help them draw up a fair sample of 10 important people in their lives. The role categories supplied as elements were:
1. Mother (or step-mother)
2. Father (or step-father)
3. Spouse or boyfriend or girlfriend
4. Someone who you admire or admired greatly
5. Someone who you are friendly with
6. Someone who likes you a great deal
7. Someone who rejects or has rejected you
8. Someone who you felt or feel sorry for
9. Someone whom you came to dislike

*In the original clinical dissertation a personality questionnaire, The Edwards personal preference schedule and a diagnostic symptom checklist, the Middlesex Hospital Questionnaire, were included in the assessments for before and after therapy and are fully discussed in the dissertation.

10. One other person who has been very important to you in your life who is not already included

Eight constructs were then elicited by asking the person to select three people he had listed and say in what important way two were alike and thereby different from the third. If the person found this difficult they could take only two people on their list and say in what way they were alike or different as people. This was often found to be easier.

Four self constructs were supplied. These were:

1. Like me in character (Self)
2. Like I would like to be (Ideal Self)
3. Like I used to be (Past Self)
4. Like I will probably become (Prospective Self)

This was done to explore self-ideal self discrepancy, self-esteem and optimism as regards change.

Two constructs were elicited from each person by asking what they saw as their main problems and deriving from this two bi-polar constructs. This was done to explore the nature of the problem in the person's *own terms* and their meaning in relation to the construct system as a whole.

I then focused attention on specific aspects of the grid to see if certain kinds of more detailed analysis would provide useful clinical information.

Self—ideal self discrepancy: this was based on the correlation between the constructs *like me* and *like I would like to be*. It was hypothesised that a moderate level of correlation between 0.2 and 0.7 would be a good prognostic sign, whereas a negative or an extremely high positive correlation might indicate something wrong (e.g. Ryle and Breen, 1972a). Thus, a huge discrepancy may indicate considerable dissatisfaction with oneself, whereas a high degree of correlation may indicate an unusual degree of complacency. Subjects were ranked from smallest to greatest discrepancy.

Level of intercorrelation between the self constructs: the difference between the number of significant self construct links (correlations) from first testing to retest was calculated. The difference scores were then ranked from largest increase through zero to largest decrease. This measure was felt to correspond to Kelly's notion of "tight" versus "loose" construing, in this instance with reference to the self constructs. A large increase in self construct links would represent a tightening in self construing, a large decrease would represent a loosening in self construing.

Problem construct variance: the amount of variance which each construct in the matrix accounted for was calculated by adding together the correlations of each construct (squared and multiplied by 100 to give percentage variance accounted for) with all other constructs in turn. The difference in the variance which these "problem" constructs (13 and 14) accounted for from test to retest was calculated and then added. The totals were then ranked from greatest to least change in variance for each person. This procedure was designed to find out how central the "problem" constructs were in relation to the rest of each person's construct system. It was hypothesised that a shift in centrality would indicate a positive change in that it might well represent a loss of involvement in the problem.

Degree of change—all constructs: each construct relationship from first to second grid was examined to see if it had become or had ceased to be statistically significant (rho 0.64 on a two-tail test). If such was the case it was counted as a change. The constructs were then ranked from most to least in terms of total number of significant changes.

Articulation—segmentation: based on the classification of Makhlouf-Norris and her co-workers (1970) an articulated system is one with more than one cluster linked by one or more constructs. A segmented system is one that consists of a number of clusters which are independent (see p. 68). A principal components analysis gave the number of clusters per grid and then the number of independent clusters was counted. These were ranked from lowest to highest number of independent clusters.

Therapists' grid predictions

Therapists were asked to specify what would constitute improvement for each person. To complete the Ideal Outcome Grid, the therapist was shown the person's first grid and transcript of the first interview and asked to draw up a hypothetical grid comprising correlations between constructs which would represent changes (or no change) felt to be desirable if the person were to resolve his or her problems.

Later on in the year, near the end of therapy, each therapist was again shown each person's first grid and asked to draw up a hypothetical matrix of correlations which would show how they thought group members had actually changed during the course of therapy (Predicted Actual Outcome Grid). These Ideal Outcome and Actual Outcome Prediction Grids could then be compared with each person's actual post-therapy grids to see (a) how the person had changed, (b) if the person had improved in the way each therapist thought desirable and (c) whether the person had changed in the way the therapist thought they had.

Outcome measures

In order to add more traditional measures of outcome to this process study, the therapists were asked to rank the six group members on both degree of change and degree of improvement. The research worker did the same, giving six ranked measures of improvement and change. These three measures of change and the three measures of improvement were then averaged to yield a further two ranked measures of improvement and change.

In addition, group members were ranked according to whether they were thought to need further treatment. It was measures such as these which made it difficult to include the therapists in the outcome matrix so they were finally omitted from it.

Statistical methods

Intercorrelation of Grid measures with Outcome measures: these measures gave 20 ranked scores in all. That is, the group members were ranked in relation to one another on all the different measures giving a matrix of 20 × 6. Tied ranks were used where necessary. Rank order correlations were computed for all possible pairs and a matrix of intercorrelations (Spearman rho's) was derived.

Grid Comparisons: the difference between the following pairs of grids was analysed for each person.

(1) First grid test (Grid 1) and retest grid (Grid 2)
(2) Grid 2 and prediction of actual change by therapist D
(3) Grid 2 and prediction of actual change by therapist R
(4) Grid 2 and Ideal Outcome Grid (Grid IO)

For each grid the matrix of relationships between constructs was rank ordered from the highest positive correlation through zero to the highest negative correlation. For the pairs of grid matrices specified above the two rank orders were correlated and the resulting Spearman rho was regarded as a global measure of the degree of similarity between the two patterns of construct relationships reflected by the grids.

An identical procedure was carried out on the construct relationships involving construct 13 (the first problem construct) and the construct relationships involving construct 14 (the second problem construct) separately.

MR. H: AGE 41. MARRIED

He had attempted suicide and suffered severe depression because his wife was going to leave him. He was extremely jealous of the wife and threatened on several occasions to kill her and her lover.

The therapists felt that one of the problems was that he never looked into the "whys" of the situation—why he needed his marriage to be just so and why it would be death if she left him. It was always his wife's fault. He had had a very strict Welsh Chapel upbringing and had very rigid and conventional ideas about relationships (for example, that a woman's place is in the home).

It was felt that by joining the group he was saying that he would not do anything drastic for the time being.

MR. H's FIRST INTERVIEW

The following are extracts from the first interview with Mr. H.

"I used to go out quite a lot with my wife and daughter but now we only go out two or three times a year so I'm much more *withdrawn*. My wife works in the evenings. Really the only time we have together is the weekends. My wife is *gregarious* and that presents conflicts. I don't like to feel that my wife and her friends are a bit *insensitive* because they are *gregarious*—it seems a bit irrational. But when they are always laughing and joking and running about in the early hours of the morning I tend to think they are insensitive. They seem to have a terrible need for meeting new people, boozing, pub crawling, party after party. I think it's not real—it's too *sophisticated*. I think my friends are more in keeping with the normal kind of life. I like to go out with my *family*.

"My father was very *violent*. I was rather violent as a teenager. I ceased to be violent after I was married but I certainly wouldn't think it wrong to strike a man if that is the only way you can express what you feel about him. I may be underneath a very violent person. I wouldn't care what other people thought about me—I only care about my daughter. I don't think life is worth living. My daughter was the one who found me after I took an overdose. She had a terrible shock . . . I would like to take revenge on my wife's friends—I'd use a knife. I just can't stand the idea that another man would touch her.

"Her friends are *very sophisticated* and *very sarcastic*. There is one man who is a friend of my wife, he is particularly sarcastic.

"I used to be able to *take a challenge*. A sarcastic person might say that there was a challenge to work my marriage out. Perhaps I should have worked at it and been more sociable . . . I think it's too late . . .I have a choice . . . Either to continue to live accepting a way of life which is totally opposed to my idea of how to live or I have to leave and get a divorce. At the moment I can't leave. On the other hand if I stayed and couldn't change anything I would be destroyed . . .".

Mr. H's first grid

After this interview with Mr. H, the first role repertory grid was completed by him. The statistically significant correlations between constructs used in that grid are shown in Fig. 17.

These same construct relationships can be seen expressed in diagrammatic form in Fig. 18.

Therapists' Ideal Outcome Grids

When Mr. H's first grid had been analysed in terms of its interconstruct correlations, each of the two therapists looked at each correlation in turn and predicted the change, or lack of change, that would ideally be expected in his second grid to be completed at the end of treatment. This procedure involved more than 90 predictions for each patient. There are three basic ways in which a correlation could be viewed in relation to some future ideal—it could remain the same, it could be reduced to statistical insignificance, or it could be increased in size either positively or negatively.

Mr. H's Ideal Outcome Grid completed by therapist D can be seen in Fig.

	2	3	4	5	6	7	8	9	10	11	12	13	14
1 like me — not like me	0.8		0.7	0.98			0.9	0.7	0.8	0.7		0.7	0.8
2 kind — nasty		0.6	0.8	0.8			0.7	0.8	0.8	0.9	−0.7	0.8	
3 not pushy — pushy			0.9		0.8			0.8	0.8	0.8		0.8	0.7
4 not sophisticated — sophisticated					0.8			0.9	0.9	0.9	−0.7	0.9	0.7
5 like I would like to be						0.6	0.9	0.7		0.8		0.7	0.7
6 doesn't like social life — does								0.9	0.9	0.7		0.9	0.7
7 violent — non violent													
8 like I used to be								0.8	0.7	0.7		0.8	0.8
9 not sarcastic — very sarcastic									0.96	0.8		0.8	
10 like I will probably become										0.8		0.96	0.8
11 likes family life — doesn't											−0.7	0.8	
12 would accept challenge — wouldn't													
13 sensitive — insensitive													0.8
14 withdrawn — gregarious													

Fig. 17. Matrix of significant construct intercorrelations (r >0.56) grid of Mr. H. on first testing.

19. If you compare this with Mr. H's first grid (Fig. 17) you will see that therapist D thought that, ideally, (a) there should be no change in his view of himself as being *sensitive* (constructs 1 and 13) or in his liking for family life (constructs 1 and 11); (b) Mr. H should come to see himself less like he used to be (reflected in a reduction in correlation between constructs 1 and 8 from 0.9 to non-significance); and (c) he should come to see himself as gregarious (reflected in a change in correlation from +0.8 to —0.6 on constructs 1 and 14).

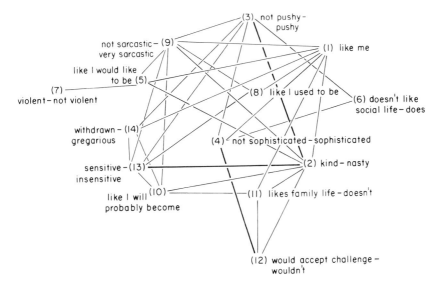

Fig. 18. Diagram of significant construct relationships in the grid of Mr. H on first testing.

Sometimes two predictions affected one score. For example, therapist D actually thought an ideal outcome for Mr. H. would be for *like me—not like me* to change from being correlated +0.8 with *withdrawn—gregarious* to being correlated —0.8. However, the therapist also predicted an overall lowering of the level of intercorrelation of all constructs in the grid, so the predicted correlation of —0.8 became —0.6, which then incorporated both predictions.

Mr. H's second grid

At the end of treatment Mr. H. completed his grid for a second time. The significant correlations from this can be seen in Fig. 20. These are also shown in diagrammatic form in Fig. 21.

	2	3	4	5	6	7	8	9	10	11	12	13	14
1 like me — not like me	0.6		0.6	0.6	0.6	-0.6	0.7		0.8	0.7		0.7	-0.6
2 kind — nasty				0.7	0.6	-0.7	0.6	0.6	0.7	0.8		0.7	
3 not pushy — pushy			0.7		0.7					0.9		0.7	0.6
4 not sophisticated — sophisticated					-0.6		0.6	0.8	0.6	0.9	-0.6	0.8	
5 like I would like to be					0.6	-0.6			0.7	0.7		0.6	
6 doesn't like social life — does						0.6	0.6		0.6			0.6	0.6
7 violent — non violent							-0.6						
8 like I used to be								0.7		0.6	0.6	0.6	0.7
9 not sarcastic — very sarcastic										0.6		0.7	
10 like I will probably become										0.7		0.7	-0.6
11 likes family life — doesn't											-0.6	-0.8	
12 would accept challenge — wouldn't													0.6
13 sensitive — insensitive													-0.6
14 withdrawn — gregarious													

Fig. 19. Ideal Outcome correlation matrix by therapist D for Mr. H.

	2	3	4	5	6	7	8	9	10	11	12	13	14
1 like me — not like me	0.6			0.6				0.6		0.8		0.7	0.8
2 kind — nasty			0.9	0.9				0.6	0.7	0.8		0.6	
3 not pushy — pushy						0.6							
4 not sophisticated — sophisticated													
5 like I would like to be								0.7	0.8	0.6		0.6	
6 doesn't like social life — does													0.8
7 violent — non violent								−0.6					
8 like I used to be													
9 not sarcastic — very sarcastic													
10 like I will probably become													0.7
11 likes family life — doesn't													
12 would accept challenge — wouldn't													
13 sensitive — insensitive													
14 withdrawn — gregarious													

Fig. 20. Matrix of significant construct intercorrelations ($r_s > 0.56$) in the grid of Mr. H on second testing.

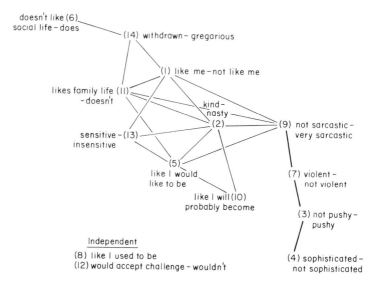

Fig. 21. Diagram of significant construct relationships in the grid of Mr. H on second testing.

Therapists' Predicted Actual Change Grids

Also at this time, both therapists completed a grid consisting of the correlations they thought would actually appear in Mr. H's second grid. The significant correlations that therapist D predicted for Mr. H. on his second grid can be seen in Fig. 22.

Change between Grids 1 and 2 for Mr. H

The level of overall correlation between Grids 1 and 2 was significant $p<.01$. Mr. H had an extremely tight construct system to begin with which loosened to a moderate level of intercorrelation. His self construct system which had been very highly inter-related also loosened whilst still being well defined. However, *like I used to be* became independent suggesting that he coped with the considerable change he had gone through by repressing or denying the past. His "problem" constructs (13 and 14) also underwent major changes, neither being significantly related to their former positions (see Table XI). On the first grid, one end of the bi-polar constructs *insensitive* and *gregarious* defined his view of his wife and her lover about whom he felt violent. After he divorced and remarried, the opposite ends of these constructs, i.e. *sensitive* and *withdrawn* became key constructs in defining himself.

Therapists' predictions

Therapist R's predictions of change were highly accurate ($p<.001$). However the predictions of therapist D were not at all accurate. Again this could have

	2	3	4	5	6	7	8	9	10	11	12	13	14
1 like me — not like me	0.7			0.8			0.7		0.6				
2 kind — nasty			0.7	0.7					0.7	0.6		0.6	
3 not pushy — pushy			0.7		0.7			0.7	0.7		0.6	0.6	
4 not sophisticated — sophisticated								0.8	0.7	0.7		0.7	0.7
5 like I would like to be										0.7		0.6	
6 doesn't like social life — does								0.8	0.7			0.7	
7 violent — non violent													
8 like I used to be								0.7	0.7	0.6		0.7	0.7
9 not sarcastic — very sarcastic								0.7					
10 like I will probably become								0.7					
11 likes family life — doesn't													0.6
12 would accept challenge — wouldn't													
13 sensitive — insensitive													0.7
14 withdrawn — gregarious													

Fig. 22. Predictions in terms of inter-construct correlations of actual grid change for Mr. H by Therapist D.

Table XI

Spearman rho correlations between different grids completed by the same person.

	First and second grid	Construct 13 on first and second grid	Construct 14 on first and second grid	Therapist D's prediction grid and second grid	Therapist R's prediction grid and second grid	Ideal outcome and second grid
Mr A	0.76	0.87	0.70	0.69	0.82	0.75
Mrs B	0.48	−0.55	0.52	0.39	0.33	0.35
Mr D	0.14	−0.76	0.77	0.20	0.14	0.31
Miss E	0.57	0.90	0.42	0.53	0.40	0.12
Miss F	0.56	0.74	0.63	0.36	0.54	0.19
Mr H	0.27	−0.10	0.11	0.17	0.38	0.21
Therapist R	0.85	0.31	0.63	0.73	0.84	0.79
Therapist D	0.31	−0.31	−0.66	0.25	0.22	0.15

levels of significance (one-tail)

r_s 0.205 <0.05
r_s 0.267 <0.01
r_s 0.338 <0.001

been affected by the fact that Mr. H. dropped out of the group for the last three months. Neither therapist predicted that *like I used to be* would become independent nor that the construct *violent* (construct 7) would become integrated in the direction that it did, although some integration was predicted.

Ideal Outcome: therapist D ranked him most improved of the group and therapist R ranked him second. The correlation between his second grid and ideal grid was only just significant (p<.05). The main areas of discrepancy were in *like I used to be* (construct 8) where it was thought desirable that it be more integrated into the construct system. They also erred in their prediction of the construct where it was considered desirable that he should become less withdrawn and more gregarious (construct 14) in order to begin a new social life. However this construct was showing signs of becoming more peripheral in his second grid, along with *doesn't like social life* (construct 6) showing a gradual move after his remarriage towards becoming less withdrawn and unsociable.

The therapists also felt it was desirable that he develop more negative attitudes towards violence but instead he dissociated it from his self constructs and it becomes a peripheral construct oddly defined as related to *not pushy* and *very sarcastic*. However this was felt to be an acceptable alternative.

Secuelae: Mr. H. did not feel he needed further treatment and the therapists concurred with this.

Mr. H's second interview

The following are extracts from the second interview with Mr. H. at the end of treatment.

"I am alright now if I don't open the box. I don't think about it (the past) too much and I don't see my ex-wife at all now. I'm the same as I was basically—perhaps a bit mellowed with age. I still stand by my views, I believe that *family life* is the most important thing and it made me very angry (in the group) when they got together and battered away at their parents—in some way they must be responsible too. In the same way one can't go on blaming the other person in the marriage for what is going on. It takes two people to make the situation and we had to look at ourselves as well.

"I think I was a very *violent* young man. I took after my father in temperament. I think now I might have a row with somebody or lose my temper but not in a physical way . . . but if somebody went too far I guess I would . . . it's still basically there.

"Well, I always did *accept a challenge*. Of course I would only consider something within my own limits and wouldn't take on something I didn't think I couldn't achieve. Of course the last time I met you I couldn't take a challenge at all. I didn't even see the point in living or breathing.

"I think the group did help at the time, or they appeared to. It might have been the combination of things. I think I got support from several quarters, from my colleagues, from the group and from my brother. I wouldn't like to say which one had more influence."

MISS E: AGE 25. SINGLE

She had an illegitimate daughter of whom she was very fond although she felt very guilty about it and about not being a good mother. Her parents however had taken over the child and seemed to prevent her from being a proper mother even though Miss E lived at home with them and did not work.

She had attempted suicide a number of times. She had no friends and the therapists saw her as being very afraid of people. Therapist D said that what seemed to frighten her was their capacity to see how unworthy she was and consequently she always seemed on the defensive in an aggressive, bolshy sort of way. Her great defence was denial. She was always saying "I don't know" or "I don't care". For her it seemed to be the ultimate degradation to admit that you need people. She was equally always accusing other people of not caring and of course most people were not prepared to stay around to prove that they did. Her disastrous relationships with women and men alike had something of a self-fulfilling prophecy in them.

She dropped out of the group after two months but returned towards the end of the year.

Miss E's first interview

The following are extracts from the first interview with Miss E at the start of treatment.

"*Guilt* is the more important problem. I always feel terribly guilty about everything, my past, things I do now. I feel everything I do is wrong and still is. If I do exactly what I want I'll be letting someone down, so either way . . . I always feel I'm letting my daughter down. I'm not a good mother. I'm never at home and I always feel she is missing out somewhere. She is terribly disturbed at the moment because she is terribly jealous of someone. That makes me feel worse and I get irritable and cross and then if I smack her I feel very guilty about it . . .

"I always feel *inadequate.* I always feel that I can't do anything right, even the simplest things in the home—cooking, washing, ironing. That is what happened when I was married. I couldn't be affectionate or anything of that sort either . . .

"I lived in total isolation until recently. Things changed when I started an affair with someone much older than myself. Now I can cook, wash, the lot. I talk to the people he has over. He is more like the father figure I would want to have—terribly affectionate and kind—my father is never affectionate.

"I'm terribly *aggressive* at home, with my parents. I won't let anything drop or pass by. My father makes me particularly angry. He is a great snob and extremely right wing . . .

"I am *emotional*—my father isn't. I suppose I relate it to being compassionate and caring about things. When my father sees a car crash he is delighted because it wasn't him . . . I'd like him to be more affectionate and compassionate . . . I feel closer to my father than I do to my mother. He's got a good brain and I admire his *confidence*. My mother isn't very confident about mixing with people.

"I think I'm pretty *dishonest*. I twist things round. Lie to make things easier at home . . . I'm very *possessive* too.

"I would like to feel more *adequate*. I used to feel terribly shy and hopeless at everything".

Miss E's first grid

After this interview with Miss E, the first role repertory grid was completed by her. The statistically significant correlations between constructs used in that grid are shown in Fig. 23 below.

These same construct relationships can be seen expressed in diagrammatic form in Fig. 24.

Miss E's second grid

At the end of treatment Miss E completed her grid for the second time. The significant correlations from this can be seen in Fig. 25. These are also shown in diagrammatic form in Fig. 26.

Change between Grids 1 and 2 for Miss E

The two grids are highly significantly related ($p < .001$). Whilst the pattern of linkages has remained similar, part of the structure has tightened considerably and a number of constructs have become independent. The part of the structure which has tightened is around the self constructs. This might, on first glance, be seen as positive change from her previous somewhat loose and fragmented self construct system. However, on closer inspection most of her self constructs are negatively defined, for example *inadequate* and *lacks confidence*. Table XI shows that her problem construct *inadequate* (13) remained virtually unchanged (0.9).

The constructs which have tended to become independent are mostly those which she used for evaluating other people. One could speculate that after she dropped out early on in the group, her increasing social isolation and her statement that other people seemed unreal may have had something to do with those constructs becoming less meaningful and usable. Unfortunately, what is absolutely clear to her is her bad qualities and lack of progress. She was also very pessimistic about improvement (*like I will probably become* is also related to all her negative self constructs as well as *like me*).

	2	3	4	5	6	7	8	9	10	11	12	13	14
1 like me — not like me													
2 introvert — extravert					−0.7			0.7					
3 narrow-minded — broad-minded				−0.8									
4 unemotional — emotional						−0.7		0.7					
5 (not) like I would like to be				0.6									
6 honest — dishonest								−0.8				−0.7	
7 lacks confidence — confident											0.7		−0.9
8 like I used to be													
9 not possessive — possessive													
10 like I will probably become													
11 aggressive — unaggressive													
12 sincere — insincere													
13 inadequate — adequate													
14 guilt — lacks guilt													

Fig. 23. Matrix of significant construct intercorrelations ($r_s > 0.56$) in the grid of Miss E on first testing.

Therapists' predictions

Actual Change: Miss E was ranked least improved by therapist R and 5th by therapist D. Both predicted, with a high degree of accuracy, what this lack of improvement involved ($p<.001$ in both cases). More specifically, therapist D predicted something of the fragmentation in certain constructs which took place and was generally more accurate than therapist R. These predictions are extremely accurate in view of the fact that Miss E dropped out (for most of the group) but this can probably be accounted for by the fact that she did return to the group, giving the therapists some opportunity to assess her current mental state.

Ideal Outcome: her second grid was not significantly related to the Ideal Outcome Grid showing again that very few of the changes thought desirable took place.

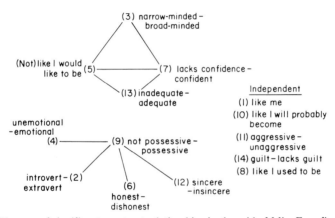

Fig. 24. Diagram of significant construct relationships in the grid of Miss E on first testing.

Miss E's second interview

The following are extracts from the second interview with Miss E at the end of treatment.

"*Inadequate* is the more important problem. I feel I can't mix with people. I don't know what to say and feel stupid . . . I'm still socially isolated, more so than before. I always feel people are better than I am or that they will think me silly or look down at me. I went back to a drug group I used to mix with, but I found their don't care attitude too much to take. I care about my daughter—the dogs even . . .

"I don't feel so *guilty* any more, not nearly as much as I used to. I still think I'm too *aggressive*, even about trivial things. But I'm more *honest* about things than I used to be. I don't lie about my daughter any more. Everybody knows about that anyway . . . I like people to be *broad-minded*.

	2	3	4	5	6	7	8	9	10	11	12	13	14
2 like me	0.7					-0.8	0.7	-0.9	0.8			0.7	
2 extravert — introvert				0.8		0.8	0.8	0.7	-0.8			-0.8	
3 narrow-minded — broad-minded													
4 emotional — unemotional													
5 like I would like to be						0.7			-0.8			-0.8	
6 honest — dishonest													
7 confident — lacks confidence								0.8	-0.95			-0.9	
8 like I used to be								-0.8	0.7			0.7	
9 possessive — not possessive									-0.9			-0.8	
10 like I will probably become												0.98	
11 aggressive — unaggressive													
12 sincere — insincere													
13 inadequate — adequate													
14 guilt — lacks guilt													

Fig. 25. Matrix of significant construct intercorrelations ($r_s > 0.56$) in the grid of Miss E on second testing.

Just live and let live and not pass judgment on people all the time or be so critical. My father is very *narrow-minded*. I also think people should be more open with children. Those parents at my daughter's school are very narrow-minded. They don't tell them anything about the facts of life.

"I'm an *introvert*. Quiet, withdrawn and don't mix. Things don't seem quite real, people don't seem real. It's probably because I have so little contact with other people. I don't have much opportunity to meet people, but when I do it always turns out to be a disaster. I seem to have got much worse—more isolated.

"I left the group because they all seemed so superficial. They all had problems but no one would talk about them. I feel they didn't like me. The only one who did was C and she left".

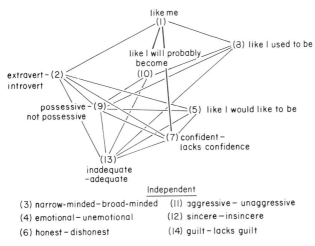

Fig. 26. Diagram of significant construct relationships in the grid of Miss E on second testing.

SUMMARIES OF CHANGE IN THE OTHER PATIENTS

Therapists and patients completed two ranked grids each, one at the beginning and one at the end of therapy, a year later. In addition there were two prediction grids for each person, including the therapists. Half were to do with "ideal" outcome and the other half with actual change. The correlations between these types of grid can be seen in Table XI.

MR. A.

He was a single man in his forties who was homosexual. However, neither he nor the therapists felt this was a problem for him. The therapists felt he had a problem of self evaluation. He also saw this but only in the context of work.

There he used to feel terrified of the prospect of some of his junior staff members being rude and that he would be unable to assert himself. In his own words "the problem that causes me most distress is fear of showing my aggression. I suppose I'm afraid of destroying my image". The therapists thought however that these fears applied equally to his relationships with his friends. It was also thought that he had dropped some of his leisure time activities because of fear of loss of face and rejection. He also saw himself as emotionally unstable (his other "problem" construct) which may partly explain his social inhibitions.

The level of correlation between his first and second grid was highly significant (p<.001). On the surface this may suggest that not much change had taken place, but in the case of Mr. A this figure is misleading. For example, his problem construct (14) *aggressive when necessary* did not change in the predicted direction but remained unrelated to the rest of the constructs. Nevertheless he did resolve the problem of aggression in a way; he simply by-passed it. "I did find that by forcing myself not to run away but to do something immediately, that I could do quite a bit and my confidence grew. I didn't have to express aggression. I just had to move around differently or just say what I wanted". In by-passing the problem of expressing aggression he had actually used different constructs as a means of solving his work problem. This points to a weakness in this form of using the grid in that fresh constructs were not elicited on retest. Only from the second interview can we see the new constructs *says what he thinks, logical, loving* and *wastes time* being used.

In several ways Mr. A did improve quite considerably. As hoped, he radically changed his conception of this problem. "A year ago I thought my problem was stress and tension at work. Partly through the group, partly through growing older and partly through conversations with a friend and partly through experiment . . . work ceased to be a problem". From the second interview it is also clear that Mr. A shifted the focus of his problems from work to leisure and personal relationships. He took up piano lessons and joined the library committee again. As far as the other "problem" construct was concerned, he stopped seeing himself as *emotionally unstable*.

Both therapists' predictions of actual change were extremely accurate (p<.001). This was far higher than for any other member of the group and perhaps indicated what the client-centred therapists called accurate empathy (Rogers, 1951). The only systematic errors were made in the construct (9) *easy-going—excitable* which both therapists thought would remain within his construct system; but which in fact became less closely linked with other constructs. It was also predicted that the other "problem" construct would become integrated but in fact did not.

The therapists ranked him second on degree of improvement. Also his second grid was significantly related to the Ideal Outcome Grid (p<.001). It was felt that the construct *like me* should be better integrated into his construct system. This seems to reflect some uncertainty about himself, possibly as a result of a crisis he was going through at the time of retesting. This also reflects a discrepancy of opinions. The therapists felt he had done well while he felt that there was still a long way to go. I saw that they were probably both right but were focusing on different aspects of his progress. He did not however ask for further treatment and nor was he offered it.

MRS. B.

She was 23, married, and had two children. She had had a happy childhood in the bosom of a warm, loving family and now she was a fairly trapped suburban housewife living a pretty isolated existence on the outskirts of London. It was from about the time of her marriage that she had had "the shakes"—a fine tremor which appeared in certain stressful situations and which had previously rendered her unable to work. She said that when she was in company she was afraid that people would see her shake and she would feel humiliated and she was convinced that people would think she was mad. She had made several suicide attempts.

The therapists felt that the problem was wider than "the shakes". They felt that her problem was having very aggressive feelings towards many people as well as her husband, her children and her relatives. However she was very proud and saw herself as well-behaved and was afraid of spoiling her self image by expressing her real feelings.

On her first grid the construct *easily angered* was linked to the construct *shaky*. However during therapy she consistently denied the suggestion that she might be "shaking with anger". Despite this she did become more accepting of expressing her anger but it was unfortunately directed at her children and not at her husband with whom she really did not get on at all well.

Her construct system was quite segmented, consisting of three independent clusters on first testing. On second testing it was only slightly less segmented (two independent clusters). The relationship between her first and second grid was, not surprisingly, highly significant (p<.001). On the positive side her self constructs were better related and better defined with more positive associated constructs.

Both therapists predicted that her system would become tighter and better integrated which was correct as far as the self constructs were concerned but incorrect as far as the total system was concerned, as in fact it loosened considerably.

Therapist R ranked her fourth and therapist D sixth in terms of improvement. The area of high discrepancy between her second grid and the Ideal Outcome Grid was in the level of correlation between constructs which the therapists felt should have been higher. It was thought that in particular the constructs *calm—easily angered, tolerant—intolerant, friendly—distant, caring—uncaring* and *dependable—dependent* should be better integrated into the construct system indicating a trend towards recognising and dealing with her emotions. However this trend did not occur.

In the second interview at the end of therapy she said that the group had helped her overcome the shakes and tension in a lot of situations, but they were still there. In her own words "I don't think I am going mad any more and I don't feel suicidal any more and I feel that I'm going to get better. It can't go on for ever".

MR. D.

He was 19 years old and single. He had attempted to commit suicide after a love affair in which his girlfriend had left him. However on interview he did not seem to be worried about it any more. He admitted that he did it to get his revenge and make her feel guilty. However he had been persuaded to seek treatment by his worried parents and a psychiatrist. He saw himself as a *reckless, moody* and *emotional* person. He seemed to be more preoccupied with the question of his intelligence and what career he should follow. He felt he was intelligent and aware of the "deeper side of life" and in the group became quite interested in the idea of becoming a psychologist. However he had quite a conflict between this and making money fast.

He seemed to have plenty of friends and soon found himself another girlfriend. He gave up the idea of becoming a psychologist when he found out how long it would take him to qualify and went to quite a well paid job at Fords, Dagenham, at which point he left the group.

He had a well articulated construct system with one main cluster and two sub-clusters well linked into the main one. His self constructs were all related to each other and seen in a good light. If anything he appeared a bit self-satisfied. *Like me* was highly related to *like I would like to be* and *like I will probably become.* In his second grid the relationships between self constructs became looser and more broadly defined which is congruent with the notion that he was finding it less necessary to defend himself by tightening up his system. Mr. D showed the most change of all group members from first to second grid. Most interesting was the complete redefinition of the self construct *like I used to be.* In his own words he saw himself becoming less emotional, less reckless, less fiery and less extreme. He now saw all these as belonging to a past self.

Despite this particular radical change from first to second grid, his second grid retains all the positive features of the first grid. It is still a well articulated system and, in addition, the self constructs are more moderately related to one another and are positively defined. He himself feels he did pretty well out of the group but left because "after a while I felt more or less at rights with myself".

However he was ranked fifth on degree of improvement by both therapists.

This seems unduly pessimistic in the light of the subsequent data. Firstly his second grid was significantly related to the Ideal Outcome Grid (p<.01). Secondly the reversal in direction of "problem" construct 13 which both therapists thought desirable, took place. The therapists also rated him very low on degree of change which was inaccurate. Nor did either therapist succeed in predicting the changes which actually took place (p<.05).

MS. F.

She was 24 years old and divorced. She had lost her mother at the age of six and had had a difficult relationship with her father and other authority figures since. The therapists felt that her father had given her the idea that she was bad, inadequate and phoney and she had tried for a long time to love him and believed he was right in most things. The result was that when she felt differently or disagreed with him or others in authority with whom she worked, she couldn't trust her own judgment or even the reality of her own feelings. She often felt unconfident and unworthy. In her own words "in my last job when criticism was asked for and I said something . . . the boss always suggested something that was more logical and I couldn't argue with it—so I just sort of agreed and was always very pleasant". However even then she cannot win "when I can't say the things that are relevant people think I'm being insincere".

She was very unhappy about her relationships. She could form a relationship but when it became too close she became overwhelmed and withdrew and then became very lonely. It was felt that her sexual relationships with women were a result of her despair over her relationships with men and not true lesbianism.

The therapists also felt that there was a faulty correspondence between the problems she presented and how she appeared to others. In the group she was seen as very warm, courageous and helpful and it was felt that she coped better with her work than she thought she did.

At the time of retesting she was going through a crisis and was quite distressed and still feeling quite unconfident. Despite this she reported feeling a bit better in her relation to people in authority including her father who she had recently stood up to. Her new relationship with a boyfriend was also going well. This change was reflected in her grids. In her first grid the central construct *anti-authority* was linked on the one hand to *spirited* and *like I would like to be* and on the other hand it was related to *lacks trust in others* and *lacks confidence in self*. In her second grid the implication dilemma was still there in the sense that *anti-authority* was still related to *lack of confidence in self* and to *spirited* but it had lost the other two conflicting implications. It had also lost some of its centrality which had shifted to her construct about trusting others, a problem area in which she had made quite a bit of headway: "I thought I couldn't trust people with showing myself—I was afraid of what they would think of me. My boyfriend helped me with this and the group as well. I have been a lot more open with them even though therapist R said we didn't have to talk about things if we didn't want to . . . If things went wrong I could always go and talk to them about it. There has been a caring attitude throughout which has really helped".

Overall though the change in her was not as great as had been hoped. Grids 1 and 2 are significantly related (p<.001). The correlation between Grid 2 and the Ideal Outcome Grids was not significant. Her construct system changed from a looser, fragmented one to a much tighter, less fragmented one which in itself seemed positive. However her three self constructs *like me, like I used to be* and *like I will probably become* remained in a tight isolated cluster totally undefined by any other constructs—perhaps reflecting her pessimism. "I think the problem is still there—the way I react to situations and feelings that I can't cope. I feel I'll never really be successful and be the kind of person I want to be".

Both therapists predicted this outcome at a high level of significance (p<.001). Therapist R was however more accurate, particularly in his prediction of her failure to resolve the authority problem. He also predicted the general level of tightening of the construct system whereas therapist D did not.

SUMMARY OF CHANGE IN THE THERAPISTS

Therapist R.

He was a man in his 40's who seemed somewhat satisfied with himself. In his first grid *like me* was highly correlated to *like I would like to be* and *like I will probably become* which was *happy, not self-centred, good, sensitive, a risk taker, logical* and *good-tempered.* His "problem" construct (13) was *secretive—trusting.* He could not decide which to be. Looking at the constructs relating to it, the problem here was that secretive was related by implication to being *static* but also to *playing safe,* which obviously had its attractions. His other "problem" construct was *applause seeking—not applause seeking.* He sometimes was the former but also felt he ought not to be. This construct was completely unrelated to the other constructs.

Therapist R had a very tight construct system which remained equally tight from first to second grid testing. Most change took place in the "problem" construct *secretive—trusting.* As a result of being in that group and being more open about himself he saw himself as becoming more trusting. In his second grid *trusting* became linked to *like me, good, not self-centred, sensitive* and *developing. Secretive* became more clearly defined as the opposite, i.e. *bad, self-centred* and so forth. He failed however to deal with his other "problem" construct, *applause seeking—not applause seeking* and this remained unrelated to the other constructs.

Both he and therapist D predicted this change to a high level of accuracy (p<.001). Also there was a very high level of correlation between his second grid and his Ideal Outcome Grid, higher in fact than anyone else in the group. One could clearly say that therapist R was doing well.

Therapist D.

She was a young, single woman in her 20s. Her grid seemed well articulated with one main cluster and two sub-clusters. An interesting feature of the main cluster was that the most central construct was *like I would like to be* which was *flexible, decisive, has sense of fun, open, strong, sensitive.* Optimistically it was also related to *like I will probably become. Like me* was only linked to *sensitive* and *like I used to be.* From this it appears that her attention was focused away from her past and present self and was directed towards the future and to change. She said herself that she was dissatisfied with the way she was.

Her "problem" constructs were *unassertive—outgoing* and *feeble—strong.* She hoped to become more outgoing and stronger. At the time of retesting she appeared to be not doing very well. The relationship between her Ideal Outcome Grid and second grid was not significant. On closer inspection the "problem" construct changed in a direction opposite to that indicated on the Ideal Outcome Grid ($r = -0.66$). In her second grid *feeble* is now more clearly linked to *like me, like I would like to be* and *like I will probably become.* The only reason I can suggest for her apparently giving up on this problem is that it also had very strong links to being *flexible* and *sensitive.* If this were so, it would be another example of an implication dilemma which makes change difficult. The "problem" construct *unassertive—outgoing* fares slightly better in that *unassertive* was now linked to *like I used to be* and appeared to now be in the past.

Change appears to be underway but still very much in process. *Like I would like to be* was still a central construct but became clearly linked to *like me* which became, in turn, better defined, that is, had more positive constructs linking on to it.

The prediction of actual change by both therapists was just significant (p<.05). Both therapists failed to predict what happened to the "problem" constructs but were slightly more accurate in predicting changes which occurred in the self constructs. Her construct system seemed to have a mixture of positive and negative features and it would appear from the considerable changes which took place in the self constructs that therapist D was herself going through a form of identity crisis.

GROUP RESULTS AND DISCUSSION

I am ever grateful to my clients for their openness and to the repertory grid for its versatility. The method of construct elicitation used provided a fair sample of the most salient and important constructs each person was using at the time of testing. I would like to focus our prime attention on the *content* of grids the constructs themselves. They are the real information that generates information, discussed by Holt (1958). Constructs contain and reveal an enormous amount of meaningful information about the person to whom they belong, which immediately gets lost the minute you translate the construct into a number. Elsewhere (1977) I have argued that numerical empiricism is over-used in psychology, to its detriment. A construct is as much a fact as is a number. There is no way we can numerically express Miss E's statement that she construes herself as *lacking confidence, inadequate, introvert* and *possessive.*

I would also like to emphasise that the interviews were absolutely crucial to understanding what the constructs meant and how they were being used in practice. It was only through the interviews that one really began to understand the changes that had taken place in the grids. These were often reflected in quite subtle shifts in emphasis in the meaning given to the constructs. It was also the only way one could get quite clear statements as to how people saw themselves and their problems.

The "problem" constructs and self constructs provided a most useful focus for analysing each person's current mental state. They were things one could look at first and which provided an organising principal as well as pointing to clinically relevant information.

The self constructs did however present some difficulties. Sometimes people objected saying that no one (of their elements) was really like them. Older people sometimes asked which past self they were supposed to refer back to. In addition, this method is open to errors of association. For example, if I rank my mother as most *like me* and my mother is *artistic, vivacious* and *a chatterbox,* I might unintentionally be rating myself as a chatterbox purely by association. In subsequent research I have found that people can psychologically handle "self", "ideal self" and "past self" better as elements. In this way each self construct is ranked independently and a more precise and detailed description of the self is obtained.

Organisation of the construct system

The measure articulation—segmentation was significantly correlated to high self/ideal self discrepancy and the need for further treatment. More specifically, articulation was related to low self ideal self discrepancy and to the lack of need for further treatment. This is congruent with Bannister and Mair's (1968) notion that a construct system which is working well is one with one main well organised cluster and one or two sub-clusters which are very often pathways along which the person can move if the need to change arises. A segmented system was found to be a poor prognostic sign, perhaps because the lack of links between clusters results in difficulty in changing (see the account of Miss E).

Two group members and one of the therapists had construct systems with only one main cluster in which correlations were very high. Makhlouf-Norris and her colleagues (1970) have described this type of system as "monolithic" and found it typical of people with obsessional neurosis. However, no one in our group was obsessional and I feel that this type of construct system is better described as a very "tight" system. From clinical experience many people's systems seem to tighten when they go through a crisis, especially if they start out with one that is well organised. It seems that Makhlouf-Norris tended to construe the organisation of a construct system as a relatively fixed entity rather like a personality trait or diagnostic category. However it is clear from this study that a construct system can go through a process of loosening and tightening (which Kelly called the creativity cycle) many times.

Predictions of Actual Change

In nine out of twelve instances the therapists managed to predict fairly accurately changes which took place in group members. Those predictions which were not significant were all related to group members who had dropped out early and with whom the therapists had had little further contact. In the light of this, the level of accuracy of prediction was extremely high. These results are an interesting reflection on the capacity of clinicians to make extremely complex multiple judgments about one person. In fact the prediction of one person's grid matrix by one therapist involved the therapist making 91 judgments which by definition had to inter-relate logically with each other. In no two cases were these predictions by any means the same. Thus the unidimensional outcome measures which psychotherapy research has frequently rested on, not only do an injustice to the complexity of the individual but also to the therapists' capacity to comprehend and make use of that complexity in therapy.

Using the process of predicting a person's grid and comparing it to the actual grid also gave specific information as to where the clinical judgments of one or both therapists were in error, even when overall predictions were fairly accurate. This could in future practice provide therapists with a way of empirically determining their "blind spots" in therapy hitherto left to the ad hoc interpretations of psychoanalysts.

The Ideal Outcome Matrices

These gave interesting information as to which patients were conforming to expectations and which were not. In five out of eight group members their grids on retest were highly significantly related to their Ideal Outcome Grids. However closer inspection gave interesting information as to the way in which the ideal might have been idealised and this reflected in unrealistic expectations of change. Perhaps psychotherapy, like politics, should be seen as the art of the possible. There were in fact several instances where a lack of correspondence between Ideal Grid and Actual Grid showed an alternative and equally valid solution to a problem, which the therapists had not thought of, and which both client and therapist ultimately felt was satisfactory (as in the case of Mr. H).

Thus while the Ideal Outcome Grid was found to be valid, it should not be seen as an "absolute" or "correct" series of judgments but in more relativistic terms as an index of the discrepancy between therapists' ideal expectations and actuality.

This is the stuff of which predictions are made. They are tentative guesses against which future events can be checked and present knowledge re-evaluated. The quality of these guesses range from blind and inaccurate lunges in the dark, to extraordinarily well informed accurate predictions. What is unpredictable is which prediction will be which. I can only conclude therefore that prediction leading to control is out of the question, whereas prediction leading to greater understanding is highly likely.

Suggestions for further research

First, arising out of a methodological criticism made earlier in this chapter, it is felt that further studies using this approach should re-elicit constructs on retest and incorporate them along with those from the first testing so that, while there is still some basis for comparison between first and second testing, new developments in the person's phenomenological world be not lost from view.

Secondly, it was also suggested that self concepts are better explored as elements than as constructs

Thirdly, it follows from the adverse criticism of the theory of conceptual structure of Makhlouf-Norris and her colleagues (1970) that in order to dispel finally the idea that grids reflect set personality traits or diagnostic categories, that there is a need to serially assess clients using the grid method plus interview over shorter intervals, say 2 to 3 months. It would be more interesting to direct enquiry into the range and type of fluctuations which occur in a person's construct system over time. This would also be a more sensitive index of change than one retest after an interval of a year.

Finally, I thought I had made this research truly reflexive by including the therapists in the sample. I then realised that I had excluded myself. Is true reflexivity only an optical illusion?

Appendix II

ANNOTATED BIBLIOGRAPHY

This is by no means an exhaustive bibliography. Its aim is to illustrate the diversity of grid usage. Later rather than earlier papers have been cited since these will yield earlier sources in their reference lists.

Grid structure and format

Adams-Webber, J. Elicited *versus* provided constructs in repertory grid technique: a review. *British Journal of medical Psychology,* 1970, **43,** 349-354.

    This review of elicited *versus* provided construct studies concluded that subjects prefer their own verbal labels but can effectively use provided labels—with the possible exception of neurotics.

Adams-Webber, J. R. An analysis of the discriminant validity of several repertory grid indices. *British Journal of Psychology,* 1970, **61,** 83-90.

    Review and reported experiment suggest that comparison studies cast doubt on whether some differently labelled grid measures really do measure "different" variables. Author suggests that the segregation of construct and figure comparisons in a structural analysis of repertory grids is unwarranted. Specifically, measures of "cognitive simplicity", "identification" and "constellatoriness" were found to be functionally similar, an observation consistent with personal construct theory.

Bannister, D. and Bott, M. Evaluating the person. *In* "New Approaches to Psychological Medicine" (Ed. P. Klein). Wiley, 1974.

    A critique of conventional testing assumptions, a discussion of grid method, an evaluation of joint grids by a married couple and a discussion of the uses of the grid for the person who completes it.

Bender, M. P. Provided versus elicited constructs: an explanation of Warr and Coffman's (1970) anomalous finding. *British Journal of social and clinical Psychology,* 1974, **13,** 329.

    No other study on extremity ratings has used the sequential method of elicitation employed by Warr and Coffman. Bender shows how this method (of only exchanging one element each time to form a new triad) produces constructs that load less highly on the first factor of a principal components analysis. He used Kelly's Self Identification Method (which he mistakenly attributes to Makhlouf-Norris) to elicit "unimportant" constructs, and triads in which only one element remains the same as the previous triad, to elicit "important" constructs. He argues that element variation is needed to yield personally significant constructs.

Caine, T. M. and Smail, D. J. Personal relevance and the choice of constructs for the repertory grid technique. *British Journal of Psychiatry,* 1967, **113,** 517-520.

    Two groups of neurotic patients were grid tested with more and less "personally relevant" constructs. They were also given tests of vocabulary, personality, and symptomatology. From the results it is argued that grids constructed from less personally relevant material give rise to higher relationship scores.

Cromwell, R. L. and Caldwell, D. F. A comparison of ratings based on personal constructs of self and others. *Journal of clinical Psychology,* 1962, **18,** 43-46.

 Forty-four subjects recalled names of six recent and six old acquaintances. Three names from each group were used in a Kelly Role Construct Repertory Test to elicit six constructs. One group then rated the remaining six people they had recalled on the construct-contrast dimensions they had produced and finally rated the same people on constructs elicited by other subjects. The second group, following the reverse order, rated first with personal constructs of others and then with their own. As predicted, ratings were more extreme from the midpoint of the scale when using one's own personal constructs as opposed to the personal constructs of another person. No effects of new *versus* old acquaintances, sequence of ratings or interactions of these variables were found.

Epting, F. Order of presentation of construct poles. What are the factors to be considered? A reply. *British Journal of social and clinical Psychology,* 1975, **14,** 427-428.

 Epting first points out that the study referred to by Gibson was a study of stability of complexity and, secondly, that Gibson has his terminology wrong. Gibson is confusing the dimension emergent *versus* implicit and construct (likeness end) and contrast. He describes several ways of ensuring that poles need not be reflected when using Bieri's complexity measure.

Epting, F., Suchman, D. I. and Nickeson, K. J. An evaluation of elicitation procedures for personal constructs. *British Journal of Psychology,* 1971, **62,** 513-517.

 The opposite method (how is this third person *opposite* to) and the difference method (how is this third person *different* from) for eliciting personal constructs were evaluated with regard to the number of bipolar constructs produced. This study is an investigation of how the constructs were used in a grid procedure and how they were reported in a structured interview. Comparing the two methods, using the grid procedure, the "opposite method" produced a greater number of bipolar constructs. Responses to the interview were incomplete. Explanations for this observed difference between methods are proposed.

Fjeld, S. P. and Landfield, A. W. Personal construct theory consistency. *Psychological Reports,* 1961, **8,** 127-129.

 A version of Kelly's Rep Test was given over a two week period to four groups each under different conditions of testing. A high degree of reliability was found in each group both supporting the rep test as a reliable research tool and suggesting that people employ the same axes of meaning even though the "objects" of these conceptual axes may change.

Isaacson, G. I. and Landfield, A. W. Meaningfulness of personal and common constructs. *Journal of Individual Psychology,* 1965, **21,** 160-166.

 Self ratings (qualities *least like me* and *most like me*) were done with Personal Construct (PC) descriptions and Butler-Haigh (BH) Q-sort statements. It was hypothesised that self ratings within the more generalised BH language would be less extreme than ratings within the more *personal* language elicited by Kelly's Role Construct Repertory Test. This hypothesis was supported in that ratings within PC language were found to be more extreme and skewed toward *most like me* whereas

BH piles up in the centre of the distribution. This investigation not only supports the greater meaningfulness of one's own personal language for understanding oneself, but also highlights the importance for the therapist of utilising a client's own language, particularly when the client is confronted by certain negative characteristics of himself.

Lansdown, R. A reliability study of the 8 × 8 repertory grid. *Journal of the Association of Educational Psychologists,* 1975.
    Children completed two small grids repeated from half an hour to more than 8 days later. Reliability reduced as time interval between testings increased.

Levy, L. H. and Dugan, R. D. A factorial study in personal constructs. *Journal of Consulting Psychology,* 1956, **20,** 53-57.
    Sets out a method of applying factor analytic techniques to the concepts formed by an individual on the Role Construct Repertory Test. Two cases are presented for illustrative purposes and the research implications of the method are discussed. A pioneer paper.

Mair, J. M. M. Some problems in repertory grid measurement: I. The use of bipolar constructs. *British Journal of Psychology,* 1967, **58,** 261-270.
    In most grid applications implicit assumptions seem to be made that elements not chosen in grid sorts using one pole of a construct dimension will be chosen in sorts based on the other pole, and that relations between constructs derived from grid sorts using one pole of a construct will be the converse of the relatons derived from sorts based on the other pole. The legitimacy of these assumptions was examined experimentally. Considerable *overlap* in element choices based on opposite poles of five construct dimensions appeared for each subject, and the practical effects of this overlap on various types of grid scores were demonstrated. Suggestions for modifications in grid usage and for further exploration of construct functions are discussed.

Mair, J. M. M. Some problems in repertory grid measurement. II. The use of whole figure constructs. *British Journal of Psychology,* 1967, **58,** 271-282.
    Whole-figure constructs (e.g. *Like self, Like Father,* etc.) have often been used in grid testing to gain an indirect assessment of a person's view of important figures in his life. Some problems in the use and interpretation of such constructs are explored. Ten male medical students provided grid results indicating that direct ratings of figures and comparable grid scores are not equivalent, and reveal various kinds of discrepancy from expectations concerning (a) relations between one whole-figure construct (*Like Self*) and personal constructs elicited to define "like" and "unlike self" characteristics; (b) relations between supplied matching highly with *Like Self* and elicited constructs defining self and non-self; (c) relations among and between elicited "like" and "unlike self" constructs. Limitations of the present grid forms are discussed in the light of the findings and interpretations of some of the discrepancies are suggested.

Metcalfe, R. J. A. Own *versus* provided constructs in a reptest measure of cognitive complexity. *Psychological Reports,* 1974, **35,** 1305-1306.
    Both cognitive complexity and cognitive differentiation scores were calculated using own and provided constructs. The two measures differed significantly from each other, suggesting they are measuring different aspects of a person's construct system. The correlations between own and provided constructs were significant on

both measures, but low. The author suggests that, although provided constructs were adequate for his purpose, the subjects' own constructs should be used if possible.

Mitsos, S. B. Representative elements in role construct technique. *Journal of Consulting Psychology,* 1958, **22,** 311-313.

The results of this study confirm the hypothesis that fulfilment of the assumption of the representativeness of the elements used on the R.C.R.T. is important. Results were most satisfactory when the role title list used included many different figures important in the subjects' lives. It was further suggested that a heterogeneous role title list (one including many different roles) tends to elicit superordinate constructs (constructs subsuming other constructs) while a homogeneous one (one calling for figures who all fill the same role) tends to elicit subordinate constructs (constructs subsumed by superordinate constructs).

Resnick, J. and Landfield, A. W. The oppositional nature of dichotomous constructs. *Psychological Record,* 1961, **11,** 47-55.

It was hypothesised that the overlap in description of the poles of "logical" constructs would be greater than that for "peculiar" constructs. The data confirms the hypothesis and supports Kelly's contention that contrasting ends of personal constructs represent similar dimensions of meaning.

Ryle, A. and Lunghi, M. W. The dyad grid: A modification of repertory grid technique. *British Journal of Psychiatry,* 1970, **117,** 323-327.

The elements in the repertory grid testing of neurotics have normally been people of significance to the subject. By using the relationships (how John sees Mary) between people as elements greater sensitivity is obtained. The use of dyad grid testing of this sort on four patients with sex role difficulties is briefly described.

Shubsachs, A. P. W. To repeat or not to repeat? Are frequently used constructs more important to the subject? A study of the effect of allowing repetition of construct in a modified Kelly repertory grid test. *British Journal of medical Psychology,* 1975, **48,** 31-37.

The aim is explained in the title. Four hundred and eighty student teachers filled out a questionnaire consisting of 2 lists each containing 15 triads of occupational titles—repetition of constructs was allowed on one test and not the other, (repetition of a construct being indicated by an R by the subject). The elicited constructs were then rated for importance on a 5-point scale. Summing of the ratings of the importance of the constructs indicated that, in general, repeated constructs were rated as more important. Several observations are expressed against accepting the conclusion that "if the subject may repeat constructs one is likely to elicit important ones more often".

Slater, P. Personal Questionnaire data treated as forming a repertory grid. *British Journal of social and clinical Psychology,* 1970, **9,** 357-370.

Data obtained by giving a personal questionnaire (Shapiro) to a patient on a series of occasions during a course of treatment for a psychiatric disorder were analysed by Slater's standard programme for analysing repertory grids. The results identify the place where the greatest fluctuations occurred in the patient's mental state (including 72 per cent of the total variation) and they provide co-ordinates for mapping the course the fluctuations followed, which proved to be a remarkably complicated one.

Slater, P. The measurement of consistency in repertory grids. *British Journal of Psychiatry*, 1972, **121**, 45-51.

A programme is described for calculating a coefficient of convergence. The procedure followed corresponds closely with Bannister's various methods for calculating "consistency scores" and the results obtained are almost exactly equivalent; but the programme extends to a far wider range of data and can be generalised if desired to compare more than two grids at a time.

Smith, S. and Leach, C. A hierarchical measure of cognitive complexity. *British Journal of Psychology*, 1972, **63**, 561-568.

A new hierarchical measure of cognitive complexity based on the repertory grid is described. This measure is considered to be both conceptually and empirically an advance over previous measures. It emphasises that the structure of a person's construct system is important, rather than merely its degree of differentiation. Three experiments are described which test the validity and reliability of the new measure. The measure is reliable and is unrelated to a measure of differentiation based on the grid. The experiment also indicates some validity for the measure.

Stringer, P. Psychological significance in personal and supplied construct systems: A defining experiment. *European Journal of Social Psychology*, 1972, **2**, 437-447.

An implication was examined of three assumptions of Personal Construct Theory. Personal and supplied construct systems were compared for their capacity to account for 34 subjects' behaviour in an independent sorting task. It was found that either construct system tended to account for a significant amount of the variance in sorting behaviour, but that more was accounted for by personal construct systems. Observations were made on the way in which this phenomenon varied between subjects, sub-tasks and parts of construct systems. The assumptions examined were held to be relevant to social perception and cognitive theories.

Grids and personal construct theory

Bannister, D. Personal construct theory: a summary and experimental paradigm. *Acta Psychologica*, 1962, **20**, 104-120.

Presents the fundamental postulate and the eleven corollaries making up the backbone of Personal Construct Theory. Aspects of construing are discussed and the Repertory Grid Test is presented, along with an experiment employing the Grid. Conclusion of the experiment is that, in a Personal Construct Theory framework, "it is theoretically and experimentally meaningful to talk of construct systems as independent of the particular elements construed".

Levy, L. H. Personal constructs and predictive behaviour. *Journal of abnormal and social Psychology*, 1956, **53**, 54-58.

In this classic study it was found that, under conditions of high invalidation, the greater amount of reconstruction occurred in constellatory constructs than in propositional constructs (those which do not fix the other realm memberships of their elements). Those constructs which were most interdependent were considered constellatory. It was concluded that there is an inverse relationship between the range of interdependency of a construct and its susceptibility to change following predictive failure. One of the only studies to attempt a grid definition of *propositional—constellatory*.

Rehm, L. Effects of validation on the relationship between personal constructs. *Journal of Personality and Social Psychology*, 1971, **20**, 267-270.

An attempt was made to demonstrate that the correlation or linkage between a pair of bipolar constructs could be influenced directly by appropriate validation. Eighty subjects rated 100 photos of people on two bipolar constructs. Two groups of 20 subjects received feedback validating either a positive or a negative linkage. A third received feedback validating constructs, but random with regard to linkage. The fourth group received no feedback. The first two procedures yielded increases in the validated linkages, while the latter two groups showed no changes. Partial evidence suggested that this effect transferred to another set of elements (real, known people) and to other means of measurement (direct and indirect semantic differentials).

Cognitive structure and complexity

Adams-Webber, J. Cognitive complexity and sociality. *British Journal of social and clinical psychology,* 1969, **8,** 211-216.
    A discussion of Bieri's definition of "cognitive complexity" within the general framework of Personal Construct Theory, and specifically in terms of the theoretical implications of Kelly's Sociality Corollary, led to the hypothesis that relatively cognitively complex persons infer the personal constructs of others in social situations more efficiently than do relatively cognitively simple persons. The results of an experiment were consistent with this hypothesis.

Bieri, J. Cognitive complexity-simplicity and predictive behaviour. *Journal of abnormal and social Psychology,* 1955, **51,** 263-268.
    The study which launched the cognitive complexity—simplicity topic. Rep tests and a Situations questionnaire were used to test the hypotheses that cognitively simple subjects are less accurate than complex subjects in predicting the behaviour of others and are more prone to see others as like themselves (assimilative projection). Results provided partial support for hypotheses.

Crockett, W. H. Cognitive complexity and impression formation. *In* "Progress in Experimental Personality Research" (Ed. B. A. Maher), Vol 2. Academic Press, New York, 1965.
    The chapter reviews the literature on definitions of cognitive complexity and its effects on the forming of impressions of others and ends with a discussion of methods of measurement and some of the accompanying problems. Crockett makes important distinction between cognitive differentiation and cognitive complexity.

Epting, F. R. The stability of cognitive complexity in construing social issues. *British Journal of social and clinical Psychology,* 1972, **11,** 122-125.
    The stability of the amount of cognitive differentiation involved in construing social issues was investigated. Using a common set of construct dimensions, three cognitive complexity instruments were built, each containing a different set of social issues. The three instruments were readministered one week later. The stability indices obtained here, on social issues, were comparable in magnitude to those reported in studies of interpersonal construing.

Gibson, M. An illustration of the effect of the order of presentation of construct poles on Bieri's measure of cognitive complexity. *British Journal of social and clinical Psychology,* 1975, **14,** 425-426.
    Taking Epting's data, Gibson demonstrated that, by reversing the poles of 2 constructs in a rated grid, cognitive complexity scores differed although cluster

patterns of constructs and elements remained the same. He points out that when Bieri's technique of measuring cognitive complexity is used, emergent poles should be compared with each other and contrast poles with each other.

Honess, T. Cognitive complexity and social prediction. *British Journal of social and clinical Psychology,* 1976, **15,** 23-31.
    The problem of "cognitive complexity" is discussed and the importance of examining the predictive validity of the different measurement techniques is stressed. The experiment examines intercorrelations between different measures of complexity and their relation to the subjects' predictions of how others' personal constructs are employed.

Kuusinen, J. and Nystedt, L. Individual versus provided constructs, cognitive complexity and extremity of ratings in person perception. *Scandinavian Journal of Psychology,* 1975, **16,** 137-148.
    Bruner and Tagiuri's concept of implicit personality theory and Kelly's theory of personal constructs were used as a basis for a hypothesis that an individual's own constructs mediate more differentiated perceptions of other people than constructs provided by the experimenter. The hypothesis was tested by using four indices of cognitive complexity and one index of extremity of ratings to measure differentiation. The individual constructs were derived by using Rep test. The provided constructs were Semantic Differential and Personality Differential scales. The subjects were 36 psychology students. Two experimenters were employed to control experimenter effect. The data did not support the hypothesis but showed that differences between individual constructs and provided constructs are dependent upon which criterion is chosen to contrast the two types of constructs, which indices are used to measure the chosen criterion, and what type of provided constructs are compared with individual constructs.

Kuusinen, J. and Nystedt, L. The convergent validity of four indices of cognitive complexity in person perception. *Scandinavian Journal of Psychology,* 1975, **16,** 131-136.
    An application of the Campbell and Fiske multimethod—multitrait analysis and factor analysis was used to study the convergent validity of the following indices of cognitive complexity: Bieri's Index, Vannoy's Interaction Variance Measure, Number of Factors, and First Factor Percentage. In the analysis the individual constructs elicited by Rep test were contrasted with two sets of provided constructs, namely Semantic Differential and Personality Differential scales. The subjects were 36 psychology students. The results indicated that the convergent type had an effect upon the intercorrelations of different indices of cognitive complexity.

Lemon, N. and Warren, N. Salience, centrality and self-relevance of traits in construing others. *British Journal of social and clinical Psychology,* 1974, **13,** -119-124.
    Salient traits were hypothesised as having importance for the individual in two respects: (i) because they allow more effective inferences to other traits (centrality); (ii) because they are typically used in characterising the self, and thus afford self-other comparison (self-relevance). The study assessed the differences between salient and non-salient traits on measures of centrality and self-relevance, and found support for both hypotheses. Centrality and self-relevance appeared to be relatively distinct features of salient traits, in that the overlap between them was fairly small.

Lester, D. Cognitive complexity of the suicidal patient. *Psychological Reports,* 1971, **28,** 158.

Four measures of cognitive complexity (8 as the grid was analysed by rows and by columns) were derived from data in Situational Resources grids of suicidal and non-suicidal students with high neuroticism scores. No differences on any of the measures was found between the two groups.

Scott, W. A. Cognitive complexity and cognitive flexibility. *Sociometry,* 1962, **25,** 405-414.

Illustrates a form of repertory grid which does not call for the use of verbal labels in a study (using nations as elements) designed to show that the greater the subject's initial complexity the greater the likelihood that he will expand his groups and gain information by such expansion.

Warr, P. B. and Coffman, T. L. Personality, involvement and extremity of judgement. *British Journal of social and clinical Psychology,* 1970, **9,** 108-121.

Persons with certain personality characteristics (e.g. authoritarianism, dogmatism, cognitive simplicity) are thought to have a general tendency to make extreme judgements on rating scales. This belief rests upon two assumptions: that extreme responding is an individually consistent characteristic across tasks, and that such a characteristic is in fact associated with such personality traits. These assumptions are examined in four separate investigations. The generality of extreme responding is adequately demonstrated, but no general relationship with personality was found. Ratings on elicited constructs were not more extreme than those on semantic differential supplied constructs.

Psychopathology

Bannister, D. Conceptual structure in though disordered schizophrenics. *Journal of Mental Science,* 1960, **106,** 1230-1249.

The first paper in the series using grids to establish that abnormally loosened construing is a central feature of thought disorder. Grids used in this study had people known personally to the subject as elements and were of the matching score variety. The measures derived from the grid were consistency (stability of the pattern of construct relationships over repeat testing), intensity (the degree of relationship between constructs), coefficient of variation, (degree of variability in strength of construct relationships within the single construct system), and social deviation (comparison of a particular pattern of constructs' relationships for a subject with the average normative pattern).

Bannister, D. The rationale and clinical relevance of repertory grid technique. *British Journal of Psychiatry,* 1965, **111,** 977-982.

The paper gives description of the method and its use in the clinical field, particularly with individual cases.

Bannister, D. The genesis of schizophrenic thought disorder: re-test of the serial invalidation hypothesis. *British Journal of Psychiatry,* 1965, **111,** 377-382.

The study presented in grid format separate constellations of constructs. For normal constructs one of the constellations was serially validated and the second serially invalidated. The intercorrelations of the validated constellation rose while in the latter the pattern of constructs relationships repeatedly changed and the strength of correlations ultimately fell. Although the formal topic of the paper is "thought disorder" the implications of the study concern validation—invalidation. It illustrates the use of grids in a process experiment.

Bannister, D. and Fransella, F. A repertory grid test of schizophrenic thought disorder. *British Journal of social and clinical Psychology*, 1965, **2**, 95-102.

The study confirms earlier findings that thought disordered schizophrenics employ loosened constructions which have low intercorrelations and low consistency on grid test. This finding is used to construct a standardised test for thought disorder for clinical use. The test differentiated thought disordered schizophrenics from non-thought disordered schizophrenics, depressives, neurotics, organics and normals.

Bannister, D. and Salmon, P. Schizophrenic thought disorder: specific or diffuse? *British Journal of medical Psychology*, 1966, **39**, 215-219.

Thought disordered subjects and normals were given two grids, one with physical objects as elements and the other with photographs of people as elements. These were designed to test the degree of structure and stability of the subjects in "thinking about people" and "thinking about objects". It was found that thought disordered subjects had lost structure much more markedly in the area of "thinking about people". The study is technically useful as an example of investigating comparison of degree of structure within different construing areas using grids which are broadly equivalent except for a difference in elements.

Bannister, D., Fransella, F. and Agnew, J. The characteristics and validity of the grid test of thought disorder. *British Journal of social and clinical Psychology*, 1971, **2**, 144-151.

A sample of 316 psychiatric admissions were given the Grid Test of Thought Disorder. Test indices were shown to relate to case note judgements and marginally to prognostic data of the "condition on discharge" type. The relationship between grid scores and diagnostic category was examined. A measure of the degree of abnormality of patterning of construct relationships (Social Deviation) was derived from the grid and shown to relate to structural thought disorder, sex and presence of a precipitating factor for the "illness".

Caine, T. M. and Smail, D. J. A study of the reliability and validity of the repertory grid technique as a measure of the hysteroid/obessoid component of personality. *British Journal of Psychiatry*, 1969, **115**, 1305-1308.

The stability of a form of the repertory grid as a measure of a known, relatively stable aspect of personality (the hysteroid/obessoid dimension) is examined. Although less stable than the validating criterion, the grid evidenced some significant reliability.

Fransella, F. Thinking in the obsessional. *In* "Obsessional States" (Ed. H. R. Beech). Methuen, London, 1974.

A construct theory explanation of obsessional neurosis was proposed based on grid results. The obsessional's world becomes increasingly meaningless as he retreats more and more into his world of symptoms. Treatment then should focus on the elaboration of his "non-symptom" constructs.

Fransella, F. The self and the stereotype. *In* "New Perspectives in Personal Construct Theory" (Ed. D. Bannister). Academic Press, London, 1977.

The grid studies showing a divorce between the self construct and group to which the person belongs (e.g. stutterer, arsonist, alcoholic, woman) is discussed in construct theory terms. Changes in the self/stereotype relationship during treatment are described in two stutterers. The measures were derived from bipolar implications grids completed on five occasions during treatment.

Fransella, F. and Adams, B. An illustration of the use of repertory grid technique in a clinical setting. *British Journal of social and clinical Psychology,* 1966, **5,** 51-62.

A modification of Repertory Grid Technique was used to study a man who had committed several acts of arson. Six grids of different types were given, designed to show its possible use in testing hypotheses derived from explanations of the behaviours of the individual patient, as a method of tracing conceptual changes in the patient resulting from psychotherapy and as a possible basis for the development of a measure of prognosis.

Fransella, F. and Crisp, A. H. Conceptual organisation and weight change. *Psychotherapy and Psychosomatics,* 1970, **18,** 176-185.

A form of repertory grid was used to study changes in attitudes to the self and others in the personal environment of two obese women during weight change. During weight loss, view of the self polarized from being evaluatively "bad" to being close to the ideal. With weight gain the view of self reverted to being "bad". After the initial weight loss, change in self construing occurred *before* change from weight loss to weight gain. The hypothesised prognostic value of degree of complexity of the construing system could not be tested as neither patient retained her weight loss. Further research will show whether the polarization of the self can be used as an indicator of forthcoming relapse and conceptual complexity as a prognostic indicator.

Fransella, F. and Crisp, A. H. Comparisons of weight concepts in groups of a) neurotic, b) normal and c) anorexic females. *British Journal of Psychiatry,* 1977, (in press).

Rank order grids, consisting of supplied and elicited constructs, were given to 40 women without weight disorders and compared with those of anorexic women. Attitudes to weight were the same for neurotic and normal women—fat is bad. Validity of the grid was indicated; the more negative the correlation between constructs *me now* and *ideal weight,* the greater the discrepancy between actual weight and stated desired weight. The degree of difference between construct/ element pairs (e.g. self now as construct and element) was suggested as a possible measure of ambivalence or conflict.

Hoy, R. M. The meaning of alcoholism for alcoholics: repertory grid study. *British Journal of social and clinical Psychology,* 1973, **12,** 98699.

The study was carried out on 14 male in-patient alcoholics in an addiction unit, who were undergoing group psychotherapy on the basis that they were self-confessed alcoholics who wished to abstain. A split-half grid was administered to each patient in standard fashion. The elements consisted of 20 photographs of the faces of anonymous males of a similar age range to that of the patients (20-57) and the constructs were supplied as being relevant to possible meanings of alcoholism, written in a bipolar form. Alcoholics viewed alcoholics as weak, sexually frustrated and lonely but did not see themselves individually in these terms.

Lifshitz, M. Long range effects of father's loss: the cognitive complexity of bereaved children and their school adjustment. *British Journal of medical Psychology,* 1976, **49,** 189-197.

Using a measure of cognitive complexity, interviewing and classroom observation the study showed that fatherless children show a tightening of diverse psychological indices. The smaller the perceived difference between self and parents, the more changeable and restless their behaviour appeared to be.

McFadyen, M. and Foulds, G. A. Comparison of provided and elicited grid content in the Grid Test of Schizophrenic Thought Disorder. *British Journal of Psychiatry*, 1972, **121**, 53-57.

Thought-disordered and non-thought-disordered subjects were given the standard grid test of thought disorder and a Kelly rep test for which elements and constructs were elicited individually. Between groups differences were broadly evident for both types of grid.

McPherson, F. M., Blackburn, I. M., Draffan, J. W., and McFayden, M. A further study of the Grid Test of Thought Disorder, *British Journal of social and clinical Psychology*, 1973, **12**, 420-427.

The performance of 36 thought-disordered schizophrenics, 24 non-thought-disordered schizophrenics, 18 manics and 33 depressives was compared on four measures derived from the Bannister-Fransella Grid Test of Thought Disorder, i.e. Intensity, Consistency, Element Consistency and Social Deviation. On all four measures, the thought-disordered schizophrenics had significantly poorer scores than the other groups. These other groups did not differ among themselves. Within a subgroup of 19 schizophrenics, each of the four measures correlated significantly with clinical ratings of the severity of thought disorder. However, when the effects of Intensity and Consistency were each partialled out, the correlation between Element Consistency and clinical ratings was reduced to insignificance, whereas when Element Consistency was partialled out, Intensity and Consistency remained significantly correlated with the ratings.

McPherson, F. M., Armstrong, J. and Heather, B. B. Psychological construing, "difficulty" and thought disorder. *British Journal of medical Psychology*, 1975, **48**, 303-315.

Two versions of the repertory grid test of thought disorder were constructed, having similar elements (photographs of people) but one of which used psychological constructs and the other non-psychological constructs. The versions had been matched for "difficulty" (defined in terms of amount of consensual agreement) and reliability. The mean Intensity and Consistency scores obtained by non-thought-disordered controls were similar. When "difficult" and "easy" versions of the test were given to normal, general psychiatric and the thought disordered groups it was found that "difficulty" had no effect on grid test scores but the use of "psychological" constructs significantly disabled the thought disordered group.

Makhlouf-Norris, F. and Norris, H. The obsessive compulsive syndrome as a neurotic device for the reduction of self-uncertainty. *British Journal of Psychiatry*, 1972, **121**, 277-288.

A group of 11 obsessional neurotics were compared to matched normal controls in terms of their personal construct systems. A measure was described which shows the integration of the concepts of self and ideal self relative to concepts of other people. Results are presented in the form of a two-dimensional self-integration plot. The "obsessional" self concepts were isolated from concepts of other people and alienated from the ideal self. The self concepts of normal people were neither isolated nor alienated.

Makhlouf, M. F., Jones, G. H. and Norris, H. Articulation of the conceptual structure in obsessional neurosis. *British Journal of social and clinical Psychology*, 1970, **9**, 264-274.

Differentiated obsessionals from "normals" by showing them to have "monolithic" or "segmented" conceptual structures and "articulated" structures respectively. A rated grid with elicited constructs from role titles was used. "Monolithic" structure is marked by one large cluster of constructs accounting for the mass of the variance; "segmented" equals several largely unrelated clusters and "articulated" several linked clusters. There is some evidence that "monolithic" or "segmented" structures are not peculiar to obsessionals but may be found generally in those suffering from neurotic disorders.

Reker, G. T. Interpersonal conceptual structures of emotionally disturbed and normal boys. *Journal of abnormal Psychology,* 1974, **83,** 380-386.

Twenty-four disturbed and 24 normal boys with a mean age of 10·5 years were asked to construe 12 persons known personally to them and 12 familiar inanimate objects on two sets of 12 5-point bipolar constructs. Subjects were also asked to arrange the people and inanimate objects into personally meaningful groups. There was significantly lower differentiation and articulation but not integration in the interpersonal conceptual structure of disturbed boys as compared with normal controls. No differences were found in construing inanimate objects. The results are interpreted as indicating that disturbed boys are handicapped by a limited interpersonal conceptual structure for anticipating and predicting their social environment.

Ryle, A. and Breen, D. A comparison of adjusted and maladjusted couples using the double dyad grid. *British Journal of medical Psychology,* 1972, **45,** 375-382.

In this study the dyad grid (which uses relationships between people rather than single persons as elements) is used as a measure of construing a partner's construing by having each partner predict the other's grid. Patients differed from controls in that they were more likely to see the relationship with the partner as resembling their relationship with their parents and that when the relationship was going badly they perceived their own role as more childlike, while that of their partner became less parent-like.

Ryle, A. and Breen, D. Some differences in the personal constructs of neurotic and normal subjects. *British Journal of Psychiatry,* 1972, **120,** 483-489.

A systematic study of certain features of repertory grid tests in relation to patient status and to scores on the Middlesex Hospital Questionnaire confirmed that there were a number of such features characteristic of neurotic as opposed to normal grids. It is suggested that these findings should add to the confidence with which repertory grid techniques are used in the clinical setting.

Smail, D. J. Neurotic symptoms, personality and personal constructs. *British Journal of Psychiatry,* 1970, **177,** 645-648.

It is hypothesised that a measure of "thinking introversion/extraversion" will be related to psychic vs. somatic symptomatology, as well as to the production by subjects (neurotic patients) of "psychological" *versus* "objective" personal constructs, and to a wider *versus* narrower range of constructs. Statistical analysis provides a good measure of support for this hypothesis, although a relationship with age is noted for some measures.

Wright, D. M. Impairment in abstract conceptualization and Bannister and Fransella's Grid Test of Schizophrenic Thought Disorder. *Journal of Consulting and Clinical Psychology,* 1973, **41,** 474.

The author argues that loose construing as defined in the Bannister—Fransella test (low Intensity and Consistency) is akin to impairment in abstract conceptualisation. Positive correlations between the grid test and the Object Sorting Test (Rapaport) in a psychiatric population supported the argument.

Wright, K. J. T. Exploring the uniqueness of common complaints. *British Journal of medical Psychology,* 1970, **43,** 221-232.

Theoretical considerations are illustrated by reference to symptoms and their personal meaning. Hinkle's "laddering" technique is described as a method which provides a way of exploring systematically aspects of a person's system of meanings. This is illustrated with examples taken from the investigation of an agoraphobic patient. The way in which the data yielded by the method can be used as a source of inference about the person and their conflicts is also illustrated.

Psychotherapy

Caplan, H. L., Rohde, P. D., Shapiro, D. A. and Watson, J. P. Some correlates of repertory grid measures to study a psychotherapeutic group. *British Journal of medical Psychology,* 1975, **48,** 217-226.

Repertory grid data provided monthly by the members of a psychotherapeutic group were related to measures of verbal behaviour during group sessions in ways which were both statistically significant and psychologically meaningful. There was evidence that the group members re-enacted earlier patterns of family relationship in their mutual interactions. For individual patient members of the group, speaking, being spoken to, and introducing several kinds of topic into the group discussion had significant associations with grid variables implicating self-esteem and patterns of identification with parents; but the correlation patterns varied between patients.

Crisp, A. H. An attempt to measure an aspect of "transference". *British Journal of medical Psychology,* 1964, **37,** 17-30.

Transference is measured by a modification of Repertory Grid Technique which focuses on the comparison of the individual's concept of "ideal dependable father" and his concepts of various Doctor figures. Predictions concerning differences in "transference score" between two social groups differing by class and a group of psychoneurotic patients during treatment are largely confirmed.

Fielding, J. M. A technique for measuring outcome in group psychotherapy. *British Journal of medical Psychology,* 1975, **48,** 189-198.

A technique for measuring a patient's progress and outcome in group psychotherapy is presented. The various measured parameters are derived from the Symptom Check List plus individualised repertory grid rating scales. This measurement model was tested on an out-patient group over 18 months and shows potential as a device for measuring outcome in diverse types of psychotherapy groups.

Fransella, F. and Joyston-Bechal, M. P. An investigation of conceptual process and pattern change in a psychotherapy group. *British Journal of Psychiatry,* 1971, **119,** 199-206.

The 8 psychoneurotic members of an analytically-oriented group and the participating and observing psychiatrist were administered a rank order form of repertory grid at 0, 3, 6, 9 and 12 months. Supplied constructs were used and the 8 patients served as elements. Various measures were derived to show ways in which group construing processes as well as construing content may be investigated, and relationships of changes in construing process and content between patients and therapists were examined. Grid and outcome measures were compared.

Landfield, A. W. Meaningfulness of self, ideal and other as related to own vs. therapist's personal construct dimensions. *Psychological Reports,* 1965, **16,** 605-608.

A modified form of rep test was used to test the hypothesis that clients at the beginning of therapy will find their own personal language dimensions more meaningful than those of the therapist. Extremity of rating was used as one measure of "meaningfulness". Results agreed with prediction.

McPherson, F. M. and Walton, H. J. The dimensions of psychotherapy group interaction: an analysis of clinicians' constructs. *British Journal of medical Psychology,* 1970, **43,** 281-290.

Seven experienced clinicians observed at least 25 meetings of a psychotherapy group and then described the intragroup interactions of the patient members, using repertory grid technique. A principal components analysis of the combined grids isolated three main independent dimensions, differentiating group members who are assertive and dominant from those who are passive and submissive; who are emotionally sensitive to other members as opposed to insensitive; and who hinder rather than aid the attainment of group goals.

Rowe, D. Poor prognosis in a case of depression as predicted by the repertory grid. *British Journal of Psychiatry,* 1971, **118,** 297-300.

A repertory grid completed by a patient, a 38-year-old woman presenting with depression, showed a dispersion of elements and constructs which indicated that this woman was unlikely to improve under treatment. Medication and ECT produced little change, but environmental manipulation maintained the patient in her own home with minimum supportive care.

Rowe, D. An examination of a psychiatrist's predictions of a patient's constructs. *British Journal of Psychiatry,* 1971, **118,** 231-244.

A patient was given a repertory grid of 20 elements and 15 constructs and required to sort the elements on each of the constructs according to the half-split method. The patient's psychiatrist, given the patient's elements and constructs, predicted the patient's sortings. The two grids were compared on the Delta programme and analysed separately on the Ingrid 67 programme. The differences between them were found to relate to systematic errors on the psychiatrist's predictions about one construct and one element.

Ryle, A. and Lipshitz, S. Towards an informed counter-transference: the possible contribution of repertory grid techniques. *British Journal of medical Psychology,* 1974, **47,** 219-225.

The use of repertory grids to investigate the counter-transference of a therapist, a group of nurses and a social worker is described and it is argued that this technique is of potential value in training.

Ryle, A. and Lipshitz, S. Repertory grid elucidation of a difficult conjoint therapy. *British Journal of medical psychology,* 1976, **49,** 281-285.

The conjoint therapy of a couple was monitored over 30 sessions by two forms of repertory grid. Little change was apparent from the sessions and grid evidence showed that the mutual perceptions of the couple and therapists remained static. However, the background grid, which included parental relationships and the couple's relationship under the two conditions of "going well" and "going badly" showed that some reconstruction had occurred and demonstrated the psychological mechanism of the couple's relationship which had prevented change.

Ryle, A. and Lunghi, M. W. The measurement of relevant change after psychotherapy: use of repertory grid testing. *British Journal of Psychiatry*, 1969, **115,**
1297-1304.

    The psychotherapeutic treatment of a psychoneurotic patient is described. The
clinical evaluation of this patient was matched with the results of repertory grid
testing. The aims of treatment were defined in terms of changes in the construct
system and in the dispersion of the self and of significant other people in this system.
Re-testing established that such changes had occurred.

Sechrest, L. V. Stimulus equivalence of the psychotherapist. *Journal of Individual
Psychology,* 1962, **18,** 172-176.

    Using Kelly's Rep Test 35 psychotherapy patients noted similarities between
psychotherapists and various persons from their environments. In general,
therapists were described as being similar to those persons whom they did, in fact,
resemble in age, sex and occupational status. Therapists' similarities to family
members were not marked. This pattern did not change during the course of
therapy—thus the Freudian transference hypothesis was not supported.

Smail, D. J. A grid Measure of empathy in a therapeutic group. *British Journal of
medical Psychology,* 1972, **45,** 165.

    An attempt to measure empathy in a small therapy group by means of grid
technique is described. The experiment was conducted in two stages so that the
relevance of grid measures could be maximised. Empathy scores are validated
against patients' and therapists' ratings, as well as being related to a questionnaire
measure of thinking-introversion. Positive relationships are demonstrated between
all these measures.

Tyler, F. B. and Simmons, W. L. Patients' conception of their therapist. *Journal of
clinical Psychology,* 1964, **20,** 112-133.

    This study used a role construct repertory test to show that mental hospital
patients see psychologists, nurses and activity therapists as "persons" and social
workers and physicians on the basis of their "task".

Watson, J. P. A repertory grid method of studying groups. *British Journal of
Psychiatry,* 1970, **117,** 309-318.

    A modified repertory grid method of studying groups is described. It is suggested
that the technique can provide information about interpersonal relationships in
groups, psychological features of individual group members and changes occurring
in persons having group therapy.

Watson, J. P. A measure of therapist-patient understanding. *British Journal of
Psychiatry,* 1970, **117,** 319-321.

    The degree of understanding, and the dimensions of misunderstanding,
between a doctor and a patient have been examined during an eight month period,
using a repertory grid method. The patient completed an identical grid on four
occasions, and on each occasion the doctor supplied a grid of guesses of the
patient's ratings.

Watson, J. P. Possible measures of change during group psychotherapy. *British
Journal of medical Psychology,* 1972, **45,** 71.

    A modified repertory grid technique was used in a preliminary study of changes
occurring during group psychotherapy. The results show that measurable changes
take place during treatment and are usually greater among patients than therapists.

Wijesinghe, O. B. A. and Wood, R. R. A repertory grid study of interpersonal perception within a married couple's psychotherapy group. *British Journal of medical Psychology,* 1976, **49,** 287-293.

An attempt was made to elucidate the dominant construct patterns within a group of 4 married couples having out-patient psychotherapy. A comparison was also made between the ability of a person to construe the construction processes of his or her spouse and the therapist's ability to construe the construction processes of that particular spouse. Constructs related to discussing problems, showing feelings and dominance were important for inter-group perceptions but opinion polarized as to the implications of these constructs for effective group functioning. There was reasonably high agreement between husbands and wives on perception of similarity in construing processes as well as in areas of shared perception. The therapist was able to predict much more accurately than the spouses constructs relating to emotional expression.

Person perception and interpersonal relationships

Adams-Webber, J. R., Schwenker, B., and Barbeau, D. Personal constructs and the perception of individual differences. *Canadian Journal of Behavioural Science,* 1972, **4,** 218-224.

The repertory grid method was used to investigate the hypothesis that skill in inferring the personal constructs of others is related to the level of differentiation achieved by an individual in structuring his social environment in terms of his own construct system. It was found that if subjects characterised close personal associates in a way that was consistent with the structure of their own self concepts, then they were less accurate in discriminating between the two new acquaintances in terms of the latter's own previously elicited personal constructs. On the other hand, subjects who differentiated between themselves and close associates on the grid performed such discriminations more accurately.

Bender, M. P. To smile at or avert the eyes from: the formation of relationships among students. *Research in Education,* 1969, **2,** 32-51.

Using implications and resistance-to-change grids, construing of others was investigated in terms of care and peripheral constructs. Ten hypotheses were tested derived from the idea that personal identity needs confirmation by others and our construing of strangers is determined by whether or not we decide he is likely to confirm our identity if we interact with him further. These hypotheses were generally supported.

Bender, M. P. Does construing people as similar involve similar behaviour towards them? A subjective and objective replication. *British Journal of social and clinical Psychology,* 1974, **15,** 93-95.

Fifteen couples who had lived together at least 6 months completed a grid with elicited constructs. One spouse was asked to think of interacting with 3 of the elements at a time and asked to indicate toward which 2 people his behaviour was most similar. Each then completed the grid in this manner but in terms of the spouse's behaviour. There was a highly significant relationship between pairs of people eliciting more similar behaviour indicated by person and spouse indicating some *validity* for these grid measures.

Benjafield, J. and Adams-Webber, J. R. Assimilative projection and construct balance in the repertory grid. *British Journal of Psychology,* 1975, **66,** 169-173.

The relationship between the degree to which people see others as like themselves (assimilative projection) and the frequency with which they use positive adjectives to describe people was examined in the context of changing role perspectives. The assimilative projection scores of those persons who use a preponderance of positive over negative adjectives were found to be influenced by changes in role perspectives. By contrast, the assimilative projection scores of those persons whose use of adjectives was less "maldistributed" were stable across roles. The results have implications for repertory grid methodology, specifically for the practice of controlling for maldistribution.

Carlson, R. Sex differences in ego functioning: exploratory studies of agency and communion. *Journal of Consulting and Clinical Psychology*, 1971, **37**, 267-277.
    An interesting use of the Rep Test in which self, being differentiated from or placed with others, was used as a measure of agency-communion (Bakan's Dimension from his Duality of Human Existence). Male or female differences were found in the predicted direction of greater male "agency".

Coleman, P. G. Interest in personal activities and degree of perceived implications between personal constructs. *British Journal of social and clinical Psychology*, 1975, **14**, 93-95.
    Reported interest in personal and non-personal activities, measured by a 24-item questionnaire comprising questions dealing with the individual's liking for various activities was related to the number of implications that subjects perceived between their own constructs. A comparison was made between results obtained by this method of directly asking for implications between constructs and by a method of measuring simplicity of construct structure from the repertory grid.

Duck, S. W. Similarity and perceived similarity of personal constructs as influences on friendship choice. *British Journal of social and clinical Psychology*, 1973, **12**, 1-6.
    A mixed-sex group of 40 student teachers was given a sociometric test and the Rep Test, and was then asked to provide for each construct a list of people who shared it. The Rep Test analysis produced two mean similarity scores for each subject: one from observable similarities with friends ("friendship pairs") and one from similarities with non-friends ("nominal pairs"). Significant differences were found between these means. It was also found from the last test that subjects tended to over-estimate the similarities between themselves and their chosen friends.

Ryle, A. and Lipshitz, S. Recording change in marital therapy with the reconstruction grid. *British Journal of medical Psychology*, 1975, **48**, 39-48.
    In this grid the elements were the relationship of husband to wife and wife to husband rated on successive occasions in terms of 18 "behaviour" and 15 "feeling" constructs. Changes in the views of the couple reported were plotted over 11 occasions of testing which preceded marital therapy sessions.

Developmental psychology

Applebee, A. N. Developmental changes in consensus in construing within a specified domain. *British Journal of Psychology*, 1975, **66**, 4, 473-480.
    Developmental changes in the amount of social consensus in grid ratings are investigated in six samples of school children spanning the age range 6—17. The grids studies use supplied constructs and elements elicited to represent various categories of stories (e.g. favourite, hard). On these grids there is increasing concensus in construing across the age span studied. This consensus is substantially

higher for patterns of inter-construct relationships (the *structure* of the system) than for ratings of specific elements on specific constructs (the *implications* of the system).

Applebee, A. N. The development of children's responses to repertory grids. *British Journal of social and clinical Psychology,* 1976, **15,** 101-102.

Grids applied to subjects aged 6, 9, 13 and 17 indicate that with increasing age, more constructs are used, there is somewhat more equal elaboration of both poles of each construct, there is the recognition of more "shades of grey".

Salmon, P. Differential conforming as a developmental process. *British Journal of social and clinical Psychology,* 1969, **8,** 22-31.

The hypothesis was tested, that when confronted with two different reference groups, peers versus adults, exerting opposite social pressures, children will conform to that group embodying the values with which they have most identified. The rep grid was used as the measure of value identification of *ideal self* and *actual self.* The significant relationship was found between ideal self and the construct *tough* predicting peer conformity and ideal self and *obedient* predicting conformity with adults. These results suggest the rep grid is a relatively sensitive instrument.

Learning

Lifshitz, M. Quality Professionals: Does training make a difference? A personal construct theory study of the issue. *British Journal of social and clinical Psychology,* 1974, **13,** 183-189.

A shortened group form of the Construct Repertory Test was used to study common characteristics and changes that take place in outlook during training. The personal perceptions and attitudes of a group of good social-work students, as compared to their older and more experienced supervisors, were studied in a design based on Kelly's personal construct theory (1955). Significant differences ($p < .01$) were found between the superordinate constructs of the two groups. The student group used most often concrete descriptive categories, such as age, sex and profession.

Philip, A. E. and McCulloch, J. W. Personal construct theory and social work practice. *British Journal of social and clinical Psychology,* 1968, **7,** 115-121.

The study demonstrates the feasibility of investigating the conceptual processes involved in case-work assessment using Kelly's theory of personal constructs. Two random samples of 25 patients were drawn from a cohort of 511 persons who had attempted suicide in Edinburgh. The concepts used by a psychiatric social worker to describe these patients were intercorrelated and analysed using McQuitty's Elementary Linkage Analysis. Two main types of construct were elicited; the first relating to the impact of the patient on the psychiatric social worker; the second reflecting the professional formulation of the case.

Runkel, P. J. and Damrin, D. E. Effects of training and anxiety upon teachers' preference information about students. *Journal of Educational Psychology,* 1961, **52,** 254-261.

The hypothesis of this study was that there would be a U-shaped curvilinear relationship between training and the cognitive complexity of the teachers' understanding of students' problems. This hypothesis was confirmed. Complexity was measured by the unfolding technique of Coombs, which is essentially a grid format.

Ryle, A. and Breen, D. Change in the course of social work training: a repertory grid study. *British Journal of medical Psychology,* 1974, **47,** 139.

Grids with self-client, self-supervisor relationships as elements were given to social work students in training. In most cases individual change, as recorded in grid re-tests, was in a direction indicating at least partial resolution of problems. The study of many of the individual grids underlined the importance of the tutor—student and supervisor—student relationships as models for the student—client relationship. Less predictably, the grids also demonstrated, that the student—client relationships echoed the student—parent relationship. The role of supportive son or daughter may be a common antecedent to the career choice of a "helping" profession, but this must generate certain difficulties. The fact that the relationships between self and parents were among those showing much reconstruction during the course suggests that these problems were being faced. Of the group changes recorded, those involving construct correlations are a little hard to interpret, but it looks as if the more affectively charged constructs are least stable through time, whereas those relating to role are more stable. The evidence of greater role confidence and the evidence of greater complexity of construing, without greater conformity after the course experience, are both encouraging.

Language

Agnew, J. and Bannister, D. Psychiatric diagnosis as a pseudo-specialist language. *British Journal of medical Psychology,* 1973, **46,** 69-73.

Eight consultant psychiatrists completed grids using their patients as elements and both formal diagnostic categories and lay descriptive terms as constructs Results indicate that the psychiatrists are no more stable and have no greater interjudge agreement in using diagnostic terms than they achieve with everyday language. Additionally, the two languages appear to "mix". It is concluded that psychiatric nosology is not a true specialist language.

Lemon, N. Linguistic development and conceptualisation; a bilingual study. *Journal of Cross-Cultural Psychology,* 1975, **6,** 173-188.

A rating form of grid was used to investigate the effect of development in a weaker language on conceptualisation in that language. Form 2 and Form 4 secondary school children in Tanzania were administered grids with elements consisting of either persons or countries in both English and Swahili. Comparison of English and Swahili grids showed that language deficit reduces the polarization of judgements made using constructs articulated in the weaker language, although no differences in construct relationships were observed. Differences in integration of construct relationships and polarization of judgement appeared to relate to the social appropriateness of each language for conceptualising the elements in question. Implications of these results for the relationship between language and conceptualisation are discussed.

Mair, J. M. M. Prediction of grid scores. *British Journal of Psychology,* 1966, **57,** 187-192.

The study assessed the capacity of grids to measure the relationships between constructs against dictionary meaning, rather than within the more complex domain of personal or private meaning. The grid appears effective in this context.

Warren, N. Social class and construct systems: examination of the cognitive structure of two social class groups. *British Journal of social and clinical Psychology,* 1966, **4,** 254-263.

The study successfully uses a modification of Kelly's grid technique (measuring Intensity) to test the theory that differences in linguistic coding are associated with social class groupings.

Unusual elements and topics

Feldman, M. M. The body image and object relations: exploration of a method utilizing repertory grid techniques. *British Journal of medical Psychology,* 1975, **48,** 317-332.

    The study demonstrates a new approach to the study of body image. It shows how an application of the repertory grid method allows one to determine properties of the body representation of Self, Mother, Father, Partner and Ideal Self. The way in which these representations relate to each other can be studied in detail and inferences can be made regarding aspects of the individual's object relations. In order to illustrate the possibilities of the approach, the results from two normal female subjects and two patients with anorexia nervosa are presented and discussed.

Fransella, F. and Bannister, D. A validation of repertory grid technique as a measure of political construing. *Acta Psychologica,* 1967, **26,** 97-106.

    Seventy-four normal adults were given a form of repertory grid test in which they rank ordered personal acquaintances on evaluative, political party and political "brand-image constructs. They also gave their 1st, 2nd and 3rd choice vote (British General Election, 1964), their degree of voting certainty and degree of interest in politics. It was found that (a) voting behaviour was predictable from evaluative/ political party construct relationships (intercorrelations), (b) anticipated relationships between evaluative and political constructs emerged and that (c) the pattern of evaluative construct interrelationships was in line with "common sense" expectations. The concept of "brand-image" was shown to be operationally definable in terms of repertory grid measures and possible indices of notions like "degree of interest in politics" and "certainty of voting intention" were noted.

Orley, J. The use of grid technique in social anthropology. *In* "Explorations of Intrapersonal Space: the measurement of intrapersonal space by grid technique", (Ed. P. Slater). Wiley, London, 1976.

    The elements were six classes of spirits in Ganda mythology. The method for construing these elements by the Ganda villagers is unusual. Orley took a pair of spirits at a time and asked to which spirit the construct most applied. There were 15 pairs in all and 18 constructs.

Salmon, P., Arnold, J. M. and Collyer, Y. M. What do the determinants determine: the internal validity of the Rorschach. *Journal of Personality,* 1972, **36,** 33-38.

    To investigate the internal validity of Rorschach profile analysis, a repertory grid technique was used with 47 undergraduate subjects. The elements of the grid were Rorschach cards. A significant common pattern of construct relationships emerged but it was not the pattern assumed in conventional profile analysis of Rorschach protocols.

Stringer, P. The use of repertory grid measures for evaluating map formats. *British Journal of Psychology,* 1974, **65,** 23.

    Effects of colour and base on construing urban planning maps are examined using measures of grid structure and content. Four sets of seven redevelopment plans, differing in colour and/or base, were shown to random samples of 50 local women. Individuals construed the plans in a typical rep grid procedure. Differentiation measures, including percentage variance of grid elements and principal components, and construct-type frequencies are compared across map sets by analysis of covariance, using biographical variables as covariates. Some effects of colour on plan construing are demonstrated, though for base the evidence is equivocal. Information available in the grid-structure measures is illustrated further.

Appendix III

BOOK LIST

Adams-Webber, J. R. (In press). "Personal Construct Theory Research since 1955". Wiley, New York.

Bannister, D. (Ed.) (1970). "Perspectives in Personal Construct Theory". Academic Press, London and New York.

Bannister, D. (Ed.) (1977). "New Perspectives in Personal Construct Theory". Academic Press, London and New York.

Bannister, D. and Mair, J. M. M. (1968). "The Evaluation of Personal Constructs". Academic Press, London and New York.

Bannister, D. and Fransella, F. (1971). "Inquiring Man". Penguin, Harmondsworth.

Bieri, J., Atkins, A. L., Briar, S., Leaman, R. L., Miller, H. and Tripodi, T. (1966). "Clinical and Social Judgement: the discrimination of behavioural information". Wiley, New York.

Bonarius, J. C. J. (1965). Research in the Personal Construct Theory of George A. Kelly. *In* "Progress in Experimental Personality Research" (Ed. B. A. Maher). Academic Press, New York and London.

Bonarius, J. C. J. (1971). "Personal Construct Psychology and Extreme Response Style". Swets and Zeitlinger, Amsterdam.

Breen, D. (1975). "The Birth of a First Child: towards an understanding of femininity". Tavistock Publications, London.

Canter, D. (1974). "Psychology for Architects". London Applied Science Publishers.

Duck, S. W. (1973). "Personal Relationships and Personal Constructs". Wiley, London.

Epting, F. (In press). "Personal Construct Theory Psychotherapy". Wiley, London and New York.

Fransella, F. (1972). "Personal Change and Reconstruction". Academic Press, London and New York.

Fransella, F. (1975). Studying the individual. *In* "Methods of Psychiatric Research" (Eds P. Sainsbury and N. Kreitman) 2nd edition. Oxford University Press, London.

Fransella, F. (1975). "Need to Change?". Methuen, London.

Fransella, F. (1976). The theory and measurement of personal constructs. *In* "Recent Advances in Clinical Psychiatry 2" (Ed. K. Granville-Grossman). Churchill Livingstone, London.

Hagan, R. (1976). "Personality Theory: The Personological Tradition". Prentice-Hall, New Jersey.

Hjelle, L. A. and Ziegler, D. J. (1976). "Personality Theories". McGraw Hill, New York.

Kelly, G. A. (1955). "The Psychology of Personal Constructs" Vols I and II. Norton, New York.

Kelly, G. A. (1969). "Clinical Psychology and Personality: the Selected Papers of George Kelly" (Ed. B. A. Maher). Wiley, New York.

Landfield, A. W. (1971). "Personal Construct Systems in Psychotherapy". Rand McNally, New York.

Livesley, W. J. and Bromley, D. B. (1973). "Person Perception in Childhood and Adolescence". Wiley, New York.

Nash, R. (1973). "Classrooms Observed". Routledge and Kegan Paul, London.

Pervin, L. A. (1975). "Personality: Theory, Assessment and Research", 2nd edition. Wiley, New York.

Ravenette, A. T. (1968). "Dimensions of Reading Difficulties". Pergamon Press, Oxford.

Ryle, A. (1975). "Frames and Cages". Sussex University Press.

Slater, P. (Ed.) (1976). "Explorations of Intrapersonal Space", Vol. I. Wiley, London.

"Nebraska Symposium on Motivation—Personal Construct Theory". (1975). University of Nebraska Press.

Appendix IV

PERSONAL CONSTRUCT THEORY

(a) *Fundamental Postulate:* A person's processes are psychologically channelized by the ways in which he anticipates events.

(b) *Construction Corollary:* A person anticipates events by construing their replications.

(c) *Individuality Corollary:* Persons differ from each other in their construction of events.

(d) *Organisation Corollary:* Each person characteristically evolves, for his convenience in anticipating events, a construction system embracing ordinal relationships between constructs.

(e) *Dichotomy Corollary:* A person's construction system is composed of a finite number of dichotomous constructs.

(f) *Choice Corollary:* A person chooses for himself that alternative in a dichotomised construct through which he anticipates the greater possibility for extension and definition of his system.

(g) *Range Corollary:* A construct is convenient for the anticipation of a finite range of events only.

(h) *Experience Corollary:* A person's construction system varies as he successively construes the replications of events.

(i) *Modulation Corollary:* The variation in a person's construction system is limited by the permeability of the constructs within whose ranges of convenience the variants lie.

(j) *Fragmentation Corollary:* A person may successively employ a variety of construction subsystems which are inferentially incompatible with each other.

(k) *Commonality Corollary:* To the extent that one person employs a construction of experience which is similar to that employed by another, his psychological processes are similar to those of the other person.

(l) *Sociality Corollary:* To the extent that one person construes the construction processes of another he may play a role in a social process involving the other person.

GLOSSARY OF TERMS

Formal aspects of constructs

Range of Convenience. A construct's range of convenience comprises all those things to which the user would find its application useful.

Focus of Convenience. A construct's focus of convenience comprises those particular things to which the user would find its application maximally useful. These are the elements upon which the construct is likely to have been formed originally.

Elements. The things or events which are abstracted by a person's use of a construct are called elements. In some systems these are called objects.

Context. The context of a construct comprises those elements among which the user ordinarily discriminates by means of the construct. It is somewhat more restricted than the range of convenience, since it refers to the circumstances in which the construct emerges for practical use, and not necessarily to all the circumstances in which a person might eventually use the construct. It is somewhat more extensive than the focus of convenience, since the construct may often appear in circumstances where its application is not optimal.

Pole. Each construct discriminates between two poles, one at each end of its dichotomy. The elements abstracted are like each other at each pole with respect to the construct and are unlike the elements at the other pole.

Contrast. The relationship between the two poles of a construct is one of contrast.

Likeness End. When referring specifically to elements at one pole of a construct, one may use the term "likeness end" to designate that pole.

Constrast End. When referring specifically to elements at one pole of a construct, one may use the term "constrast end" to designate the opposite pole.

Emergence. The emergent pole of a construct is that one which embraces most of the immediately perceived context.

Implicitness. The implicit pole of a construct is that one which embraces constrating context. It contrasts with the emergent pole. Frequently the person has no available symbol or name for it; it is symbolised only implicitly by the emergent term.

Symbol. An element in the context of a construct which represents not only itself but also the construct by which it is abstracted by the user is called the construct's symbol.

Permeability. A construct is permeable if it admits newly perceived elements to its context. It is impermeable if it rejects elements on the basis of their newness.

Constructs classified according to the nature of their control over their elements

Preemptive Construct. A construct which preempts its elements for membership in its own realm exclusively is called a preemptive construct. This is the "nothing but" type of construction—"If this is a ball it is nothing but a ball."

Constellatory Construct. A construct which fixes the other realm memberships of its elements is called a constellatory construct. This is stereotyped or typological thinking.

Propositional Construct. A construct which carries no implications regarding the other realm memberships of its elements is a propositional construct. This is uncontaminated construction.

General diagnostic constructs

Preverbal Constructs. A preverbal construct is one which continues to be used, even though it has no consistent word symbol. It may or may not have been devised before the client had command of speech symbolism.

Submergence. The submerged pole of a construct is the one which is less available for application to events.

Suspension. A suspended element is one which is omitted from the context of a construct as a result of revision of the client's construct system.

Level of Cognitive Awareness. The level of cognitive awareness ranges from high to low. A high-level construct is one which is readily expressed in socially effective symbols; whose alternatives are both readily accessible; which falls well within the range of convenience of the client's major constructions; and which is not suspended by its superordinating constructs.

Dilation. Dilation occurs when a person broadens his perceptual field in order to reorganise it on a more comprehensive level. It does not, in itself, include the comprehensive reconstruction of those elements.

Constriction. Constriction occurs when a person narrows his perceptual field in order to minimize apparent incompatibilities.

Comprehensive Constructs. A comprehensive construct is one which subsumes a wide variety of events.

Incidental Constructs. An incidental construct is one which subsumes a narrow variety of events.

Superordinate Constructs. A superordinate construct is one which includes another as one of the elements in its context.

Subordinate Constructs. A subordinate construct is one which is included as an element in the context of another.

Regnant Constructs. A regnant construct is a kind of superordinate construct which assigns each of its elements to a category on an all-or-none basis, as in classical logic. It tends to be non-abstractive.

Core Constructs. A core construct is one which governs the client's maintenance processes.

Peripheral Constructs. A peripheral construct is one which can be altered without serious modification of the core structure.

Tight Constructs. A tight construct is one which leads to unvarying predictions.

Loose Constructs. A loose construct is one leading to varying predictions, but which retains its identity.

Constructs relating to transition

Threat. Threat is the awareness of an imminent comprehensive change in one's core structures.

Fear. Fear is the awareness of an imminent incidental change in one's core structures.

Anxiety. Anxiety is the awareness that the events with which one is confronted lie mostly outside the range of convenience of his construct system.

Guilt. Guilt is the awareness of dislodgment of the self from one's core role structure.

Aggressiveness. Aggressiveness is the active elaboration of one's perceptual field.

Hostility. Hostility is the continued effort to extort validational evidence in favor of a type of social prediction which has already been recognised as a failure.

C-P-C Cycle. The C-P-C Cycle is a sequence of construction involving, in succession, circumspection, preemption, and control, and leading to a choice precipitating the person into a particular situation.

Impulsivity. Impulsivity is a characteristic foreshortening of the C-P-C Cycle.

Creativity Cycle. The Creativity Cycle is one which starts with loosened construction and terminates with tightened and validated construction.

References

Those references with asterisks also appear in the Annotated Bibliography.

*Adams-Webber, J. (1969). Cognitive complexity and sociality. *British Journal of social and clinical Psychology* **8**, 211-216.

*Adams-Webber, J. (1970a). An analysis of the discriminant validity of several repertory grid indices. *British Journal of Psychology* **61**, 83-90.

*Adams-Webber, J. (1970b). Elicited versus provided constructs in repertory grid technique: a review. *British Journal of medical Psychology* **43**, 349-354.

*Adams-Webber, J., Schwenker, B. and Barbeau, D. (1972). Personal constructs and the perception of individual differences. *Canadian Journal of Behavioural Science* **4**, 218-224.

*Agnew, J. and Bannister, D. (1973). Psychiatric diagnosis as a pseudo specialist language. *British Journal of medical Psychology* **46**, 69.

Allison, B. (1972). The development of personal construct systems. Unpublished manuscript, Memorial University, St. John's, Newfoundland, Canada.

*Applebee, A. N. (1975). Developmental changes in consensus in construing within a specified domain. *British Journal of Psychology* **66**, 4, 473-480.

*Applebee, A. N. (1976). The development of children's responses to repertory grids. *British Journal of social and clinical Psychology* **15**, 101-102.

Arthur, A. Z. (1966). Response bias in the semantic differential. *British Journal of social and clinical Psychology* **5**, 103-107.

Baillie-Grohman, R. (1975). The use of a modified form of repertory grid technique to investigate the extent to which deaf school leavers tend to use stereotypes. Unpublished M.Sc. dissertation, University of London.

Bannister, D. (1959). An application of personal construct theory (Kelly) to schizoid thinking. Unpublished PhD. thesis, University of London.

*Bannister, D. (1960). Conceptual structure in thought disordered schizophrenics. *Journal of Mental Science* **106**, 1230-1249.

Bannister, D. (1962a). The nature and measurement of schizophrenic thought disorder. *Journal of Mental Science* **108**, 825-842.

*Bannister, D. (1962b). Personal construct theory: a summary and experimental paradigm. *Acta Psychologica* **20**, 104-120.

Bannister, D. (1963). The genesis of schizophrenic thought disorder: a serial invalidation hypothesis. *British Journal of Psychiatry* **109**, 680-686.

*Bannister, D. (1965a). The rationale and clinical relevance of repertory grid technique. *British Journal of Psychiatry* **111**, 977-982.

*Bannister, D. (1965b). The genesis of schizophrenic thought disorder: re-test of the serial invalidation hypothesis. *British Journal of Psychiatry* **111**, 377-382.

*Bannister, D. and Bott, M. (1974). Evaluating the person. *In* "New Approaches to Psychological Medicine" (Ed. P. Kelin). Wiley, London.

*Bannister, D. and Fransella, F. (1965). A repertory grid test of schizophrenic thought disorder. *British Journal of social and clinical Psychology* **2**, 95-102.

Bannister, D. and Fransella, F. (1966). "Grid Test of Thought Disorder". Psychological Test Publications, Barnstaple.

Bannister, D. and Mair, J. M. M. (1968). "The Evaluation of Personal Constructs". Academic Press, London.

*Bannister, D. and Salmon, P. (1966a). Schizophrenic thought disorder: specific or diffuse? *British Journal of medical Psychology* **39**, 215-219.

Bannister, D. and Salmon, P. (1966b). A measure of intransitivity within resistance-to-change grids. Unpublished manuscript.

Bannister, D. and Salmon, P. (1967). Measures of superordinacy. Unpublished manuscript.

*Bannister, D., Fransella, F. and Agnew, J. (1971). Characteristics and validity of the grid test of thought disorder. *British Journal of social and clinical Psychology* **10**, 144-151.

Bannister, D., Adams-Webber, J. R., Penn, W. I. and Radley, A. R. (1975). Reversing the process of thought disorder: a serial validation experiment. *British Journal of social and clinical Psychology* **14**, 169-180.

Barton, E. S., Walton, T. and Rowe, D. (1976). Using grid technique with the mentally handicapped. *In* "Explorations of Interpersonal Space" (Ed. P. Slater), Vol. I. Wiley, London.

Bateson, G., Jackson, D., Haley, J. and Weakland, J. (1956). Towards a theory of schizophrenia. *Behavioural Science* **4**, 251.

*Bender, M. P. (1969). To smile at or avert the eyes from: the formation of relationships among students. *Research in Education* **2**, 32-51.

*Bender, M. P. (1974). Provided versus elicited constructs: an explanation of Warr and Coffman's (1970) anomolous finding. *British Journal of social and clinical Psychology* **13**, 329.

*Bender, M. P. (1976). Does construing people as similar involve similar behaviour towards them? A subjective and objective replication. *British Journal of social and clinical Psychology* **15**, 93-95.

*Benjafield, J. and Adams-Webber, J. R. (1975). Assimilative projection and construct balance in the repertory grid. *British Journal of Psychology* **66**, 169-173.

Bergin, A. E. (1972). The evaluation of therapeutic outcomes. *In* "Handbook of Psychotherapy and Behaviour Change" (Eds A. E. Bergin and S. L. Garfield). Academic Press, London and New York.

*Bieri, J. (1955). Cognitive complexity—simplicity and predictive behaviour. *Journal of abnormal and social Psychology* **51**, 263-268.

Bieri, J., Atkins, A. L., Briar, S., Leaman, R. L., Miller, H. and Tripodi, T. (1966). "Clinical and Social Judgment: the Discrimination of Behavioural Information". Wiley, New York.

Bonarius, J. C. J. (1965). Research in the personal construct theory of George A. Kelly: role construct repertory test and basic theory. *In* "Progress in Experimental Personality Research" (Ed. B. A. Maher) Vol. 2, 2-46. Academic Press, New York and London.

Bonarius, J. C. J. (1971). "Personal Construct Psychology and Extreme Response Style". Swets and Zeitlinger, N. V., Amsterdam.

Brierley, D. W. (1967). The use of personality constructs by children of three different ages. Unpublished PhD. thesis, University of London.

Brown, R. W. (1958). Is a boulder sweet or sour? *Contemporary Psychology* **3**, 113-115.

*Caine, T. M. and Smail, D. J. (1967). Personal relevance and choice of constructs for the repertory grid technique. *British Journal of Psychiatry* **113**, 517-520.

*Caine, T. M. and Smail, D. J. (1969). A study of the reliability and validity of the repertory grid technique as a measure of the hysteroid/obsessoid component of personality. *British Journal of Psychiatry* **115**, 1305-1308.

*Caplan, H. L., Rhode, P. D., Shapiro, D. A. and Watson, J. P. (1975). Some correlates of repertory grid measures used to study a psychotherapeutic group. *British Journal of medical psychology* **48**, 217-226.

*Carlson, R. (1971). Sex differences in ego functioning: exploratory studies of agency and communion. *Journal of consulting and clinical Psychology* **37**, 267-277.

Carr, J. E. (1970). Differentiation similarity of patient and therapist and the outcome of psychotherapy. *Journal of abnormal Psychology* **76**, 361-369.

Cattell, R. B. (1966). "Handbook of Multivariete Experimental Psychology". Rand McNally, Chicago.

*Coleman, P. G. (1975). Interest in personal activities and degree of perceived implications between personal constructs. *British Journal of social and clinical Psychology* **14**, 93-95.

Coombs, C. H. (1964). "A Theory of Data". Wiley, New York.

*Crisp, A. H. (1964). An attempt to measure an aspect of "Transference". *British Journal of medical Psychology* **37**, 17-30.

*Crockett, W. H. (1965). "Cognitive Complexity and Impression Formation in Progress in Experimental Personality Research" (Ed. B. A. Maher) Vol. 2. Academic Press, New York and London.

*Cromwell, R. L. and Caldwell, D. F. (1962). A comparison of ratings based on personal constructs of self and others. *Journal of clinical Psychology* **18**, 43-46.

Cronbach, L. J. (1946). Response sets and test validity. *Educational and Psychological Measurement* **6**, 475-494.

Draffan, J. W. (1973). Randomness in grid test scores. *British Journal of medical Psychology* **46**, 391.

*Duck, S. W. (1973). Similarity and perceived similarity of personal constructs as influences on friendship choice. *British Journal of social and clinical Psychology* **12**, 1-6.

Duck, S. and Spencer, C. (1972). Personal constructs and friendship formation. *Journal of Personality and Social Psychology* **23**, 40-45.

*Epting, F. R. (1972). The stability of cognitive complexity in construing social issues. *British Journal of social and clinical Psychology* **11**, 122-125.

*Epting, F. R. (1975). Order of presentation of construct poles. What are the factors to be considered? A reply. *British Journal of social and clinical Psychology* **14**, 427-428.

*Epting, F. R., Suchman, D. I. and Nickeson, K. J. (1971). An evaluation of elicitation procedures for personal constructs. *British Journal of Psychology* **62**, 513-517.

Fager, R. E. (1962). Program for the analysis of repertory grids on the 1620 IBM computer. Unpublished manuscript, Syracuse University.

*Feldman, M. M. (1975). The body image and object relations: exploration of a method utilizing repertory grid techniques. *British Journal of Medical Psychology* **48**, 317-332.

*Fielding, J. M. (1975). A technique for measuring outcome in group psychotherapy. *British Journal of medical Psychology* **48**, 189-198.

*Fjeld, S. P. and Landfield, A. W. (1961). Personal construct theory consistency. *Psychological Reports* **8**, 127-129.

Foulds, G. A., Hope, K., McPherson, F. M. and Mayo, P. R. (1967). Cognitive disorder among the schizophrenias. I: The validity of some tests of thought process disorder. *British Journal of Psychiatry* **113**, 1361-1368.

Fransella, F. (1965). The effects of imposed rhythm and certain aspects of personality on the speech of stutterers. Unpublished PhD. thesis, University of London.

Fransella, F. (1969). The stutterer as subject or object? *In* "Stuttering and the Conditioning Therapies" (Eds B. B. Gray and G. England). Monterey Institute for Speech and Hearing, California.

Fransella, F. (1970). . . . . and then there was one. *In* "Perspectives in Personal Construct Theory" (Ed. D. Bannister). Academic Press, London and New York.

Fransella, F. (1972). "Personal Change and Reconstruction: Research on a Treatment of Stuttering". Academic Press, London and New York.

*Fransella, F. (1974). Thinking in the obsessional. *In* "Obsessional States" (Ed. H. R. Beech). Methuen, London.

Fransella, F. (1975). Studying the individual. *In* Methods of Psychiatric Research" (Eds P. Sainsbury and N. Kreitman) (2nd Ed.). Oxford University Press, London.

Fransella, F. (1976). The theory and measurement of personal constructs. *In* "Recent Advances in Clinical Psychiatry" (Ed. K. Granville-Grossman). Churchill Livingstone, London.

*Fransella, F. (1977). The self and the stereotype. *In* "New Perspectives in Personal Construct Theory" (Ed. D. Bannister). Academic Press, London and New York.

*Fransella, F. and Adams, B. (1966). An illustration of the use of repertory grid technique in a clinical setting. *British Journal of social and clinical Psychology* **5**, 51-62.

*Fransella, F. and Bannister, D. (1967). A validation of repertory grid technique as a measure of political construing. *Acta Psychologica* **26**, 97-106.

*Fransella, F. and Crisp, A. H. (1970). Conceptual organisation and weight change. *Psychotherapy and Psychosomatics* **18**, 176-185.

Fransella, F. and Crisp, A. H. (1971). Conceptual organisation and weight change. *In* "Recent Research in Psychosomatics" (Ed. R. A. Pierlot). S. Karger, Basel.

*Fransella, F. and Crisp, A. H. (1977). Comparisons of weight concepts in groups of a) neurotic b) normal and c) anorexic females. *British Journal of Psychiatry* (in press).

*Fransella, F. and Joyston-Bechal, M. P. (1971). An investigation of conceptual process and pattern change in a psychotherapy group. *British Journal of Psychiatry* **119**, 199-206.

Frith, C. E. and Lillie, F. J. (1972). Why does the repertory grid test indicate thought disorder? *British Journal of social and clinical Psychology* **11**, 73-78.

*Gibson, M. (1975). An illustration of the effect of the order of presentation of construct poles on Bieri's measure of cognitive complexity. *British Journal of social and clinical Psychology* **14**, 425-426.

Guertin, W. H. (1973). SORTO: Factor analyzing Q sorts of Kelly's personal construct productions. *Journal of Personality Assessment* **37**, 69-77.

Hall, M. F. (1966). The generality of cognitive complexity-simplicity. Unpublished doctoral dissertation, Vanderbilt University.

Hamilton, D. L. (1968). Personality attributes associated with extreme response style. *Psychological Bulletin* **69**, 192-203.

Harris, G. C. (1962). Some Rao-Guttman relationships. *Psychometrika* **21**, 185-190.

Haynes, E. T. and Phillips, J. P. N. (1973). Inconsistency, loose construing and schizophrenic thought disorder. *British Journal of Psychiatry* **123**, 209-217.

Hays, W. L. (1958). An approach to the study of trait implications and trait similarity. *In* "Person Perception and Interpersonal Behaviour" (Eds R. Taguiri and L. Petrullo). Stanford University Press, Stanford.

Heather, N. (1976). The specificity of schizophrenic thought disorder: a replication and extension of previous findings. *British Journal of social and clinical Psychology* **15**, 131-137.

Heider, F. (1946). Attitude and cognitive organisation. *Journal of Psychology* **2**, 107-112.

Hemsley, D. R. (1976). Problems in the interpretation of cognitive abnormalities in schizophrenia. *British Journal of Psychiatry* **129**, 32-35.

Hinkle, D. (1965). "The Change of Personal Constructs from the View point of a Theory of Construct Implications". Unpublished Ph.D. thesis, Ohio State University.

Hjelle, L. A. and Ziegler, D. J. (1976). "Personality Theories: Basic Assumptions, Research, and Applications". McGraw-Hill, New York.

Holt, R. R. (1958). Clinical and statistical prediction: a reformulation and some new data. *Journal of abnormal and social Psychology* **56**, 1-12.

*Honess, T. (1976). Cognitive complexity and social prediction. *British Journal of social and clinical Psychology* **15**, 23-31.

Honess, T. (1977a). An implication grid suitable for use in developmental research. Unpublished manuscript, University of Exeter.

Honess, T. (1977b). A comparison of the implication and repertory grid techniques. Unpublished manuscript, University of Exeter.

Honikman, B. (1976). Construct theory as an approach to architectural and environmental design. *In* "Explorations of Interpersonal Space" (Ed. P. Slater), Vol. I. Wiley, London.

*Hoy, R. M. (1973). The meaning of alcoholism for alcoholics: a repertory grid study. *British Journal of social and clinical Psychology* **12**, 98-99.

Hudson, R. (1974). Images of the retailing environment: an example of the use of the repertory grid methodology. *Environmental Behaviour* **6**, 470-494.

Hunt, D. E. (1951). Studies in role concept repertory: conceptual consistency. Unpublished M.A. thesis, Ohio State University.

Isaacson, G. I. (1966). A comparative study of the meaningfulness of personal and common constructs. Unpublished doctoral dissertation, University of Missouri.

*Isaacson, G. I. and Landfield, A. W. (1965). Meaningfulness of personal and common constructs. *Journal of Individual Psychology,* **21**, 160-166.

Judkins, M. (1976). Introspective dialogue technique. Unpublished manuscript, Royal Free Hospital, London.

Kear-Colwell, J. J. (1973). Bannister-Fransella grid performance: relationships with personality and intelligence. *British Journal of social and clinical Psychology* **12**, 78-82.

Kelly, G. A. (1955). "The Psychology of Personal Constructs", Vols 1 and 2. Norton, New York.

Kelly, G. A. (1961). The abstraction of human processes. Proceedings of the 14th International Congress of Applied Psychology, Munksgaard, Copenhagen.

Kelly, G. A. (1963). Comments on Aldous, the personable computer. *In* "Computer Simulation of Personality" (Eds S. Tomkins and S. Messick). Wiley, New York.

Kelly, G. A. (1969). The role of classification in personality theory. *In* "Clinical Psychology and Personality: the Selected Papers of George Kelly" (Ed. B. Maher). Wiley, New York.

Kelly, G. A. (1970). Behaviour is an experiment. *In* "Perspectives in Personal Construct Theory" (Ed. D. Bannister). Academic Press, London and New York.

Kelly, J. V. (1963). A program for processing George Kelly's Rep Grids on the IBM 1620 computer. Unpublished manuscript, Ohio State University.

Kelsall, P. N. and Strongman, K. T. (1977). Emotional experience and the implication grid. *British Journal of Medical Psychology* (in press).

*Kuusinen, J. and Nystedt, L. (1975a). The convergent validity of four indices of cognitive complexity in person perception. *Scandinavian Journal of Psychology* **16**, 131-136.

*Kuusinen, J. and Nystedt, L. (1975b). Individual versus provided constructs, cognitive complexity and extremity of ratings in person perception. *Scandinavian Journal of Psychology* **16**, 137-148.

Laing, R. D. and Esterson, A. (1964). "Sanity, Madness and the Family". Tavistock, London.

*Landfield, A. W. (1965). Meaningfulness of self, ideal and other as related to own versus therapist's personal construct dimensions. *Psychological Reports* **16**, 605-608.

Landfield, A. W. (1968). The extremity rating revisited within the context of personal construct theory. *British Journal of social and clinical Psychology* **7**, 135-139.

Landfield, A. W. (1971). "Personal Construct Systems in Psychotherapy". Rand McNally, Chicago.

Landfield, A. W. and Barr, M. A. (1976). Ordination: a new measure of concept organization. Unpublished manuscript, University of Nebraska-Lincoln, U.S.A.

*Lansdown, R. (1975). A reliability study of the 8 × 8 repertory grid. *Journal of the Association of Educational Psychologists.*

Lauterbach, W. (1972). The measurement of conflict and its correlation with mood. Unpublished Ph.D. thesis, University of London.

Lauterbach, W. (1975a). Assessing psychological conflict. *British Journal of social and clinical Psychology* **14**, 43-47.

Lauterbach, W. (1975b). Covariation of conflict and mood in depression. *British Journal of social and clinical Psychology* **14**, 49-53.

Leitner, L. M., Landfield, A. W. and Barr, M. A. (1975). Cognitive complexity: a review and elaboration within personal construct theory. Unpublished manuscript, University of Nebraska.

*Lemon, N. (1975). Linguistic developments and conceptualisation. *Journal of Cross-Cultural Psychology* **6**, 173-188.

*Lemon, N. and Warren, N. (1974). Salience, centrality and self-relevance of traits in construing others. *British Journal of social and clinical Psychology* **13**, 119-124.

*Lester, D. (1971). Cognitive complexity of the suicidal patient. *Psychological Reports* **28**, 158.

*Levy, L. H. (1956). Personal constructs and predictive behaviour. *Journal of abnormal and social psychology* **53**, 54-58.

*Levy, L. H. and Dugan, R. D. (1956). A factorial study in personal constructs. *Journal of Consulting Psychology* **20**, 53-57.

Levy, P. (1972). Concept-scale interaction in semantic differential research: solutions in search of a problem. *British Journal of Psychology* **63**, 235-236.

Lidz, T. (1964). "The Family and Human Adaptation". Hogarth.

*Lifshitz, M. (1974). Quality professionals: does training make a difference? A personal construct theory study of the issue. *British Journal of social and clinical Psychology* **13**, 183-189.

*Lifshitz, M. (1976). Long range effects of father's loss: the cognitive complexity of bereaved children and their school adjustment. *British Journal of medical Psychology* **49**, 189-197.

Little, B. R. (1967). Age and sex differences in the use of psychological, role and physicalistic constructs. Unpublished manuscript, University of Oxford.

Little, B. R. (1968). Factors affecting the use of psychological versus non-psychological constructs on the Rep. Test. *Bulletin of the British Psychological Society* **21**, 34.

*McFadyen, M. and Foulds, G. A. (1972). Comparison of provided and elicited grid content in the grid test of schizophrenic thought disorder. *British Journal of Psychiatry* **121**, 53-57.

McPherson, F. M. (1969). Thought-process disorder, delusions of persecution and "non-integration" in schizophrenia. *British Journal of medical Psychology* **42**, 55-57.

McPherson, F. M. and Buckley, F. (1970). Thought-process disorder and personal construct subsystems. *British Journal of social and clinical Psychology* **9**, 380-381.

*McPherson, F. M. and Walton, H. J. (1970). The dimensions of psychotherapy group interaction: an analysis of clinicians' constructs. *British Journal of medical Psychology* **43**, 281-290.

McPherson, F. M., Buckley, F. and Draffan, J. W. (1971). "Psychological" constructs, thought-process disorder and flattening of affect. *British Journal of social and clinical Psychology* **10**, 267-270.

*McPherson, F. M., Blackburn, I. M., Draffan, J. W., McFayden, M. (1973). A further study of the grid test of thought disorder. *British Journal of social and clinical Psychology* **12**, 420-427.

*McPherson, F. M., Armstrong, J. and Heather, B. B. (1975). Psychological construing, "difficulty" and thought disorder. *British Journal of medical Psychology* **48**, 303-315.

McQuitty, L. (1966). Single and multiple hierarchical classification by reciprocal pairs and rank order types. *Educational Psychology Measurement* **26**, 253-265.

Mair, J. M. M. (1964). The derivation, reliability and validity of grid measures: some problems and suggestions. *British Psychological Society Bulletin* **17**, 55.

*Mair, J. M. M. (1966). Prediction of grid scores. *British Journal of Psychology* **57**, 187-192.

*Mair, J. M. M. (1967a). Some problems in repertory grid measurement: 1. The use of bipolar constructs. *British Journal of Psychology* **58**, 261-270.

*Mair, J. M. M. (1967b). Some problems in repertory grid measurement: II. The use of whole figure constructs. *British Journal of Psychology* **58**, 271-282.

Mair, J. M. M. (1970). Psychologists are human too. *In* "Perspectives in Personal Construct Theory" (Ed. D. Bannister). Academic Press, London and New York.

Mair, J. M. M. and Boyd, P. (1967). A comparison of two grid forms. *British Journal of social and clinical Psychology* **6**, 220.

Mair, J. M. M. and Crisp, A. H. (1968). Estimating psychological organisation, meaning and change in relation to clinical practice. *British Journal of medical Psychology* **41**, 15-29.

*Makhlouf-Norris, F. and Norris, H. (1972). The obsessive compulsive syndrome as a neurotic device for the reduction of self-uncertainty. *British Journal of Psychiatry* **121**, 277-288.

*Makhlouf-Norris, F., Jones, H. G. and Norris, H. (1970). Articulation of the conceptual structure in obsessional neurosis. *British Journal of social and clinical Psychology* **9**, 264-274.

*Metcalfe, R. J. A. (1974). Own vs. provided constructs in a reptest measure of cognitive complexity. *Psychological Reports* **35**, 1305-1306.

*Mitsos, S. B. (1958). Representative elements in role construct technique. *Journal of Consulting Psychology* **22**, 311-313.

Mitsos, S. B. (1961). Three versions of the F scale and performance on the semantic differential. *Journal of abnormal and social Psychology* **62**, 433-434.

Morris, J. B. (1977). Towards a personal science. *In* "New Perspectives in Personal Construct Theory" (Ed. D. Bannister). Academic Press, London and New York.

Morse, E. L. (1966). An exploratory study of personal identity based on the psychology of personal constructs. Unpublished Ph.D. thesis, Ohio state University.

Nie, N. W., Hull, C. H., Jenkins, J. G., Steinbrenner, K. and Bent, D. H. (1975). "Statistical Package for the Social Sciences". McGraw Hill, New York.

Norris, H. and Makhlouf-Norris, F. (1976). The measurement of self-identity. *In* "The Measurement of Intrapersonal Space" (Ed. P. Slater) Vol. 1. Wiley, London.

Nystedt, L., Ekehammar, B. and Kuusinen, J. (1976). Structural representations of person perception: a comparison between own and provided constructs. *Scandinavian Journal of Psychology* **17**, 223-233.

O'Donovan, D. (1965). Rating extremity: pathology or meaningfulness? *Journal of Educational Psychology* **22,** 279-289.

*Orley, J. (1976). The use of grid technique in social anthropology. *In* "Explorations of Interpersonal Space: Vol. I, The Measurement of Intrapersonal Space by Grid Technique" (Ed. P. Slater). Wiley, London.

Orley, J. H. and Leff, J. P. (1972). The effect of psychiatric education on attitudes to illness among the Ganda. *British Journal of Psychiatry* **121,** 137-141.

Osgood, C. E., Suci, G. J. and Tannenbaum, P. M. (1957). "The Measurement of Meaning". University of Illinois Press, Urbana.

Pedersen, F. A. (1958). Consistency data on the role construct repertory test. Unpublished manuscript, Ohio State University.

*Philip, A. E. and McCulloch, J. W. (1968). Personal construct theory and social work practice. *British Journal of Social and Clinical Psychology* **7,** 115-121.

Presley, A. S. (1969). "Slowness" and performance on the grid test for thought disorder. *British Journal of social and clinical Psychology* **8,** 79-80.

Radley, A. R. (1974). Schizophrenic thought disorder and the nature of personal constructs. *British Journal of social and clinical Psychology* **13,** 315-327.

Ravenette, A. T. (1964). Some attempts at developing the use of the repertory grid in a Child Guidance Clinic. *In* "The Theory and Methodology of George Kelly" (Ed. N. Warren). Unpublished manuscript.

Ravenette, A. T. (1968). The situations grid: a further development of grid technique with children. Unpublished manuscript, London Borough of Newham.

Ravenette, A. T. (1975). Grid techniques for children. *Journal of Child Psychology and Psychiatry* **16,** 79-83.

*Rehm, L. (1971). Effects of validation on the relationship between personal constructs. *Journal of personality and social Psychology* **20,** 267-270.

*Reker, G. T. (1974). Interpersonal conceptual structures of emotionally disturbed and normal boys. *Journal of abnormal Psychology* **83,** 380-386.

*Resnick, J. and Landfield, A. W. (1961). The oppositional nature of dichotomous constructs, *Psychological Record* **11,** 47-55.

Rogers, C. R. (1951). "Client-centered Therapy". Houghton Mifflin, Boston.

Rosie, A. (1976). The role of personal construct theory in understanding classroom talk. Unpublished M.Sc. thesis, University of London.

*Rowe, D. (1971a). An examination of a psychiatrist's predictions of a patient's constructs. *British Journal of Psychiatry* **118,** 231-244.

*Rowe, D. (1971b). Poor prognosis in a case of depression as predicted by the repertory grid. *British Journal of Psychiatry* **118,** 297-300.

Rowe, D. (1977). "The Experience of Depression". Wiley, London. (In press.)

Rummell, R. J. (1970). "Applied Factor Analysis". Northwestern University Press, Evanston.

*Runkel, P. J. and Damrin, D. E. (1961). Effects of training and anxiety upon teachers' preference information about students. *Journal of Educational Psychology* **52,** 254-261.

*Ryle, A. and Breen, D. (1972a). Some differences in the personal constructs of neurotic and normal subjects. *British Journal of Psychiatry* **120,** 483-489.

*Ryle, A. and Breen, D. (1972b). A comparison of adjusted and maladjusted couples using the double dyad grid. *British Journal of medical Psychology* **45,** 375-382.

Ryle, A. and Breen, D. (1972c). The use of the double dyad grid in the clinical setting. *British Journal of medical Psychology* **45,** 383-389.

*Ryle, A. and Breen, D. (1974). Change in the course of social work training: a repertory grid study. *British Journal of medical Psychology* **47,** 139.

*Ryle, A. and Lipshitz, S. (1974). Towards an informed counter-transference: the possible contribution of repertory grid techniques. *British Journal of medical Psychology* **47**, 219-225.

*Ryle, A. and Lipshitz, S. (1975). Recording change in marital therapy with the reconstruction grid. *British Journal of medical Psychology* **48**, 39-48.

*Ryle, A. and Lipshitz, S. (1976). Repertory grid elucidation of a difficult conjoint therapy. *British Journal of medical Psychology* **49**, 281-285.

*Ryle, A. and Lunghi, M. W. (1969). The measurement of relevant change after psychotherapy: use of repertory grid testing. *British Journal of Psychiatry* **115**, 1297-1304.

*Ryle, A. and Lunghi, M. W. (1970). The dyad grid: a modification of repertory grid technique. *British Journal of Psychiatry* **117**, 323-327.

Salmon, P. (1967). The social values and conformity behaviour of primary schoolboys, in relation to maternal attitudes. Unpublished Ph.D. thesis, University of London.

*Salmon, P. (1969). Differential conforming of the developmental process. *British Journal of social and clinical Psychology* **8**, 22-31.

Salmon, P. (1976). Grid measures with child subjects. *In* "Explorations of Intra-personal Space" (Ed. P. Slater), Vol. 1. Wiley, London.

Salmon, P., Bramley, J. and Presley, A. S. (1967). The word-in-context test as a measure of conceptualization in schizophrenics with and without thought disorder. *British Journal of medical Psychology* **40**, 253-259.

*Salmon, P., Arnold, J. M. and Collyer, Y. M. (1972). What do the determinants determine: the internal validity of the Rorschach. *Journal of Personality* **36**, 33-38.

*Scott, W. A. (1962). Cognitive complexity and cognitive flexibility. *Sociometry* **25**, 405-414.

*Sechrest, L. V. (1962). Stimulus equivalence of the Psychotherapist. *Journal of Individual Psychology* **18**, 172-176.

Shepard, R. N. (1972). A taxonomy of some principal types of data and multi-dimensional methods for their analysis. *In* "Multidimensional Scaling: Theory and Applications in the Behavioural Sciences" (Eds R. N. Shepard, A. Kemball Romney and S. B. Nerlove) Vol. 1. Seminar Press, London.

Shepard, R. N., Kemball Romney, A. and Nerlove, S. B. (1972). "Multidimensional Scaling: Theory and Application in the Behavioural Sciences". Seminar Press, London.

*Shubsachs, A. P. W. (1975). To repeat or not to repeat? Are frequently used constructs more important to the subject? A study of the effect of allowing repetition of constructs in a modified Kelly repertory test. *British Journal of medical Psychology* **48**, 31-37.

Slade, P. and Kjeldsen, A. (1976). "Conflict Grid Analysis". Unpublished manuscript.

Slater, P. (1964). "The Principal Components of a Repertory Grid". Vincent Andrew, London.

Slater, P. (1968). Summary of the output DELTA. Unpublished manuscript, St. George's Hospital, London.

*Slater, P. (1970). Personal questionnaire data treated as forming a repertory grid. *British Journal of social and clinical Psychology* **9**, 357-370.

*Slater, P. (1972). The measurement of consistency in repertory grids. *British Journal of Psychiatry* **121**, 45-51.

Slater, P. (ed.) (1977). "The Measurement of Interpersonal Space by Grid Technique", Vol. 2. Wiley, London (in press).

*Smail, D. J. (1970). Neurotic symptoms, personality and personal constructs. *British Journal of Psychiatry* **117**, 645-648.

*Smail, D. J. (1972). A grid measure of empathy in a therapeutic group. *British Journal of medical Psychology* **45**, 165.

*Smith, S. and Leach, C. (1972). A hierarchical measure of cognitive complexity. *British Journal of Psychology* **63**, 561-568.

Spelman, M. S., Harrison, A. W. and Mellsop, G. W. (1971). Grid test for thought disorder in acute and chronic schizophrenics. *Psychological Medicine* **1**, 234-238.

Sperlinger, D. (1976). Aspects of stability in the repertory grid. *British Journal of medical Psychology* **49**, 341-347.

*Stringer, P. (1972). Psychological significance in personal and supplied construct systems: a defining experiment. *European Journal of Social Psychology* **2**, 437-447.

*Stringer, P. (1974). A use of repertory grid measures for evaluating map formats. *British Journal of Psychology* **65**, 23-34.

Tripodi, T. and Bieri, J. (1963). Cognitive complexity as a function of own and provided constructs. *Journal of Psychological Reports* **13**, 26.

*Tyler, F. B. and Simmons, W. L. (1964). Patients' conception of their therapist. *Journal of clinical Psychology* **20**, 112-133.

Vannoy, J. S. (1965). Generality of cognitive complexity-simplicity as a personality construct. *Journal of personality and social Psychology* **2**, 385-396.

*Warr, P. B. and Coffman, T. L. (1970). Personality, involvement and extremity of judgement. *British Journal of social and clinical Psychology* **9**, 108-121.

*Warren, N. (1966). Social class and construct systems: examination of the cognitive structure of two social class groups. *British Journal of social and clinical Psychology* **4**, 254-263.

*Watson, J. P. (1970a). A repertory grid method of studying groups. *British Journal of Psychiatry* **117**, 309-318.

*Watson, J. P. (1970b). A measure of therapist-patient understanding. *British Journal of Psychiatry* **117**, 319-321.

*Watson, J. P. (1972). Possible measures of change during group psychotherapy. *British Journal of medical Psychology* **45**, 71.

Watson, J. P., Gunn, J. C. and Gristwood, J. (1976). A grid investigation of long-term prisoners. *In* "The Measurement of Intrapersonal Space by Grid Technique" (Ed. P. Slater). Wiley, London.

*Wijesinghe, O. B. A. and Wood, R. R. (1976). A repertory grid study of inter-personal perception within a married couple. *British Journal of medical Psychology* **49**, 287-293.

Wilcox, J. W. (1972). "A Method of Measuring Decision Assumptions". M.I.T. Press, Cambridge, Mass.

Williams, E. (1971). The effect of varying the elements in the Bannister-Fransella grid test of thought disorder. *British Journal of Psychiatry* **119**, 207-212.

Wilson, P. (1976). Dimensional analysis of rep-grids. Unpublished manuscript, Royal Free Hospital School of Medicine, London.

*Wright, D. M. (1973). Impairment in abstract conceptualization and Bannister and Fransella's Grid Test of Schizophrenic Thought Disorder. *Journal of Consulting and Clinical Psychology* **41**, 474.

*Wright, K. J. T. (1970). Exploring the uniqueness of common complaints. *British Journal of medical Psychology* **43**, 221-232.

AUTHOR INDEX

SUBJECT INDEX

A

Aggression, 2
Articulation, grid score of, 68, 95, 109

B

Bi-polar Impgrid, 9, 30, 49-52, 58-59, 63, 74, 78, 84, 96
  and children, 58-59, 78
  and rank grid, 78, 84
  and reliability, 78
Bi-polarity, 2, 5, 47, 49, 63, 64, 70, 84, 104-105

C

Children, 13, 16, 54-55, 56, 57, 58, 78, 84, 85, 98-99, 117
  and bi-polar Impgrids, 58-59, 78
  and elements, 13, 16, 54
  and elicitation, 54-55, 58
  and grid reliability, 78, 84, 85
  and grid validity, 98-99
Classification, of constructs, 21, 90
Cognitive Balance Theory, 71
Cognitive complexity, 22, 61-62, 65, 101, 106, 109, 114
Cognitive differentiation, 61-62, 65, 101, 106, 109, 114
Cognitive integration, 62-69, 107
  and articulation, 68, 95, 109
    between self and others, 68-69
  and extremity ratings, 63-64, 65
  and ordination, 64
  and organisation corollary, 62
  and saturation, 52, 62-63
COIN, computer programme, 79
Commonality corollary, 7, 21, 97
Computer programmes, 36, 51, 68, 62, 73-77, 79, 81, 109
  COIN, 79
  DELTA, 79
  FRAN 2, 51
  INGRID, 36, 68, 72, 73, 109

Kelly's non-parametric factor analysis, 73
McQuitty's cluster analysis, 74
Statistical Package for the Social Sciences, 40, 74-76
Concepts, 6
Conflict, 69-72, 107
Consistency, measures and, 61, 79-81, 89, 101, 107
Constellatory construing, 8, 63, 100, 116
Construct theory, 4, 7-9, 10, 11, 22, 23, 52, 59, 62-65, 68, 93, 96, 97, 100, 101-102, 104-110, 113-119, 133
  and dependency, 52-53
  and diagnosis, 59
  and grid technique, 23, 104-110
  and Hinkle's theory of implications, 62-63
  and propositionality, 8, 61, 63, 100, 116
  and superordinacy, 62-68, 93
  and validation, 100-102
Construct theory, corollaries,
  commonality, 7, 21, 97
  individuality, 7, 19, 97
  organisation, 8, 17, 62
  range, 6, 13, 30, 55, 56, 57-58, 65, 68, 93, 103, 105
  sociality, 8, 97
Constructs,
  balanced/imbalanced triads, 71-72
  and bi-polarity, 2, 5, 47, 49, 63, 64, 70, 84, 104-105
  and change, 39, 45, 47, 49, 62, 82, 96
  and classification, 21, 90
  and concepts, 6
  constellatory, 8, 63, 100, 116
  and context, 6, 8, 59, 106, 116
  core role, 9, 118
  and definition of, 5
  as discriminations, 2, 13
  elicited, 13, 14-19, 21, 54-56, 62, 63, 86, 106-107
  and hierarchical linkage, 2, 3, 8, 62,